WITHDRAWN
UTSA LIBRARIES

Rethinking Enterprise Policy

Also by Simon Bridge:

UNDERSTANDING ENTERPRISE, ENTREPRENEURSHIP AND SMALL BUSINESS
(first and second editions with Ken O'Neill and Stan Cromie, third edition with Ken O'Neill and Frank Martin)

UNDERSTANDING THE SOCIAL ECONOMY AND THE THIRD SECTOR
(with Brendan Murtagh and Ken O'Neill)

Rethinking Enterprise Policy

Can Failure Trigger New Understanding?

Simon Bridge

© Simon Bridge 2010

All rights reserved. No reproduction, copy or transmission of this publication may be made without written permission.

No portion of this publication may be reproduced, copied or transmitted save with written permission or in accordance with the provisions of the Copyright, Designs and Patents Act 1988, or under the terms of any licence permitting limited copying issued by the Copyright Licensing Agency, Saffron House, 6–10 Kirby Street, London EC1N 8TS.

Any person who does any unauthorized act in relation to this publication may be liable to criminal prosecution and civil claims for damages.

The author has asserted his right to be identified as the author of this work in accordance with the Copyright, Designs and Patents Act 1988.

First published 2010 by
PALGRAVE MACMILLAN

Palgrave Macmillan in the UK is an imprint of Macmillan Publishers Limited, registered in England, company number 785998, of Houndmills, Basingstoke, Hampshire RG21 6XS.

Palgrave Macmillan in the US is a division of St Martin's Press LLC, 175 Fifth Avenue, New York, NY 10010.

Palgrave Macmillan is the global academic imprint of the above companies and has companies and representatives throughout the world.

Palgrave® and Macmillan® are registered trademarks in the United States, the United Kingdom, Europe and other countries

ISBN 978–0–230–23558–8   hardback

This book is printed on paper suitable for recycling and made from fully managed and sustained forest sources. Logging, pulping and manufacturing processes are expected to conform to the environmental regulations of the country of origin.

A catalogue record for this book is available from the British Library.

Library of Congress Cataloging-in-Publication Data

Bridge, Simon.
   Rethinking enterprise policy : can failure trigger new
  understanding? / Simon Bridge.
     p. cm.
  ISBN 978–0–230–23558–8
 1. Industrial policy.   2. Entrepreneurship—Government policy.
 3. Small business—Government policy.   I. Title.
HD3611.B8775 2010
354'.234—dc22

                                                           2010023773

10 9 8 7 6 5 4 3 2 1
19 18 17 16 15 14 13 12 11 10

Printed and bound in Great Britain by
CPI Antony Rowe, Chippenham and Eastbourne

Contents

List of Tables	vi
List of Figures	vii
List of Illustrations	ix
List of Cases	x
Preface	xi
Acknowledgements	xiii
1 Introduction	1
Part I The Current Models and Approaches	
2 Government Agenda	17
3 Models of the Influences on Entrepreneurship	37
4 The Problem: The Facts Do Not Fit the Theory	63
Part II Exploring the Position	
5 Different Perspectives	81
6 Perspectives on Entrepreneurship and Enterprise	95
7 Nature or Nurture?	118
8 Comparisons	134
Part III An Alternative Model	
9 An Enterprise is a Goal-Realisation Device	149
10 The Basis of Choice	160
11 The Social Dimension	177
12 An Alternative Approach	194
13 A View Forward	214
Index	223

List of Tables

2.1	The possible components of a policy framework	19
3.1	Attributes and resources, and how they are acquired	47
3.2	Interpretation of components of the GEM conceptual model	49
3.3	Policy areas with an impact on the five factors	55
4.1	Variations in business start-up rates across the UK	74
5.1	Organisations and activities which are neither in the public nor the private sector	85
6.1	E-numbers: Interpretation and some comparable uses	107
9.1	Reasons why people might want to work	151
9.2	Some of the means by which people can obtain resources for life	153
9.3	Different kinds of entrepreneurs	154
9.4	How enterprise (and entrepreneurship) might be viewed from venture and people perspectives	157
11.1	Some domains of social capital	184
11.2	The components of social capital?	189

List of Figures

1.1	The transition route from data to wisdom	12
2.1	A diagram of a policy framework	18
2.2	The OECD/EUROSTAT framework for entrepreneurship indicators	27
3.1	The perceived key business start-up needs	39
3.2	A hierarchy of enterprise needs	42
3.3	A formula for entrepreneurial success	44
3.4	Shane's model of the entrepreneurial process	46
3.5	Intentions model of entrepreneurial potential (simplified)	46
3.6	Attributes and resources model	47
3.7	GEM conceptual model (the total process)	49
3.8	The determinants of nascent entrepreneurship	51
3.9	Stevenson's portrayal of the entrepreneurship system	52
3.10	Comprehensive model of factors leading to entrepreneurial activity	53
3.11	Factors impacting entrepreneurship	54
3.12	Casson's demand and supply of entrepreneurs	56
3.13	The layers of the small business support network	57
3.14	A default assumption about influences on entrepreneurship?	58
3.15	Simple form of the OECD/EUROSTAT framework for entrepreneurship indicators	60
4.1	Invest NI presentation of GEM TEA measurements	68
4.2	Plot of UK and Northern Ireland GEM TEA indicators 2000–8	69
5.1	An economic development agency's world view?	89
5.2	An individual's world view at the start of working life?	90
6.1	Two dimensions of entrepreneurship: Stage and type	105

6.2	E-numbers: A categorisation of enterprise and entrepreneurship	108
7.1	Mechanisms through which genetic factors might influence entrepreneurship	126
9.1	What you see is not everything	156
10.1	A 'default' model of the impact of an influence on crime	173
10.2	Predictions of the incidence of criminality in a society	174
12.1	The 'default' assumption about influencing entrepreneurship?	201
12.2	A possible model of the level of entrepreneurship	202
12.3	Diagrammatic presentation of Ajzen's Theory of Planned Behaviour	208

List of Illustrations

1.1	Terminology: Is it enterprise or entrepreneurship?	2
2.1	Examples of the prominence of enterprise and entrepreneurship in government policy	17
2.2	'Small Business', 'Entrepreneurship' and 'Enterprise' policy	20
2.3	Stevenson's summary of policy evolution	24
6.1	Recognising the process for what it is, rather than what we would like it to be	113
7.1	Can the supply of entrepreneurs be increased?	127
8.1	An example of bridging the research–practice divide	139
8.2	What is the basis of policy?	143
10.1	Examples of the assumption of individual risk–return analysis	166
10.2	The social brain	170
11.1	Measuring social capital	184
11.2	An analogy with vitamins?	187
11.3	Who are a person's peers?	190
11.4	Entrepreneurship capital	190
12.1	Enterprise and deprivation: The rationale for UK public policy	195
12.2	The bias of the 'classic' dissertation	200
12.3	Entrepreneurship and the Theory of Planned Behaviour	207

List of Cases

2.1	The city of Montreal	29
2.2	An earlier enterprise initiative in Northern Ireland	31
3.1	The development of enterprise support in Northern Ireland	38
4.1	Accelerating Entrepreneurship: A case study in interpreting indicators	68
4.2	Some findings from the Richard Report	72
5.1	The influence of agency agenda	88

Preface

Two years ago, assisted by Ken O'Neill and Frank Martin, I finished preparing the third edition of *Understanding Enterprise, Entrepreneurship and Small Business*. In the first two editions, when trying to summarise our chapter on the effectiveness of enterprise policy, we concluded that 'there appears to be no strong body of evidence to say that intervention works, but also there is no clear evidence that it doesn't'. For the third edition, however, which we wrote in 2008, we changed that and said that there now appear to be several studies which suggest that much intervention has failed and that

> it seems reasonable to conclude that, overall, the evidence is that the methods so far applied have not worked in that they have not had the effect intended in improving rates of entrepreneurship or levels of business performance. Despite the similarity of policies and interventions across the world, there are few proven examples of successful 'best practice'. The adoption of interventionist policies appears to be due more to a 'me too' approach than any rigorous examination of their impact. If governments still want to intervene, and they will, and if they want to achieve more than just being seen to do something, they will need to change their intervention methods. For this they will need new models of what actually influences entrepreneurs and enterprises. Doing more of the same seems unlikely to yield significantly different results.

That statement still seems to be accurate, but it is clearly not the end of the story. It, leads, for instance, to successive questions such as, if current methods do not work, why, and what will work? This book is an attempt to explain why and to suggest other avenues to explore in a search for new methods. It takes as its starting point the view that often a shortage of enterprise, and/or of entrepreneurship, is diagnosed as a key factor in economic underperformance and that, on this assumption, governments and their development agencies have tried to raise the levels of enterprise, especially in countries or regions with relatively weak economies.

However, as indicated above, the evidence now seems to suggest that those efforts have not worked. In order to effect an economic cure, more enterprise may have been prescribed but it is not being delivered. The diagnosis therefore required is why enterprise does not respond to policies to increase it in the way that the originators of those policies both desired and assumed. This book looks at current models of enterprise and of the factors that are thought to influence it and then at a number of different perspectives on this subject. From them it derives an alternative model, based on current understandings of human behaviour, which does appear to be consistent with many observations of enterprise.

That model offers an explanation for why current enterprise promotion policies may be misguided and thus provides a diagnosis for their failure. But, just as in medicine, diagnosing why a supposed cure does not work does not mean that an alternative prescription is developed and ready. However it does suggest that continuing with the old cure is likely to waste resources, and it indicates new avenues to explore in a search for working solutions.

This book is illustrated by, among others, a number of examples from Northern Ireland because that is where I have been working on enterprise-related tasks for over a quarter of a century. One consequence is that I have my own memories and personal records for that period, and they provide a record of the evolution of Northern Ireland's enterprise policy in a way that it would probably not now be possible to assemble from official sources. If anyone feels that I have misinterpreted the evidence, I am sorry, but I have tried to present the story as I saw it.

Thank You

I have been encouraged and helped in my search by many people, both directly in face-to-face conversations and indirectly through articles, papers and books. I hope therefore that I have given appropriate acknowledgement for all such contributions, for which I am very grateful.

There are however two people to whom I owe a particular debt of gratitude. One is my wife Irene who has tolerated the time I have spent on writing the book, even to the extent of taking my laptop with me on holiday so that I could apply myself without the danger of phone-call interruptions. The other is my former co-author Ken O'Neill who, although not responsible for any of the content of this book, has nevertheless provided essential support, guidance and encouragement and invaluable, and seemingly innumerable, constructive reviews. I would not like to have tried it without that help.

Acknowledgements

The author and publishers gratefully acknowledge the following for permission to reproduce copyright material in this book:

Mark Casson, Allan Gibb, Ji-Hee Kim et al., Norris Krueger, Scott Shane and Lois Stevenson for permission to reproduce material from their work.

Cambridge Alumni Magazine for permission to quote from one of its articles.

The Danish Ministry of Economic and Business Affairs for permission to use the FORA model.

Edward Elgar Publishing for permission to use material from Scott Shane, *A General Theory of Entrepreneurship* and Mark Casson, *The Entrepreneur: An Economic Theory*.

Elsevier for permission to reproduce material from the *Journal of Business Venturing*.

The copyright holders, who kindly granted permission to reproduce material on the Global Entrepreneurship Monitor (GEM) conceptual model, and the authors, national teams, researchers, funding bodies and other contributors who have made this possible.

OECD for permission to reproduce its material.

The Random House Group for permission to quote from Philip Ball, *Critical Mass: How One thing Leads to Another* published by Arrow Books.

Sage Publications for permission to reproduce material from the *International Small Business Journal*.

Senate Hall Academic Publishing for permission to reproduce material from the *International Journal of Entrepreneurship Education*.

Springer Publishers for permission to reproduce material from Anders Lundström and Lois Stevenson, *Entrepreneurship Policy: Theory and Practice*.

SystemsWiki (www.systemswiki.org) for permission to use material from its site.

University of Chicago Press for its Fair Use Policy under which excerpts from 'The Experiential Aspects of Consumption' are quoted.

1
Introduction

Today enterprise and entrepreneurship often feature in government policies, usually because they appear to be seen as some sort of universal cure which can be administered to improve economic performance. In this context the words enterprise and entrepreneurship have come to be used apparently with similar meanings and often interchangeably. This prescription of enterprise and entrepreneurship as an economic cure seems to be based on the beliefs that enterprise and/or entrepreneurship are good for us, and that because we know how to grow more of them, governments and others should take steps to promote them. These beliefs are reflected, for instance, in the introduction to a report on the 'World Entrepreneurship Summit' held in 2008 which, in calling for more action to promote entrepreneurship across the world, said that

> we have plenty of research that tells us that entrepreneurship is important and what we need to do to get more entrepreneurs. We have policies aplenty to create entrepreneurial cultures, to deepen our scientific and technological knowledge and to widen access to education, finance and the internet.[1]

This quotation indicates both that entrepreneurship is important and that we know how to get more of it. These assertions are simply stated without qualification, as if they were justified assumptions which need no further explanation, but it might be worthwhile reflecting on their validity. The first assertion is that entrepreneurship is important and there have been a number of studies which help to confirm this, not least because of the apparent link between entrepreneurship and economic development. Also, as a senior venture capitalist is reputed to have said

> You may not be able to get the economic models to prove that entrepreneurship creates economic growth, but I'll tell you one thing. You won't get growth without it.[2]

However, just because entrepreneurship is supposed to be good for us, the second assertion, that we know how to get more of it, does not necessarily follow. Despite any suggestions to the contrary, the research which has indicated the importance of entrepreneurship has not been followed by a similar effort to confirm that we do indeed know how to get more entrepreneurs. Instead there is now evidence to the contrary in a number of studies which suggest that the policies followed by many governments to promote entrepreneurship are not working. The statement quoted above may reflect therefore what many people believe to be the current state of knowledge in this area but it may, nevertheless, make an assumption about getting more entrepreneurship which is not justified.

Illustration 1.1 Terminology: Is it enterprise or entrepreneurship?

There was a time when the word entrepreneurship was used to refer almost exclusively to the process of the formation and/or growth of private-sector businesses. At the same time the word enterprise was sometimes also used in a similar narrow way to refer just to business but sometimes with a broader meaning of the exercise, in any context, of a set of attributes and behaviours such as creativity, perseverance, self-belief and achievement orientation. Now however the word entrepreneurship is sometimes used in that broad way so that, in some situations, the two are, in practice, interchangeable. For instance:

'The European Enterprise Awards recognise and reward excellence in initiatives that support entrepreneurship at regional level.'[3]

It seems, sometimes, that even those responsible for delivering enterprise and entrepreneurship programmes do not know which aspect of this subject they are trying to cover. The meanings of the two words have evolved, and are still evolving, and neither of them now has a single narrow definition but they are instead each used with a spectrum of meanings, with considerable overlap between the two spectra. As a result confusion is sometimes to be expected.

> It is probably therefore necessary to add this note on vocabulary. In keeping with common usage, this book does not try to impose specific narrow definitions of the words enterprise and entrepreneurship, not least because it often quotes from the usage of others, which do not conform to any single definition. It might be helpful to have other more narrowly defined words with which to convey different shades of meaning but none are readily available. New words might be invented but enterprise and entrepreneurship are the words that are most often used by other writers in this field and quotes from the other literature will include them. This book therefore uses these words, despite the potential for confusion, but tries, when necessary, to indicate which meaning is appropriate at any particular point. (See, however, Chapter 6 for more on this point and a possible categorisation of the different meanings.)

Introduction – we do not always know the right solution

George Washington was probably killed by his doctors. He contracted a nasty sore throat and breathing problems after being out on his horse in freezing weather and died two days later. His reported symptoms are consistent with an acute inflammation of the epiglottis but his doctors bled him. When he did not respond, they bled him some more. Because four such bleedings removed over half his blood in the space of about ten hours, it seems that it was not the inflammation but the loss of blood that killed him; although the inflammation probably did not help.[4]

Why was he bled? At that time bloodletting had long been the accepted cure for many complaints. It appears to be one of the oldest medical practices. It was first recorded in ancient Egypt, but its widespread use in Western medicine probably owes its origins to the Hippocratic doctors in the Greek-speaking world whose teachings were rediscovered, after the Dark Ages, from Islamic sources. Before them the sources from which medical help was sought or expected were probably mainly diviners and witch-doctors, and their medicine would have been seen to belong more to the realm of religion and the spirits than to science. It seems that it was in the fifth century BC with the Hippocratic doctors that an essentially secular medicine first appeared, based apparently on observation rather than superstition. The technique of treating some conditions by bleeding the patient had therefore a logical rationale based on a classical corpus of knowledge. It was derived from an observation-based theory, it was clearly wanted by patients and believed in by doctors, and it would seem that it frequently appeared to work, in that the patients, having been bled, got better.

Although subsequently it has been largely discredited, at that time the practice of bloodletting was widely believed to be the correct prescription for a wide range of medical problems. We may now think that it was wrong but what this medical story tells us is that rational people following accepted best practice do not necessarily apply a good solution. Could this also apply to policies which attempt to increase levels of enterprise (and entrepreneurship) as the cure for a range of apparent economic and social ills?

Promoting enterprise

The 1980s and 1990s were supposedly the decades of the 'enterprise culture'. Before that, in the 1970s, there had been a change. Although then many people could still remember the period of unemployment that had been a problem in many countries in the depression of the 1930s, it seemed that subsequently full employment had become the norm. This had been achieved, apparently, by the effort required for the Second World War and then sustained by the effects of that war and the application of Keynesian economics. Therefore it was worrying when, in the 1970s, the level of unemployment once again started to rise. In the UK, for instance, the unemployment figure had stayed relatively low at half a million or fewer from the end of the conflict until the early 1970s, but between 1974 and 1985, the figure rose sixfold to three million. The UK and other governments were anxious to do what they could to stimulate the creation of more jobs.

For those jobs governments increasingly looked to small businesses. Just at the time of the 1970s rise in unemployment, David Birch had been doing some research in America which indicated that, contrary to many people's expectations, it was small businesses, rather than big businesses, which were at that time the main creators of jobs in the US economy. What Birch said was that firms which employed 100 people or fewer had, in the early 1970s, created 80 per cent of the new net jobs. It was not that big businesses did not create jobs; they did, but overall they lost almost as many jobs as they created.[5] Small businesses, on the other hand, created significantly more jobs than they lost and so their net effect was job creation. Birch's findings did not receive immediate and universal acceptance as they were counter-intuitive and relied on dynamic statistical analysis. But some of the other researchers who tried to replicate his work reported similar findings, the validity of which began to be accepted.

The statistical debate may still be continuing, but, right or not, Birch's conclusions were taken up and used to inform government policy.

The combination therefore of a need for more employment and the apparent identification of small businesses as a source of employment led many to follow a policy of promoting the establishment and growth of small businesses. To start with such policies were often labelled enterprise policies, but, by the late 1990s, the terminology had started to change and the emphasis was put on entrepreneurship. Earlier the term entrepreneurship had been used almost exclusively to refer to the process of starting and running a business, which was indeed the focus of many of the early enterprise programmes. However, just as enterprise sometimes referred to small business and sometimes to a wider concept of 'a group of qualities and competencies that enable individuals, organisations, communities, societies and cultures to be flexible, creative, and adaptable in the face of, and as contributors to, rapid social and economic change',[6] so too entrepreneurship began to acquire a wider meaning. In Northern Ireland, for instance, the government's *Entrepreneurship and Education Action Plan* of 2003 said that it considered entrepreneurship to be 'the ability of an individual, possessing a range of essential skills and attributes, to make a unique, innovative and creative contribution in the world of work, whether in employment or self-employment'.[7]

Thus people have talked about small business policies, enterprise policies and entrepreneurship polices, but it was not always clear if those different labels conveyed intended distinctions between the policies or were essentially referring to the same thing. Some observers, for instance, have suggested that while both small business policies and entrepreneurship policies might be enterprise policies, small business policies were generally designed to stimulate the growth of the existing small business base, and entrepreneurship policies were generally designed to encourage more people to start businesses. Because those objectives require different approaches, any attempt to address both with the same policy would probably fail to achieve either. Nevertheless often such advice does not appear to have been followed.

In policy terms, then, it is not always clear whether references to entrepreneurship are just using a new label for what might have been formerly labelled enterprise or are intended to refer specifically to a somewhat different policy target. Nevertheless, despite a lack of clarity in the terminology, since the last decade of the twentieth century there has been a popular policy focus on entrepreneurship and, along with that, a wider research and practitioner interest in those policies.

Lois Stevenson[8] listed a number of reasons for this growing interest in entrepreneurship policy:

- There is need for an increased rate of new firm formation, because of a desire for jobs, productivity improvements, innovation renewal, and links with economic growth.
- SME (Small and Medium-sized Enterprise) policies have not been sufficient.
- There is a need for policy re-orientation to foster a "dynamic".
- There is a supply side drive for new entrepreneurs – a shift from an employee mentality.
- There is limited knowledge about the construction of an entrepreneurship policy.
- There are better data, international comparisons (GEM), new research (for instance in nascent entrepreneurs), a focus of think tanks (OECD, EU), and the convergence of interdisciplinary research – all contributing to a growing capability.
- Recent efforts to benchmark entrepreneurship policy.

As Stevenson's first point suggests, most entrepreneurship policies are now aimed at stimulating the creation of new businesses for a wider set of reasons than just creating jobs. Similarly those policies designed to stimulate the growth of already established businesses often recognise a wider set of objectives. While the initial reason was job creation, and that is possibly still the main reason, other economic and social benefits of small businesses are also recognised, such as:

- Small businesses provide a productive outlet for the energies of those enterprising people who set great store by economic independence.
- Many small firms act as specialist suppliers to large companies.
- Small firms provide competition, both actual and potential, and provide some check on monopoly profits.
- Competition also widens choice for consumers and small businesses can supply specialist niches.
- The small-firm sector is the traditional breeding ground for innovation and for new industries.
- The small business sector is also perceived to offer a means of social and community cohesion.[9]

Often these enterprise and/or entrepreneurship policies have been pursued in and for places where there has been significant relative deprivation. These are often the areas where unemployment is highest and thus the areas which might most be in need of new jobs. Inward investment was not ignored as a possible source of help for these areas but, possibly following the analogy that if you give people a fish, you feed them for a day whereas if you teach them to fish, you feed them for life, encouraging the creation of new businesses in those areas has helped them to establish more lasting solutions.

Where some form of target was indicated for such policies, it frequently involved the concept of 'convergence'. In the UK, by the middle of the 1990s, the strength of the economy had been restored and overall unemployment had fallen again, and the focus of government was no longer on raising the overall UK average level of enterprise and/or entrepreneurship, but on raising its level in the more deprived areas. Given that the level of enterprise and/or entrepreneurship in such areas was low, as indicated for instance by the rate of business start-ups and recently by GEM (Global Entrepreneurship Monitor) surveys, the aim, it was sometimes declared, should be to raise it so that it 'converged' with the national average.

Thus many countries or regions followed enterprise or entrepreneurship policies which they hoped would contribute to an improvement in the relative position of the more deprived areas. If you were a government with a deprivation problem, it was what you did and in doing it you followed many of what have become the classical methods. Those methods included business-start advice and training, financial support, incubation premises and mentoring, and such approaches had a good pedigree. They were apparently developed from, or supported by, what was described as 'an explosion of research into entrepreneurship and the small and medium enterprise',[10] and so were supposedly 'evidence based'. The assistance provided was also apparently welcomed by its recipients who reported that it had helped them and that they had started or grown businesses a result. So, if enterprise (including entrepreneurship and small businesses) provided what was needed, if the methods followed were the established way of promoting enterprise, and if the recipients of the assistance provided by those methods reported that it was helpful and led to more business, should that not have been good policy?

The problem is that it does not seem to have worked. For instance, according to its action plan for small business, the UK government had committed itself to making the UK the best place in the world to start and grow a business[11] and, in a supporting document, claimed that several independent surveys had found that it does, now, have one of most favourable regulatory environments for starting a business. If that was what mattered, then it might be expected that business formation rates would be high as a result, yet the same document admits that the UK continues to lag behind the US and many countries in Europe in terms of entrepreneurial activity.[12] As one observer has commented: 'All governments recognise the importance of SMEs and wish to promote them. ... Most instruments used by governments to promote SMEs fail to achieve their objectives, or have only a very minor impact'.[13] Are these enterprise policies therefore like the medical practice of bloodletting: policies apparently based on classical theory and evidence but nevertheless wrong?

The 'evidence base' for bloodletting

The Hippocratic corpus of medical knowledge was also supposedly 'evidence' based. It explained health and illness broadly in terms of shifting balances of the four life-sustaining humours which were thought to be present in every body. They were: blood – the source of vitality; choler – the gastric juice indispensable for digestion; phlegm – which included the various colourless secretions and which acted as a lubricant and coolant; and bile or melancholy – not seen on its own but darkening the other humours. Among them, the four major fluids accounted for the visible and tangible phenomena of physical existence. It could be observed that if a man lost a lot of blood, for instance through a wound obtained in battle, then his body became cold and dry, and eventually he died. Blood, it was therefore supposed, made the body hot and wet, and similarly choler made it hot and dry, phlegm cold and wet, and bile cold and dry.[14]

This thinking was thus in accord with observations of the body and the liquids in it and had ready explanations when people fell sick. Illness, it said, resulted when one of the fluids either built up or diminished. If a body had too much blood, possibly because of a faulty diet, it became hot and wet, whereas too little blood led to fainting, coma and even death. Someone who was feverish and was too hot and wet was therefore thought to have too much blood.

Such thinking did not end suddenly. It changed gradually, following a number of discoveries such as that of the circulation of blood and of the difference between poison, diet deficiency and germs as causes of disease. It now seems strange to relate that the concept of some illnesses being caused by invading germs is very recent. Diseases such as malaria and cholera were once thought to have been caused by bad air. London's Victorian sewers were originally built to reduce the threat of cholera by removing the sewage that was the source of bad air before it was discovered that cholera was water borne and that the sewers worked by removing the source of pollution of water supplies. The link between mosquitoes and malaria was only demonstrated in about 1900. It was this slow, piece-meal development of medical understanding that eroded the perceived rationale for bleeding and indicated alternative approaches.

Before those discoveries the prescription and application of bloodletting appeared to have much to recommend it and the suggestion that such classical approaches did not work would have been rejected by most people in the medical establishment. As late as the Franco-Prussian War of 1870–1, the French military medical staff did not believe in Lister's teaching that germs caused infections and the consequent need for antiseptic practices. Because the German staff used some of Lister's procedures in treating battle wounds, they achieved outcomes noticeably superior to the French.

The situation, however, is not black and white. Bloodletting is not always the wrong treatment, and modern medical understanding indicates that there were and are some occasions when bleeding does appear to offer real help (see example in Chapter 8). Nevertheless its former use as an almost universal cure has now been discredited as doing more harm than good. It may be relevant to note however that this change of view on the effectiveness of bloodletting did not happen suddenly and the new approach took a long time to be (more or less) universally accepted, following the accumulated input of new discoveries and new thinking.

These developments included the following, none of which alone was enough to change established thinking, but cumulatively led to new understanding of the nature of illness and better ways to prevent or cure it:

- The discovery of the circulation of blood, which in turn suggested that blood had a different function from that of the other 'humours'.
- The realisation by Lister and others of the importance of cleanliness, which in turn suggested that some illness might result from the transference of something from other ill people.
- The folk wisdom that if a dairy maid got cow pox, she would not then get smallpox, which suggested that if stimulated in the right way, the body itself could combat disease.
- The association of cholera with specific sources of water, which suggested that it was not caused by bad air but by something in bad water.

An analogy for enterprise

It has been suggested that, if the study of enterprise and entrepreneurship is a science, it is much closer to medicine than to very deterministic sciences like physics. It is in basic sciences like physics that it has been possible to derive general theories, such as Newton's law of gravity, that can provide the basic understanding which explains a wide range of known phenomena and from which other developments can be derived, in the way that the law of gravity both explained the motions of the planets and provided the basis for the calculations for getting a man to the moon. It might be nice if there was such a general theory of enterprise and/or entrepreneurship which would provide an overall model of the subject that would guide our understanding of it, whether we want to engage in it, to teach it or to intervene to promote more of it. Medicine, however, like enterprise, is an applied science and is not deterministic like physics. Instead medical understanding has developed through a series of relatively small steps rather than through large leaps such as that offered by Newton.

In this book, Chapter 2 argues that the policies applied in many countries to promote entrepreneurship use similar methods to try to achieve their aims, and Chapter 3 indicates some of the models of the influences on entrepreneurship which would seem to support those methods. Thus, like the practice of medicine 200 years ago, there is a common approach to the promotion of entrepreneurship backed by articulated theory apparently based on observation. However Chapter 4 presents evidence that these entrepreneurship policies are not working, which could mean that our understanding of entrepreneurship is only as good as was our earlier understanding of medicine. However, if like the 'humours' model in medicine which led to the prescription of bloodletting, our current models of enterprise appear not to lead to working solutions, that does not mean that alternative models are readily available. As in medicine, it might take a while to discover better ways. This book is, however, an attempt to explore where those better ways might lie.

It is, though, relevant to highlight one difference between the practice of bloodletting as a cure for ill patients and the promotion of enterprise as a cure for poor economies. When bloodletting was widely practised, fevers, with their associated high temperatures and sweating, were recognised as the signs of an illness and bloodletting was supposed to reduce them and thus to restore a patient to a healthy state. In the same way a lack of entrepreneurship is seen as a sign of a weakness in an economy and enterprise policies are designed therefore to increase entrepreneurship in order to restore economic health. But, just as bloodletting did not itself reduce temperatures and sweating, so too current enterprise polices do not increase entrepreneurship. In the case of bloodletting the cure was often applied and the level of a patient's blood was actually reduced, but it is thought that reducing the amount of blood did not cure the patient. In contrast, in the case of enterprise, this book will review evidence that policies have not increased levels of entrepreneurship. Therefore in the latter case we cannot actually see if enterprise works as a cure because the cure has not been applied to the patients. That suggests that it is in the administration of the prescribed cure that the problem currently lies and that it is our understanding that is inadequate This book does not therefore try to argue that enterprise is not the right cure, just that it is not being delivered and therefore its effectiveness as a cure is not yet established.

The development of wisdom

To respond to this challenge it will be necessary, as a first step, to recognise that our current knowledge of entrepreneurship might be limited, or even wrong, because without such a motivation we are unlikely to look for improvements. We would also need to appreciate how knowledge is developed.

> Where is the wisdom we have lost in knowledge? Where is the knowledge we have lost in information?
>
> T. S. Eliot – *The Rock*

Today T. S. Eliot might possibly have asked: 'Where is the information we have lost in data?' This book does not seek to introduce new data on enterprise. It does however try to look at some of the information that is already available to see if anything new can be learnt from it, in the hope that that might, in turn, lead to the development of new knowledge and even wisdom. Further, like the terms enterprise and entrepreneurship, terms such as knowledge and wisdom are not always used with the same precise definitions. In some situations, it seems, knowledge refers to no more than acquired information, but in other situations it indicates a development from information in order to understand what that information might be telling us. Nevertheless Figure 1.1 presents one attempt to suggest the possible links between data, information, knowledge and wisdom, based on different levels of understanding.

This path of understanding is not easy, it may take some time, and it may require different people for different stages. The original

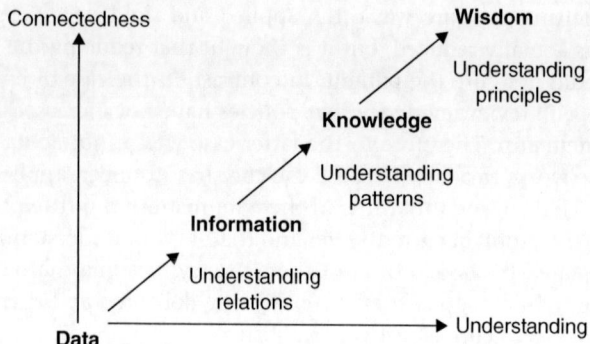

Figure 1.1 The transition route from data to wisdom
Source: G. Bellinger, D. Castro and A. Mills, *Data, Information, Knowledge and Wisdom*, 2004. Available at www.systemswiki.org/index.php?title=Data,_Information,_Knowledge_ and_ Wisdom (Accessed 15 April 2010).

researcher who obtained the data does not have to be the same person who eventually converts the outcome into knowledge or even wisdom. For instance it could be argued that it was the data on planetary motion provided by Tycho Brahe's observations, informed by Copernicus's understanding of relationships placing the sun at the centre of the solar system, which provided information for Kepler. He, in turn, using an understanding of patterns, demonstrated that the paths of planets were ellipses with the sun at one focus. It was to this knowledge that Newton then applied his understanding of principles and produced his inverse square law of gravitational attraction, which, whether it was considered to be wisdom or not, was at least a scientific law good enough to get men to the moon and back, although Einstein eventually improved on even Newton's understanding.

The declared scientific method for developing new knowledge is to start with a theory and then to test it by checking if the results of experiments conform to what the theory says they should be. If they are, then the theory can be accepted as at least a workable basis for progression and, in some cases, even a scientific 'law'. However if, at any stage, the results of the experiments do not agree with the theory, then the theory is disproved and a new theory is sought which does explain the observations. Thus theories are never proved, they are only on probation or disproved. Sometimes they are disproved because a new theory has suggested particular experiments which disprove the old one, or sometimes it just becomes clear that the old theory does not conform to reality. In the former case there is already a new theory to guide practical applications, but in the latter case it is not so simple. New theories are not generally available to order and a period of exploration may be necessary before something better can be found. Often new insight will be needed, possibly derived from an understanding of where the old theory went wrong. But, whatever the process, developing a workable new theory can take time and until it happens, the old theory may continue to be used on the grounds that some guidance is better than none, even if it is known to be inadequate.

This book and its layout

This book is not an attempt to say that the current approach has been proved to be completely wrong and utterly without relevance. It does suggest, however, that, if there is a reasonable chance that at least some current received wisdom might be wrong, then it should be worth looking for alternatives now, rather than waiting for more proof which will probably only come at the stage by which we realise 'we should have done this a long time ago'.

The book does not try to prove completely and irrefutably all the points it makes or to indicate all the evidence for them. It does try however to provide sufficient supporting evidence to indicate why there might be a *prima facie* case worthy of further consideration.

Similarly the book discusses policy implications, but it does not try to say what new policy should be. That is not primarily because policy-making is difficult but because producing new ideas is a different task from that of converting ideas into policy, and it may be helpful to reflect on, and to test, the ideas produced before conversion is attempted. The book does try however to suggest some ideas on which new policy might be based.

The book attempts to explore theories of enterprise and entrepreneurship in three stages. Following this introductory chapter, Part I considers the current models of the influences on enterprise. It looks at government agenda and their different aspects and at the various models on which current policies might be based. It then examines the evidence for the effectiveness of those policies, or rather for their lack of effectiveness, and at other evidence about levels of enterprise. Part II tries to explore the problem indicated by the ineffectiveness of current policies. It looks at enterprise, or entrepreneurship, from different perspectives, and it also considers the nature–nurture debate and other aspects of the nature of enterprise. Part III presents an alternative model of enterprise. It considers enterprise as a choice of means, not an end, and it looks at the sort of factors which might influence that choice. In particular it considers social influence and how that might relate to the concept of social capital. It reviews the possible factors identified and the extent to which they might explain the apparent variations in rates of enterprise. Finally it considers what the next step might be in this continuing exploration.

References

1. From the introduction to R. Harding, *Inaugural Report to the World Entrepreneurship Summit January 2008* (Eastbourne: Delta Economics, 2008), p. 3.
2. R. Harding, op. cit., p. 7.
3. European Enterprise Awards, http://ec.europa.eu/enterprise/entrepreneurship/smes/awards, accessed 24 February 2009.
4. S. Moalem, *Survival of the Sickest* (London: HarperCollins, 2008), and other reports.
5. D. Birch, *The Job Generation Process* (Cambridge, MA: MIT Programme on Neighborhood and Regional Change, 1979).
6. 'Towards an "Enterprising" Culture – A Challenge for Education and Training', *OECD/CERI Educational Monograph*, No. 4 (1989), p. 7.
7. *Entrepreneurship and Education Action Plan*, a joint plan developed by the Department of Enterprise, Trade and Investment, the Department of Education and the Department of Employment and Learning, published in March 2003, p. 5.
8. L. Stevenson, paper presented at *Fostering Entrepreneurship*, an Invest Northern Ireland Seminar held on 14 March 2007 at Narrow Water Castle (report by S. Bridge available on www.isbe.org.uk, accessed 16 October 2008).
9. Based on S. Bridge, K. O'Neill and F. Martin, *Understanding Enterprise, Entrepreneurship and Small Business* (Basingstoke: Palgrave Macmillan, 2009), pp. 13–14.
10. A. A. Gibb, 'SME Policy, Academic Research and the Growth of Ignorance, Mythical Concepts, Myths, Assumptions, Rituals and Confusions', *International Small Business Journal*, Vol. 18, No. 3, 2000, pp. 13–35.
11. Small Business Service, *A Government Action Plan for Small Business* (London: Department for Trade and Industry, 2004).
12. Small Business Service, op. cit., pp. 22 and 21.
13. G. Bannock, *The Economics and Management of Small Business* (London: Routledge, 2005), p. 194.
14. R. Porter, *Blood and Guts: A Short History of Medicine* (London: Penguin Press, 2002).

Part I
The Current Models and Approaches

Following the introduction in Chapter 1, Part I explores current approaches to the promotion of enterprise and the apparent validity of the models which support them.

Chapter 2 starts with a look at government agenda. Many governments pursue enterprise, entrepreneurship and/or small business policies, and there is a lot in common, not just between the aims of those policies, but between the methods and programmes used to implement them. That raises the questions of why those methods are followed and what suggests that they will achieve the desired results.

Chapter 3 looks at some of the theories and models that have been advanced to indicate or explain the enterprise process. It considers the extent to which the models are consistent with each other and with current policy. It suggests that much policy, if not actually based on these theories and models of enterprise, is influenced by them or is at least consistent with them. That therefore suggests that these models provide a theoretical basis for expecting that current policy should work.

Chapter 4 looks at the effectiveness of that policy and whether it is succeeding as the current theory would suggest. It finds that, on the contrary, the evidence suggests that much enterprise policy is not effective and levels of enterprise are not rising despite many attempts to encourage and support it. That, in turn, suggests that the current models of enterprise do not work and the chapter considers other findings about enterprise which also appear to be inconsistent with the models. Thus it seems that, in this field, the facts do not fit the theory.

2
Government Agenda

Illustration 2.1 Examples of the prominence of enterprise and entrepreneurship in government policy (emphasis added)

'The policy programme for employment, **entrepreneurship** and worklife supports the [Finnish] Government's goals of securing ... economic growth, employment and the financial basis of the welfare society.'[1]

'For ten years **enterprise** has been one of the five core drivers of the [UK] Government's strategy to lift the productivity of the economy.'[2]

'Following the spirit of the Lisbon objective, the Danish government has set an ambitious goal in the area of **entrepreneurship**; Denmark is to be a part of the European entrepreneurship elite by the year 2010 and among the countries with the highest share of high-growth start-ups by the year 2015.'[3]

'We laid out our long-term economic plan in *Advantage Canada*. It identified five Canadian objectives – related to tax-reduction, debt reduction, **entrepreneurship**, knowledge in the workforce, and infrastructure – that will help Canadians improve their quality of life and succeed on the world stage.'[4]

As Chapter 1 and Illustration 2.1 indicate, many governments pursue enterprise and/or entrepreneurship ambitions. Also, as Chapter 1 indicates, many of these policies may initially have been driven by a desire for more jobs at a time of relatively high unemployment, but, as unemployment subsequently reduced, the policies were continued for other economic reasons. Establishing the reasons for government policy is not always easy because there can be many components to a policy framework (see Figure 2.1 and Table 2.1), not all of which may be identified or declared, and the fundamental reasons (or policy drivers) for a having a policy can be different from the specified goals (or policy objectives) and from the declared justification for intervention (or policy rationale).

Thus a government might adopt an enterprise policy because it feels the need to do something to address unemployment, and the declared objective of the policy might therefore be to stimulate the creation of more businesses, in the belief or hope that those businesses will then create jobs. The justification given for the intervention might however be to address market failure because that will allow the policy to pass an economic acceptability test. In such circumstances it seems that market failure is usually an excuse for intervention rather than the reason for wanting to intervene in the first place.

Enterprise policy drivers and objectives

Figure 2.1 presents a possible framework to show the different components, and the links between them, that might together comprise government policy in a particular area. These components are described in slightly more detail in Table 2.1.

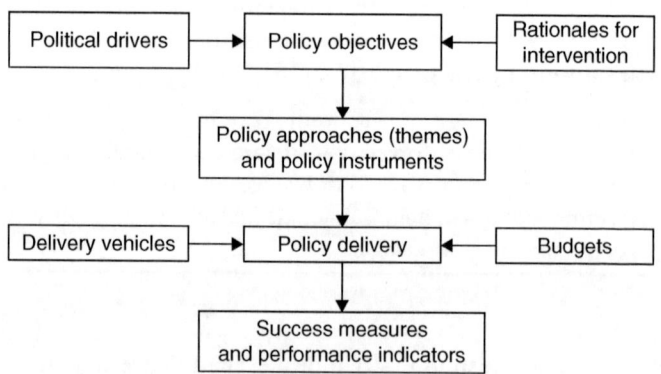

Figure 2.1 A diagram of a policy framework
Source: Based on S. Bridge, B. Murtagh and K. O'Neill, *Understanding the Social Economy and the Third Sector* (Basingstoke: Palgrave Macmillan, 2009), p. 227.

Table 2.1 The possible components of a policy framework

Political drivers
Political drivers can be interpreted as the overall political reason for having a particular policy, although this is rarely highlighted.

Policy objectives
Policy objectives are the overall aim(s) of the policy in question and they can be stated qualitatively or quantitatively. Sometimes, however, the overall aim is described in a vision or mission statement while the term 'objectives' is instead applied to a set of quantified targets for the policy.

Rationales for policy intervention
Although a government may identify certain objectives, intervention to achieve them may, overall, be counter-productive unless there is a good justification for it. The justification frequently used (whether adequately assessed or otherwise) is that of 'market failure' in that, without intervention, deficiencies in the normal working of the market will preclude the desired outcomes. (But see also Illustration 8.2.)

Policy approaches and instruments
To achieve the objectives of enterprise intervention a number of broad approaches are generally available. One (sometimes referred to as an entrepreneurship approach) concentrates on the creation of an environment favourable to the establishment and growth of enterprise and the other (sometimes referred to as a small business approach) supports the actual start-up and growth of individual enterprises. Within each approach a number of specific instruments can then be used. These approaches need not be mutually exclusive and both can be seen in the policy instruments in the UK. (See also Illustration 2.2.)

Delivery vehicles
In order to undertake the work of implementing its policy, a government needs delivery vehicles: agents which will undertake the work required to implement the policy.

Budget
Implementing the policy is also likely to require a budget to pay for it.

Policy delivery
Having put all that together, policy delivery should then take place. The effectiveness of that delivery can then be assessed through success measures and/or performance indicators.

Success measures and performance indicators
In order to be able to determine if and when the policy achieves its objectives, and therefore accomplishes its mission, actual performance needs to be measured and compared with pre-determined overall trend indicators and appropriate performance targets for each policy instrument.

Source: Based on S. Bridge, B. Murtagh and K. O'Neill, *Understanding the Social Economy and the Third Sector* (Basingstoke: Palgrave Macmillan, 2009), pp. 226–30.

Illustration 2.2 'Small Business', 'Entrepreneurship' and 'Enterprise' policy

> There can be at least three distinct policy approaches which some people now distinguish with the labels 'small business', 'entrepreneurship' and 'enterprise'. However this terminology is sometimes used loosely and/or interchangeably so these labels are not always consistently applied. Nevertheless the approaches which have been identified are:
>
> - *Small business policies*, which are policies for stimulating growth of already-established small business, variations of which have also been called a 'growth' or 'business growth' policy and a 'backing winners' policy. This sort of policy tends to focus on the businesses and what will help them to grow, not the entrepreneurs behind them.
> - *Entrepreneurship policies*, which are policies for encouraging and facilitating more people to take up self-employment. These policies are centred on people and on what will persuade or help them to start businesses, although they can be referred to as 'business start' or 'business birth-rate' policies.
> - *Enterprise policies*, which are policies for encouraging enterprise in its broad sense, much, but not all, of which may be manifest as new business starts. These policies are clearly focused on people, both as individuals and in groups, and seek to develop skills and attitudes likely to assist people to be more successful in any chosen career or endeavour.
>
> The description 'enterprise' may also be applied to policies which try to promote both entrepreneurship and small business growth, and to the development of the business sector in general. However entrepreneurship and small business policies require different approaches so, it has been suggested, policies which try to cover both are likely to fail to do either.

Source: Based on S. Bridge, K. O'Neill and F. Martin, *Understanding Enterprise, Entrepreneurship and Small Business* (Basingstoke: Palgrave Macmillan, 2009), p. 392.

Policy drivers

Illustration 2.3 indicates the varied nature of the evolution of enterprise policy which has rarely been presented in as clear a fashion as Figure 2.1 and Table 2.1 suggest. Nevertheless some drivers of enterprise

> Small and Medium-sized Enterprises (SMEs) are the backbone of Europe's economy. ... They are Europe's net job creators ... and are a guarantee of social cohesion and stability. SMEs play an important role for European growth ... (and) ... a major role in the innovation process.
>
> *Handbook on Community State Aid Rules for SMEs*[5]

and/or entrepreneurship policy can on occasion be identified or inferred. Generally the drivers are the benefits which the proposers of the policy expect or hope to gain from implementing it. These desired benefits could include one or more of the following:

- achieving economic growth
- increasing employment/reducing unemployment
- developing a more resilient economy and/or coping with economic uncertainty
- addressing/reducing/removing disadvantage and deprivation
- getting (re)elected

The following quotes indicate that each of these benefits has at some time overtly or apparently been sought in the UK and other governments' policies:

Economic growth:
'Enterprise is a talent we admire in individuals and applaud in companies. In a competitive global market, it is also a vital attribute for nations. For ten years enterprise has been one of the five core drivers of the Government strategy to lift the productivity of the economy.'[6]

Increasing employment/reducing unemployment:
'People on unemployment or incapacity benefits are heavily concentrated in deprived areas. These areas also have far lower levels of self-employment, and we need to encourage people to see self-employment as a viable alternative. Self-employment may provide opportunities for those with work-limiting disabilities.'[7]

Entrepreneurship as part of the response to economic challenge:
'The Prime Minister has today announced that he will establish a National Economic Council to provide a new approach to coordinating economic policies across government. Britain is facing immense

economic challenges ... The National Economic Council will work to help people and businesses to deal with the current economic uncertainties. ... The Council will meet frequently to assess:

- the implications of the ongoing challenges in the financial markets for the wider economy globally and nationally;
- the latest developments in global commodity markets and their impact on the UK economy;
- our objective to promote sustainable and secure energy supplies;
- the impact of global economic developments on the skills and employment that the UK needs;
- *the remaining barriers to entrepreneurship, innovation, and the opportunities for small business growth;*
- our housing and planning needs; and
- the impact across every part of the UK.'[8] (italics added)

Addressing/reducing/removing disadvantage and deprivation:
'Enterprise can be a route out of disadvantage and deprivation but we need a better understanding of what works.'[9]

'The government will promote enterprise in more deprived areas and among the disadvantaged groups that are heavily represented there, to help raise enterprise levels in the UK as whole ... Our understanding of success around enterprise in deprived areas is best informed by the self-employment rate.'[10]

'Since 2006 around £150 million has been committed to implement proposals from England's most deprived local authorities to support enterprise initiatives. A further £280 million will be committed between 2008 and 2011.'[11]

Getting re-elected:
'As a number of writers have pointed out, there has been a paucity of sophisticated, systematic evaluations of specific interventions to enhance the achievements of small businesses. The result is that many uncertainties arise in connection with the usefulness of various policies. These uncertainties permit, or even encourage, a political dimension of policy to develop. If actions appear to look good and there is no clear evidence for what they achieve, or fail to achieve, then the actions may be pursued, not for the results they bring, but for the credit that applying them will earn for those responsible.

This is politically motivated behaviour, and it is particularly prevalent when an objective is desired but its achievement cannot easily be measured. These conditions apply in small business support. There is a considerable willingness to support small businesses, combined with a lack of information on what really works. In these circumstances, intervention, if at least superficially justified, may actually be engaged in for political reasons, connected with the desire for recognition or advancement by the people involved, rather than because of any real desire to promote enterprise.'[12]

'Expressed at its crudest the argument is that ... the small business owner is significantly more likely to vote Conservative than to vote Labour. Some public policies towards small firms adopted by Conservative administrations ... will directly benefit those individuals who are currently business owners and who therefore are likely to be Conservative voters.'[13]

Policy objectives

The objectives are the things that a policy might try to do because they should in turn lead to the desired benefits. They are the targeted outputs which should then deliver desired outcomes and, for enterprise and/or entrepreneurship policies, they might include:

- Jobs – because the availability of more jobs should help to reduce unemployment.
- Business start-ups – because they should lead to the creation of greater wealth and employment. Often there is a policy focus in particular on high-tech, global and/or targeted sector business start-ups as they are thought to lead to the greatest economic contribution and therefore the best returns for intervention effort.
- Business growth – because it too should lead to more wealth and/or employment.
- Innovation – because it can be a source of ideas for new businesses or of new opportunities for established businesses.
- Entrepreneurship – because it should lead to more businesses and, in turn, to more wealth and/or jobs.
- Social enterprise and/or social capital – because they are sometimes thought to be particularly relevant to deducing deprivation and/or social exclusion.*
- Inward investment/foreign direct investment (FDI) – because that too can lead to more jobs and earnings.

Note: *But see the end of Chapter 7 in S. Bridge, B. Murtagh and K. O'Neill, *Understanding the Social Economy and the Third Sector* (Basingstoke: Palgrave Macmillan, 2009), which suggests that this might not always be the case.

Illustration 2.3 Stevenson's summary of policy evolution

Policy evolution:

Pre-1950s – twentieth-century industrial era policy:

- Assumption that a small number of large manufacturing firms was the major source of economic growth and would produce a 'trickle-down' effect.
- Government policy focus on national firm champions.
- Policies sometimes actually discouraged the emergence of new firms.
- The roles of small firms, of new firms and of the entrepreneur were overlooked.
- Stimulation of entrepreneurial activity was at best a by-product of industrial policies.

1950s – SME policies start to emerge in some countries:

- Post-war – stimulate the economy, enable small firms.
- Small Business Act 1953 (US).
- Access to finance – small business guarantee schemes and banks.

1960 – protect SMEs, level the playing field:

- Competition and anti-trust policies.

1970s – small business support measures:

- Bolton White Paper on small business (UK, 1971).
- Governments start focusing on upgrading SME management skills.
- Early small business enterprise centres.

1980s – beginning of the era of small business:

- Influence of Birch study (1979).
- Rise in self-employment rates.
- Early emergence of enterprise/entrepreneurship policy.
- White Paper on regulatory burden on small business (UK, 1985).

1990s – policy shifts:

- Storey (1994) and a policy focus on growth firms.
- More governments move to address regulatory burdens.

Mid-1990s – beginning of the era of entrepreneurship:

- High levels of unemployment in OECD countries.
- Growing research evidence of the link between new firms, job creation, innovation and productivity improvements.
- EU/OECD 1998 – issue papers on 'fostering entrepreneurship'.

2000s – almost every country seeks to become a more entrepreneurial society:

- Promotion of entrepreneurship by organisations like OECD, EU, UN.
- 'Unleashing Entrepreneurship' report, UN.
- Entrepreneurship policies more evident:
  – SME policies insufficient to drive entrepreneurship rates.
  – New policy formulation, programme measures.
  – Holistic policy frameworks.
- Growing interest in 'innovative' entrepreneurship policies.
- Thinking about policy convergence!

An emerging policy imperative:

- New firms are needed to replace exiting firms and to replace jobs lost due to exiting and downsizing firms, and for product innovation.
- Of the businesses that will be operating in ten year's time, 75–80 per cent do not exist today.
- Most of those businesses will be started by people who don't even know they are going to be the entrepreneurs of tomorrow and will start their business driven by some form of 'inspiration' or 'desperation'.
- They are largely unprepared with little know-how and experience in venturing: most will *not* have business degrees.

Source: Based on L. Stevenson, presentation to 35th International Small Business Congress, Belfast, November 2008.

The methods used – policy approaches and instruments

Government interest in promoting enterprise occurs at a number of levels:

- International level: For instance, the EU has enterprise policies.
- National level: Where it might be most obvious.
- Regional government level: For instance, in the UK, there are, or have been, enterprise policies for Northern Ireland, Scotland and Wales.
- Local authority level: Also in the UK some enterprise support is delegated to local councils.

This section considers a sample of the methods (the policy themes and/or instruments) that have been suggested and/or used at international, national, regional and local level.

International policy

The EU is one example of government at an international level which has an enterprise policy, implemented at EU level and through national governments. 'Through the Lisbon Strategy, the Community aims to foster economic dynamism and help create more and better jobs' and the aim of its enterprise policy is 'to make Europe an attractive place to invest and work in'.[14] For this its priorities have included:

- Promoting entrepreneurship by encouraging business creation and supporting SMEs during their start-up and development.
- Promoting innovation – following up technological developments, new product designs and new ways to market.
- Promoting better access to funding, support networks and programmes.
- Promoting simplification of the regulatory and administrative environment.

The OECD is another international body which has promoted enterprise and entrepreneurship. One of its working papers suggests a framework for addressing and measuring entrepreneurship, which is based (at least in part) on work done by the Danish government (which is summarised in Chapter 3). This framework is illustrated in Figure 2.2 and includes not only possible determinants of entrepreneurship, but also their possible areas of impact. However, as also noted in Chapter 3, the intention is that further analysis should be done to confirm the significance of each supposed determinant and, if necessary, to remove from the framework any determinant whose impact seems to be marginal.

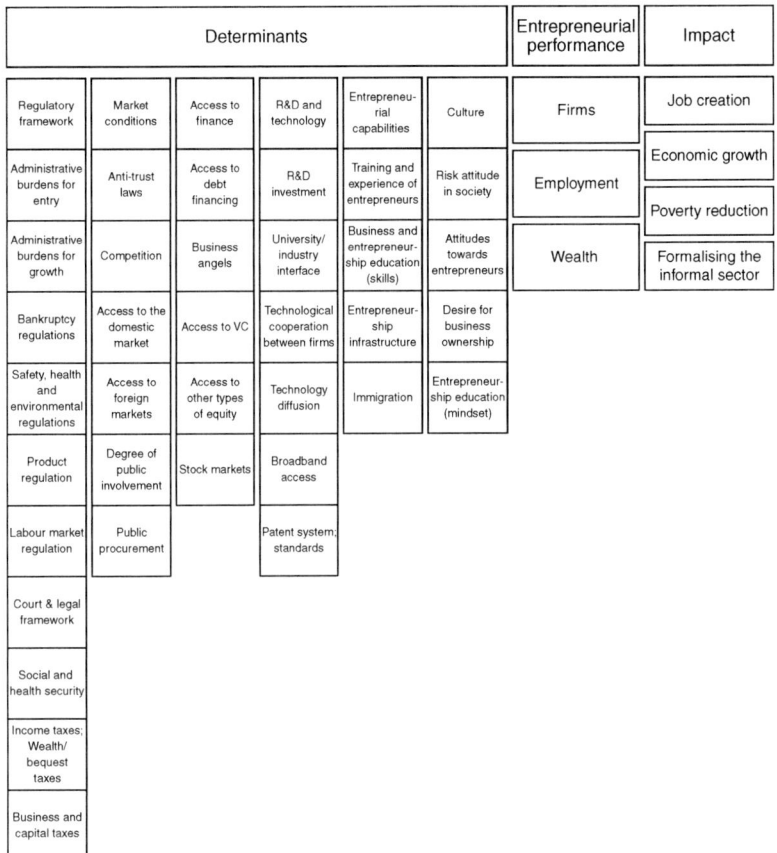

Figure 2.2 The OECD/EUROSTAT framework for entrepreneurship indicators
Source: N. Ahmad and A. Hoffman, 'A Framework for Addressing and Measuring Entrepreneurship', *OECD Statistics Working Papers*, 2008/2, OECD Publishing, doi:10.1787/243160627270, p. 20.

National policy

The UK government has probably been pursuing enterprise strategies longer than many. A summary of its SME policies in the early 1990s was provided in 1994 by David Storey:[15]

1. Macro policies (for instance interest rates and taxation)
2. Deregulation and simplification (including cutting 'red tape' and legislative exemptions)
3. Sectoral and problem-specific policies (for example, for high-tech firms, rural enterprises, community enterprises and ethnic businesses)

28 *Rethinking Enterprise Policy*

4. Finance assistance (including the Enterprise Investment Scheme, the Loan Guarantee Scheme, the Enterprise Allowance Scheme and grants)
5. Indirect assistance (such as information and advice, training, mentoring and consultancy)
6. Relationships (Small Firms Division and policy formulation)

The evolution of those policies in the 2000s is shown in the UK government's enterprise strategy of 2008 which was based around five enablers:

1. Culture: developing 'a culture in which talent can be unlocked and flourish'.
2. Knowledge and skills: ensuring 'that individuals and businesses have access to and are able to develop the best possible knowledge and skills to support the growth of their business'.
3. Access to finance: 'ensuring that people starting or growing a business have access to the appropriate level of finance'.
4. Regulatory framework: a 'targeted net reduction in the administrative burden of regulation'.
5. Business innovation: 'to promote and incentivise greater investment in research and development'.[16]

A review of recent entrepreneurship policy in the Netherlands recognised that 'entrepreneurship is the foundation upon which the economy of the Netherlands is built' and indicates that the Dutch Ministry of Economic Affairs has included among its goals 'encouraging more entrepreneurs in the Netherlands and supporting a higher quality of entrepreneurship'.[17] The report also indicates that, to achieve this, policies have focussed 'on the following fields:

- Financing;
- Technology and innovation
- Internationalisation;
- Education;
- Regulatory simplification.[18]

Regional and local policy

There are many regional and local administrations which support some form of enterprise initiatives, although often this is tied in with national policy. In Europe some of the supposedly better initiatives are nominated for the European Enterprise Award for national, regional and local authorities supporting entrepreneurship. The 13 initiatives shortlisted for the 2008 award[19] were mainly regional or local level initiatives and the methods they employed included:

- An entrepreneurship-awareness raising team made up of teachers on secondment
- Cost-free advice for women thinking of starting businesses
- A range of support services for independent entrepreneurs wishing to settle in the target area
- Networking for students and workshops with experienced entrepreneurs
- Finding placements for unemployed people
- An effective community service organisation
- Reducing statistical reporting requirements
- Using culture and folklore to provide a unique tourism experience
- A social enterprise based on traditional crafts
- Providing entrepreneurs with access to tailored professional advice
- Helping young entrepreneurs to get started
- Attracting companies developing IT services to provide employment for graduates
- Regenerating a seaside town

Other examples of local and regional initiatives are given in Cases 2.1 and 2.2 and a recent successor to the initiative described Case 2.2 is to be found in the Accelerating Entrepreneurship Strategy of Invest Northern Ireland. According to the strategy brochure, 'Stimulating higher levels of innovation and entrepreneurship in Northern Ireland is essential if we are to create a more vibrant and balanced society. This strategy proposes a framework that builds on existing achievements and support for entrepreneurs. It also aims to provide vigorous encouragement for a greater number of entrepreneurs to become involved in sustainable new business starts.'[20] (The measurement of the effectiveness of this strategy is also the subject of Case 4.1).

Case 2.1 The city of Montreal

In 2006, believing that it needed a more dynamic economy and that entrepreneurship offered an appropriate economic development strategy, the city of Montreal established a working committee with a mandate to:

- promote entrepreneurial culture,
- foster venture creation,
- provide better support for entrepreneurial success, and

- achieve a better fit between the needs of entrepreneurs and the supply of entrepreneurship services.

The committee included members from regional government, city government, academic research and support agencies. In 2007, after extensive consultation, including a 'day of reflection on entrepreneurship in Montreal', the committee presented its recommendations for a nine-point entrepreneurship development strategy and stressed that there was an urgent need for action for what would be a long-term process.

The project was intended to serve as an example of the type of structure that can be set up to develop entrepreneurship within an urban community and to show what a community can do to take charge of its own development.

The nine points in the strategy were:

1. **Promote and strengthen the entrepreneurial culture:**
   - Declaration for an Entrepreneurial Quebec
   - General public and students
   - Spokespeople
   - An event to acknowledge the efforts of support providers
   - The Quebec Entrepreneurship Contest and the Youth Entrepreneurship Challenge
   - School/business partnerships
   - An Entrepreneurial Culture Day
   - The Entrepreneurship Montreal website

2. **Encourage and develop spin-off practices:**
   - Promote spin-offs among organisations
   - Specialist moderators
   - Encourage the creation of formal spin-off programmes in businesses

3. **Foster the creation of innovative technological businesses:**
   - Support services
   - Financing
   - Technology spin-offs
   - Young Scientists Programme

4. **Develop and consolidate entrepreneurial skills:**
   - Charter of Entrepreneurial Skills

- Reference and evaluation tool for training and needs
- Pilot projects for training within the network

5. **Improve support practices and access to funding:**
   - Joint promotion of financial tools
   - Membership of financial networks
   - Syndication of funds
   - Consolidation of entrepreneurship support

6. **Enhance and strengthen business networks:**
   - Awareness and promotion activities
   - Plato feasibility study
   - Entrepreneur training project based on peer learning

7. **Encourage commitment from the business community:**
   - Commitment, a social goal
   - Creation of outlets for commitment
   - Involve private sector resources
   - Promote mentoring
   - Set up a Montreal business mentoring group
   - Set up private foundations

8. **Adjust services to special needs:**
   - Young entrepreneurs (financing, information and reception)
   - Women entrepreneurs (promotion, venture creation conditions)
   - Immigrants (service adjustments)
   - Social entrepreneurs (awareness)

9. **Reinforce the network of support services:**
   - A network of support providers
   - Use of new technology
   - Ability to meet the needs of entrepreneurs

Source: Based on a presentation by Louis Jacques Filion at the International Small Business Congress (ISBC) Belfast, November 2008.

Case 2.2 An earlier enterprise initiative in Northern Ireland

The following summary is comprised of extracts from a description, written in 1993, of Northern Ireland's enterprise strategy which was developed in the late 1980s. (See also Case 3.1 for some of the background to the development of this strategy.)

Developing enterprise in Northern Ireland

Background – is Northern Ireland enterprising?

'Northern Ireland has not had [a] small business background. Typically there have been three main sources of employment. Someone's parents and grandparents are much more likely to have worked, if they had work, for a large business in an industry such as textiles, engineering or shipbuilding. Alternatively they may have been employed on the land where many people had a subsistence existence on their own small holding which was very self-contained and not basically a trading business. Also, rather more recently, a relatively high proportion of the (working) population have been employed in the public sector. Taking the initiative themselves in the commercial world is not something in which many people have had experience or role models. Northern Ireland has not been enterprising, or at least not to the extent now needed.'

The Task – more Enterprise

'*The enterprise task*: The Enterprise Taskforce felt it was counterproductive to argue whether, on an absolute scale, Northern Ireland had an enterprising culture or not. There was however agreement that it needed to be more enterprising than it was. Their task was then to suggest ways of achieving this. They were not given a definition of what enterprise was and they decided that for their purposes it could be defined as 'the propensity of individuals to create jobs, for themselves and for others, by engaging in and developing a legitimate activity which will earn them a living or by developing their existing jobs'.

'*The proposed plan*: The basic approach proposed was twofold:

(a) To campaign to improve awareness and attitudes to enterprise.
(b) To promote the availability of an appropriate range of assistance for those who were thinking of their own business. NB: The assistance was seen as supporting the attitude change sought, rather than being the solution in its own right.'

What has been done

'In many respects Northern Ireland's efforts to address this task are still at an early stage. Many things have been started and some of the structure may have been established. It now needs time to develop, to take effect and to produce results. It is therefore too early to try to measure ultimate changes, but initial surveys were done on attitudes to provide a basis for assessing change in the future. It is however possible to indicate some of the key actions taken and describe the reason for them.'

'*Local enterprise agency network*: A network of local enterprise agencies (LEAs) has been established. ... (They have) property built or adapted to provide suitable nursery premises for small businesses ... (and) a manager to provide support and advice.'

'*Pre-start support*: The LEAs have been encouraged and assisted to offer ideas workshops, counselling and basic business skills training in their localities' (and grants were also available).'

'*The enterprise network*: The concept has thus arisen of the enterprise network in Northern Ireland. This is generally seen as a term to include the relevant government agencies, the LEAs, the business faculties in the academic institutes, the small business advisers of the banks and a wide range of other bodies and individuals who are interested in helping to promote enterprise. This again helps to place the initiative in the fabric of society.'

'*Enterprising Northern Ireland*: To assist with the task of promoting the concept of enterprise a campaign called 'Enterprising Northern Ireland' was launched.'

'*Other initiatives*: This work has been supported by a range of other initiatives including:'

- The education sector – 'to help get the message across in schools and colleges.'
- Community business – 'extra assistance ... to start community businesses.'
- Head Start – 'an annual small business competition on local commercial television.'

Source: Based on a Local Enterprise Development Unit (LEDU) briefing paper.

Comparing the methods

The summaries and cases above present just a few of the available examples of enterprise policies pursued by governments at international,

national, regional and local levels. Nevertheless they serve to support the view that such policy recipes are mainly assembled from a common set of components such as:

- Finance programmes (including loans and grants)
- Premises programmes (including incubators and nurseries)
- Advice and mentoring programmes
- Business training programmes (often teaching the business plan)
- Marketing programmes, including exporting assistance
- Management development programmes
- R&D and innovation promotion programmes
- Start-up programmes
- Awareness raising programmes (including TV advertising and road shows)
- Targeted approaches (for instance, focusing on specific industry sectors or on the promotion of exporting)
- And (although it may not be admitted) just wanting to be seen to be doing something

Thus there appears to be a lot in common between the methods selected for different programmes and in different countries, and the emphasis now seems to be more on how those methods should be put together for delivery than on how new and better methods might be identified to supplement or replace the current provision.

Putting the policy together

While the initial focus for enterprise and entrepreneurship policies might have been on what methods might be employed to promote enterprise, it has increasingly been acknowledged that the methods alone are not enough and that, to be effective, a policy has to apply them in the right way. That means, for instance according to Stevenson, that a good entrepreneurship policy should have:

- 'A clear high level statement about the importance of business dynamics to economic renewal and growth.
- A plan for accelerating entrepreneurship activity presented in one policy framework.
- A rationale, objectives, explicit targets, set policy lines of action, policy and programme priorities and measures.
- Reinforcement in other government policy documents.

- Performance indicators (e.g. for improved culture, climate, conditions for new entries, entrepreneurial activity levels) and quantified targets.
- A specific budget allocation.
- Clear responsibility for the implementation of the policy framework.'[21]

Following that recipe for a good policy might seem logical but two reasons might be suggested for why the eventual outcomes might still be disappointing. One reason is that it is not always easy to follow the recipe because, while they may be simple to state, the conditions are not always easy to apply. For example, getting the appropriate high-level endorsement and securing reinforcement across different government departments require a strong commitment to the policy from the top, which might not always be forthcoming. Therefore, despite its apparent clarity and logic, the recipe is not often followed. On this basis Stevenson has identified just Denmark, Finland, the Netherlands and the UK as countries which have holistic entrepreneurship policies covering all these components.

The second reason for possible failure, however, is that Stevenson's list could be said to put the emphasis more on doing things in the right way than on doing the right things since the list does not specify that the methods to be used should be ones that work. Does good quality just mean that the components have been properly put together or should it also mean that they are the right components? It might be supposed that this goes without saying and that these methods are being selected because they work. But that might not be the case and Chapter 3 therefore explores the models of enterprise and entrepreneurship that guide, explain or are at least consistent with the policies that are followed in order to see why these methods might have become the common ones and what logic there might be behind their selection.

Summary

Many governments want to promote entrepreneurship and in consequence have policies/programmes to promote entrepreneurship. The analysis above suggests that they do this for broadly similar reasons, and they apply similar methods in trying to achieve their aims. Their policies/programmes thus have a lot in common. Some, but not all, of them are good programmes, if good means properly put together. However that does not necessarily mean that they are using the right components.

Chapter 3 therefore looks at the way the methods have been selected and at the rationale for them.

References

1. From a resolution adopted by the Finnish Government on 5 December 2007 at www.tem.fi, accessed 17 February 2009.
2. BERR (now part of BIS), *Enterprise: Unlocking the UK's Talent* (London: HM Treasury, March 2008), p. 3.
3. A. Hoffmann and H. M. Gabr, *A General Policy Framework for Entrepreneurship* (Denmark: FORA, April 2006), at www.foranet.dk, accessed 17 February 2009.
4. Industry Canada, *Business Plan 2008–2009*, at www.ic.gc.ca, accessed 17 February 2009.
5. *Handbook on Community State Aid Rules for SMEs*, at http://europa.eu/competition/state_aid/studies_reports/sme_handbook.pdf, accessed 15 February 2009.
6. From the Foreword by Gordon Brown, Alistair Darling and John Hutton to BERR, op. cit.
7. BERR, op. cit., p. 34.
8. Press release dated 3 October 2008, at www.number10.gov.uk, accessed 13 October 2008).
9. Small Business Service (SBS), *A government action plan for small business: making the UK best place in the world to start and grow a business – the evidence base* (London: Department of Trade and Industry, HMSO, 2004), p. 59.
10. BERR, op. cit., p. 88.
11. BERR, op. cit., p. 89.
12. S. Bridge, K. O'Neill and F. Martin, *Understanding Enterprise, Entrepreneurship and Small Business* (Basingstoke: Palgrave Macmillan, 2009), p. 355.
13. D. J. Storey, *Understanding the Small Business Sector* (London: Routledge, 1994), p. 262.
14. See http://ec.europa.eu/enterprise/enterprise_policy, accessed 20 February 2009.
15. D. J. Storey, op. cit., p. 269.
16. BERR (now part of BIS), op. cit., pp. 7–9.
17. M. Bakkenes, M. Schouwstra and J. Snijders (eds), *Ten Years of Entrepreneurship Policy: A Global Overview* (Netherlands, Zoetermeer: EIM, January 2009), p. 9.
18. M. Bakkenes, M. Schouwstra and J. Snijders (eds), op. cit., p. 17.
19. See http://ec.europa.eu/enterprise/entrepreneurship/emes/awards/index/_en.htm, accessed 14 February 2009.
20. Invest Northern Ireland, *Accelerating Entrepreneurship Strategy*, June 2003, p. 4.
21. L. Stevenson, in *Fostering Entrepreneurship: A Seminar Organised by Invest Northern Ireland*, 14 March 2007, report by S. Bridge, at www.isbe.org.uk, accessed 16 October 2008.

3
Models of the Influences on Entrepreneurship

Chapter 2 indicated that many governments are pursuing enterprise, entrepreneurship and/or small business policies and that there is a lot in common, not just between the aims of those policies, but also between the methods and programmes applied to implement them. This chapter considers why these common methods are followed and explores the reasons for thinking that they would achieve the desired results.

It is often hard to identify the reasons why particular policy methods have been introduced. Chapter 2 presented at least some of the reasons why many governments want to pursue enterprise policies (the 'policy drivers') and their rationale for adopting many similar policy objectives. It also indicates that there is a lot in common between the various methods chosen by governments to try to achieve those objectives (the 'policy themes and instruments'). It does not suggest however why those particular methods have been selected.

Good practice in policymaking, such as that described in the UK government's Green Book,[1] suggests that there should be an appraisal of the different options available for pursuing a policy objective, before a particular method is selected. Little information is available however about the different options considered for enterprise policies. That might be because appraisals may not be done or may just not have been made public. If they were done it seems very probable that only a very limited number of options are considered because so few are perceived to be available. In any case public announcements and publications rarely go into this sort of detail, possibly because it is presumed that the choice of methods is obvious or that no alternatives exist. Interested observers are left therefore with the impression that methods are frequently selected on a 'me too' basis, often described as identifying and following 'best practice'.

Developing enterprise policy

Case 3.1 The development of enterprise support in Northern Ireland

The provision of specific enterprise support in Northern Ireland might be said to have started in 1972 with the creation, by the Northern Ireland government, of the Local Enterprise Development Unit (LEDU). LEDU was established as a company limited by guarantee with government funding and a remit to support small businesses. In the early 1980s, when levels of unemployment had risen and when the job creation potential of small businesses was being more widely recognised, LEDU's budget was increased and it expanded its operations. By then Northern Ireland had a Westminster-led direct rule government and that government was prepared to fund economic development efforts in Northern Ireland and the work of agencies such as LEDU, presumably because it wished to reduce unemployment in Northern Ireland which it saw as a special case and not therefore necessarily a precedent for similar levels of support in other areas of the UK.

Although LEDU's task was to encourage and support small businesses, in those days it had an annual job promotion target – and for LEDU the jobs it 'promoted' were the jobs which LEDU client businesses had promised they would create if they received funding from LEDU. LEDU thus addressed its target by negotiating packages of grant or loan assistance for small businesses which wished to start up, expand or recover from problems and then by counting the jobs which those businesses had indicated they would be creating or maintaining.

It would seem that LEDU gave grants to businesses because, when asked, struggling businesses often say that what they need is money and LEDU had indeed itself been given money in order to help such small businesses. It must therefore have seemed obvious that LEDU should try to give businesses the money they said they wanted which, from an early stage, was done in the form of grants or loans.

Later, in the 1980s, after a process of varied consultation, LEDU introduced additional forms of assistance. It introduced expansion, marketing and R&D grants, and it provided a simple grant for one- and two-person start-ups. It funded the provision of premises for small businesses and the provision of business start training. It asked the Local Enterprise Agencies (LEAs), which were providing premises for small businesses, to provide the training, because it believed that they were in a good position also to encourage and help the recipients of that training to expand their networks. The LEAs were also encouraged to establish low-interest small business loan funds. Thus, from just providing grants, and occasionally loans, LEDU expanded small business support to include broader and simpler loans, premises, training, marketing initiatives and networking. An assistance model which LEDU used at that time to explain its approach is reproduced as Figure 3.1.

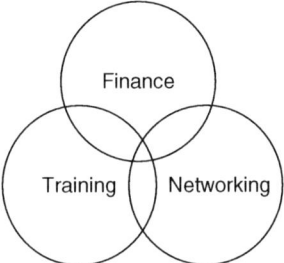

Figure 3.1 The perceived key business start-up needs

During the late 1980s, LEDU widened its approach from supporting people who wished to start and/or run small businesses to embrace encouraging more people to start businesses, which it did under its 'Enterprising Northern Ireland' campaign. In 2002 however LEDU was merged with the Northern Ireland Industrial Development Board (IDB) which had been responsible for assisting larger businesses and for inward investment/foreign direct investment (FDI), and with other parts of the government economic support structure, to form Invest Northern Ireland (Invest NI). The new organisation was responsible for supporting a much wider range of businesses than the small businesses which were LEDU's remit and it also inherited something of a focus on FDI. Nevertheless, in 2003, Invest NI launched its Accelerating Entrepreneurship Strategy, which was essentially a repackaging of the enterprise promotion methods pursued by LEDU, although it was able to apply more resources to that task. In support of this strategy, for instance, Invest NI launched its 'Go For It' campaign which has used media campaigns and advertising, including TV advertising, to encourage people to think of starting businesses and to inform them of the assistance available to support such enterprise. The range of that assistance has however, if anything, been reduced as start-up grants are much more limited and the conscious encouragement of networking has largely been dropped. Invest NI has continued, however, to support other initiatives such as schools' enterprise and entrepreneurship education in Northern Ireland's universities.

A reflection

This is a history of the provision, in a region of the UK, of support initially for established small businesses but which later expanded to include encouraging the creation of more small businesses. Thus LEDU engaged in what has been called small business policy (supporting businesses once started) to which it later added entrepreneurship policy (encouraging more start-ups) although it did not make a clear distinction between the two. The methods it used seem initially to have been based on providing small businesses with the money that they said they needed, although it might be argued that people will ask for what they want, but that is not necessarily what they need. LEDU did not appear to have questioned whether the tool it had been given was the right tool for its purpose; it just used it without considering either initially or later whether it could be converted into a better tool. Indeed, its methods of grant finance soon became established practice which those involved saw no reason to question.

Later there was some wider consultation. The Northern Ireland Department of Economic Development's 'Pathfinder' process in the mid 1980s included an enterprise taskforce which sought the advice of academics and others with an international perspective. Specialist consultants were also asked to help design the Enterprising Northern Ireland initiative. Thus Northern Ireland did attempt to broaden its sources of advice and to learn from, and to follow, international best practice. That 'best practice' was presented and adopted however as the right and only thing to do, not as one option among others which merited continuous appraisal.

In the quarter of a century since then there has been little change to the approach. The components may be presented in a different way and the relative emphasis on different ones may have been changed. One or two may have been dropped, but no new ones have been added. But essentially the methods being used now by Invest NI were being used formerly by LEDU. The initial reasons for adopting some of them may however have been forgotten. For instance in Northern Ireland the LEAs were originally chosen as the vehicle for delivering enterprise training because they had, or were developing, seed funds and they could provide access to local networks. Thus, if they were asked to deliver the training also, they could provide all the components of Figure 3.1 in a sort of one-stop-shop. However a recent evaluation of the enterprise training provided in Northern Ireland by the LEAs does not appear to have explored the extent to which the people receiving the training were also being helped to access funding or being linked into local networks, although it was the potential for such links that was a key reason for delivering the training in that way.

(See also Case 2.2 for a description of the strategy.)

Source: Based on the author's personal experience and records.

The author's personal experience (reflected in Case 3.1) of developing a regional enterprise promotional strategy in the 1980s and 1990s was that the methods pursued were a combination of what seemed obvious, what had already been done (which was itself probably based on what had seemed to be the obvious thing to do), and what appeared to be best practice elsewhere which was probably also originally based on the same apparently obvious methods (as summarised for example in Figure 3.1). New staff recruited to an economic development organisation rarely brought in new methods, often because they had not done such work before. They tended to follow what their colleagues were doing, and what their predecessors had done, trusting that the organisation knew what it was doing. If the reasons for selecting the methods in the first place had been recorded, such records were not consulted, and probably were not available. For instance, without the author's own memory and records, Case 3.1 would have been very hard to reconstruct because the organisational memories are actually very short-term, any surviving relevant files have gone into storage, many of the organisations concerned have changed and, in any case, none of the people involved are still doing the same jobs.

So what appears to have been the rationale for early enterprise policy and why were the early methods chosen and followed? The development history related in Case 3.1 may be typical. Assistance probably started as an *ad hoc* response to perceived needs: if struggling businesses said that they needed money then loan or grant schemes were introduced, if a sufficient budget was available. If those businesses did not appear then to have the skills to manage their money, or to expand their businesses, training courses were introduced to give them some understanding of financial management and bookkeeping or an introduction to marketing and selling, supported often by mentoring in some form. If premises for start-ups were in short supply then incubation schemes were started or subsidy schemes were introduced to encourage the commercial market to provide them.

However asking what was needed rarely produced a coherent picture. Even when supposed experts were consulted, it appeared that there was a close correlation between people's areas of expertise and what they suggested was needed: thus trainers indicated that the main need was training, bankers talked about finance initiatives, and advertisers proposed promotion campaigns. The author was involved in a consultation exercise undertaken to inform the early policies of NESTA (the UK's lottery-funded National Endowment for Science, Technology and the Arts). For this task over 80 people were interviewed to ascertain their views about the gaps in support for scientific, technical or artistic endeavour. A wide range of responses were obtained, including the contradictory views, stated definitively by different people, that almost invariably the main problem was a lack of money and that money was not the problem. It was to make sense of such a variety of answers that the model in Figure 3.2 was initially proposed. It suggests that there is a hierarchy of development needs, with 'higher'-level needs being masked until lower-level needs were satisfied and with money not being a core need but a means through which the actual needs might be addressed. This, it was suggested, is like a glider sitting on the ground which needs help from a

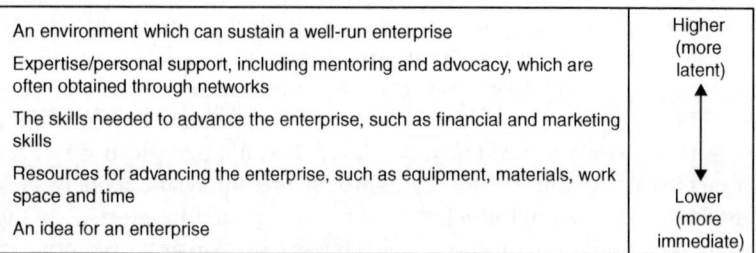

Figure 3.2 A hierarchy of enterprise needs
Source: S. Bridge, K. O'Neill and F. Martin, *Understanding Enterprise, Entrepreneurship and Small Business* (Basingstoke: Palgrave Macmillan, 2009), p. 372.

winch or tow to get it into the air but, once it is up there, its pilot then hopes then to find his or her own lift to keep it aloft. If, however, the glider pilot does not have the skills needed, once launched, to find lift, then he or she descends and once again asks for external help. Thus just providing the launch assistance requested will not provide lasting help until the skills need is also addressed.

Criticism has been made that 'too often public policy is made without regard to empirical research but in conformity with a misconceived conventional wisdom or ideological fixation'.[2] Trying to satisfy the apparent needs at one or more different levels in that hierarchy seems to explain many early enterprise policies, and basing policy on reported needs seems to be the extent to which it has been 'evidence based'. In the UK an attempt to clarify the link between evidence and policy was made by the government's Small Business Service (SBS) which, in 2004, published *The Evidence Base*[3] for a government action plan for small business. In its foreword the document indicates that the SBS's aim 'is to ensure that all decisions which affect small business are only taken after reviewing the evidence on what is needed and what actually works – and where the lessons learned in the delivery of products and services are fed back into the further development of policy'. The introduction then states that

> this paper sets out a more detailed analysis of the evidence base underpinning the Action Plan. It aims to provide a resource which policy makers and analysts across government and external researchers in the small business field can draw upon, and to make transparent the evidence on which policy is made.

However, despite that declaration, it has been argued that the document was mainly a presentation of evidence *about* the policies that were being followed and that it offered little, if any, evidence *for* why they should be followed. It did not, for instance, present:

- Evidence for why enterprise/entrepreneurship and/or small business should be promoted, which will in turn depend on:
  - Evidence for what people want or need
  - If that is jobs, evidence for what sort of jobs (and for what are 'quality' jobs)
  - Evidence that enterprise/entrepreneurship and/or small business will provide what is sought

- Evidence that enterprise/entrepreneurship and/or small business can usefully be promoted.
- Evidence for how enterprise/entrepreneurship and/or small business can be promoted.
- Evidence that enterprise/entrepreneurship and/or small business are being successfully promoted.[4]

Thus early policies seem to have been based, not on evidence about what worked, but on assumptions that providing the help that people apparently said they needed would work. However the hierarchy model and glider analogy suggest that people might not always know what they really need, and there seems to be little evidence that traditional policies consciously followed models other than common or 'best' practice.

A selection of models

> In contrast with physics, entrepreneurship has no great theories.
>
> Bill Bygrave[5]

Nevertheless models have been developed and some of them are described here. As might be expected the early ones tended to be simpler and later ones more complex as more apparently relevant factors have been identified for inclusion. Figure 3.1 was one particularly early model which simply links three possible areas of need and therefore of possible scope for assistance. It is though a significant move forward from the 'give them money' approach of some earlier assistance measures although it does not indicate as wide a range of possible need as Figure 3.2 which, unlike many models, also indicates a sequence of needs.

Figure 3.3 presents a formula for entrepreneurial success which, like Figure 3.1, was developed in the 1980s. It too suggests that there are

Entrepreneurial success	= New venture idea + Entrepreneurial know-how + Entrepreneurial know-who

Figure 3.3 A formula for entrepreneurial success
Source: R. Peterson and R. Rondstadt, 'A Silent Strength: Entrepreneurial Know Who', *The 16th ESBS/EFMD/IMD Report* (86/4), p. 11.

three components of success, two of which are the same as, or close to, those indicated in Figure 3.1. The 'know-who' is the same as networking and the 'know-how' can be interpreted as both the relevant technical skill for the particular business and general business skills. Unlike Figure 3.1, however, Figure 3.3 does not include money as a need, so it has that in common with Figure 3.2. The 'new venture idea' in Figure 3.3 might be both the idea of having a business in the first place and then a business idea to pursue, so this model would support both promotion of business start-up as the thing to do and then the provision of ideas workshops for those who want to do it. However, although the model in Figure 3.3 was apparently available when Figure 3.1 first informed the development of policy in Northern Ireland (see Case 3.1), it was not then known by the people responsible and so was not immediately used by them.

Although it has not been specifically highlighted as a model, Armstrong has suggested that a core tenet of what he calls the enterprise ideology is 'that enterprise is a natural expression of the human spirit' and that 'from this it follows that its absence is always due to its suppression, either by hostile systems of ideas, by regulative restriction or by a denial of the material upon which it can operate'.[6] Such thinking, he suggests, led to the measures proposed in the UK Department of Trade and Industry White Paper on Competitiveness of 1998 which he describes as being 'consistent with the belief that enterprise is a natural human behaviour which will emerge spontaneously once the barriers are removed'.[7]

Another model has been provided by Scott Shane who attempted to provide a 'general theory' of entrepreneurship. In his book of that name[8] he suggests that

> the entrepreneurial process begins with the perception of the existence of opportunities or situations in which resources can be recombined for a potential profit. Alert individuals, called entrepreneurs, discover these opportunities, and develop ideas for how to pursue them, including the development of a product or service that will be provided to customers. These individuals then obtain resources, design organisations or other modes of opportunity exploitation or develop a strategy to exploit the opportunity.

He then suggests a model of the entrepreneurial process which is reproduced in Figure 3.4. This approach assumes that entrepreneurship starts with alert individuals who spot business opportunities. It does not,

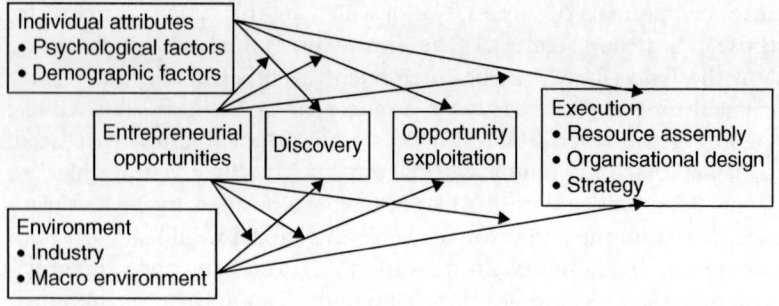

Figure 3.4 Shane's model of the entrepreneurial process
Source: S. Shane, *A General Theory of Entrepreneurship* (Cheltenham: Edward Elgar, 2003), p. 11.

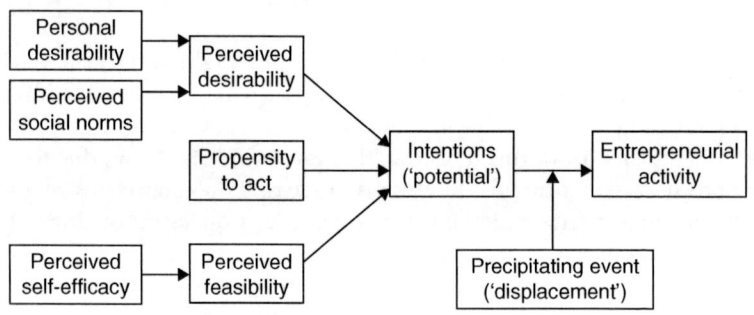

Figure 3.5 Intentions model of entrepreneurial potential (simplified)
Source: N. F. Krueger, 'Prescription for Opportunity: How Communities Can Create Potential for Entrepreneurs' (Washington DC: Small Business Foundation of America, Working Paper 93-03, 1995), p. 10.

however, suggest what might encourage or cause individuals to be alert because they want to find business opportunities and does not therefore indicate how more people might be encouraged to be entrepreneurial.

A model which does look at the individual and at what might lead him or her to engage in entrepreneurial activity was described by Krueger. His diagram is reproduced in Figure 3.5 and suggests that if an individual is to have the intention, given a suitable trigger, to engage in entrepreneurial activity, then he or she should see it as personally desirable, as socially desirable and as personally feasible. This model does not seem to have been used by many policymakers because, although some programmes seek to present entrepreneurship as attractive and feasible, the issue of 'social norms' does not seem to have been picked up.

Krueger's model also includes the propensity to act which is a personal attribute and the approach presented in Figure 3.6 corresponds with a

Figure 3.6 Attributes and resources model
Source: S. Bridge, K. O'Neill and F. Martin, *Understanding Enterprise, Entrepreneurship and Small Business* (Basingstoke: Palgrave Macmillan, 2009), p. 84.

Table 3.1 Attributes and resources, and how they are acquired

Attributes	**Resources**
Attitude	Ideas
Self-confidence	Technical skills
Enthusiasm	Interpersonal and communication skills
Diligence and perseverance	Information, and access to it
Initiative	Network
Independence	Finance
Persuasiveness	Experience, e.g. of small business, of marketing and of planning
Positive outlook	
Perception	Track record and credibility
Attitude to risk	
Direction	
How acquired	
Attributes can be acquired from both nature and nurture. The nurture influences can include family, education, culture, work experience, role models, peers, economic structure, lifestyle and stages of life.	Resources are acquired through many of the processes of working and living. They will, however, be more readily acquired if this acquisition is planned and targeted.

Source: S. Bridge, K. O'Neill and F. Martin, *Understanding Enterprise, Entrepreneurship and Small Business* (Basingstoke: Palgrave Macmillan, 2009), p. 85.

view of enterprise, and of enterprising behaviour, that is based on the attributes and resources an individual may possess at any point in time. As indicated in Table 3.1, attributes may include self-confidence, diligence, perseverance, interpersonal skills and innovative behaviour. Resources may include finance, experience, knowledge, skills, a network and a track record. It is suggested that it is the interaction among these factors that produces a rational response, on the basis of available information, when the opportunity occurs for a business start-up.

This view, however, also acknowledges that there is inertia in individual behaviour and that it may take a 'precipitating event', a discontinuity in work or in life, to trigger a review of an individual's situation. Whether this review will lead to an individual trying his or her own enterprise will then depend on the attributes and resources he or she has accumulated, together with his or her perception of environmental factors such as the availability of encouragement, and support such as advice, grants and training. The implications of this view are that the start-up decision will be affected by the attributes and resources acquired prior to the trigger for taking the decision, and that there is scope for initiatives to enhance the acquisition of those attributes and resources.

The model in Figure 3.6, developed for an earlier book co-written by this author, was in effect an attempt to present a model which summarised what were then thought to be the key influences on enterprise and entrepreneurship. If policy seemed to follow this model, it was not because policy was based on this model but because both policy and the model were based on the same thinking which was then current.

The models considered so far have looked at enterprise and/or entrepreneurship in individuals. The Global Entrepreneurship Monitor (GEM) research programme took a broader view and was derived from a conceptual model summarising the major causal mechanisms thought to effect national economies. This model is illustrated by Figure 3.7 and the components of the model are interpreted in Table 3.2.

The GEM approach was apparently derived from the overall model presented in Figure 3.7 which suggests various factors which might influence the level of entrepreneurship in a country or region. Also GEM originally stated that it planned to explore three questions, one of which was what makes a country entrepreneurial. Subsequently, however, that question in its original form has been dropped and the objectives of uncovering the factors determining the levels of entrepreneurial activity and identifying policies that may enhance the level of entrepreneurial activity have been assumed instead. However successive GEM reports have said little directly about these objectives. GEM's main model explaining the level of entrepreneurship might now be said to be a U-shaped curve indicating that the level of entrepreneurship is normally high in countries with low *per capita* GDP, is then low in countries with a medium level of *per capita* GDP, and rises again in countries with relatively high *per capita* GDP. However that is a best-fit

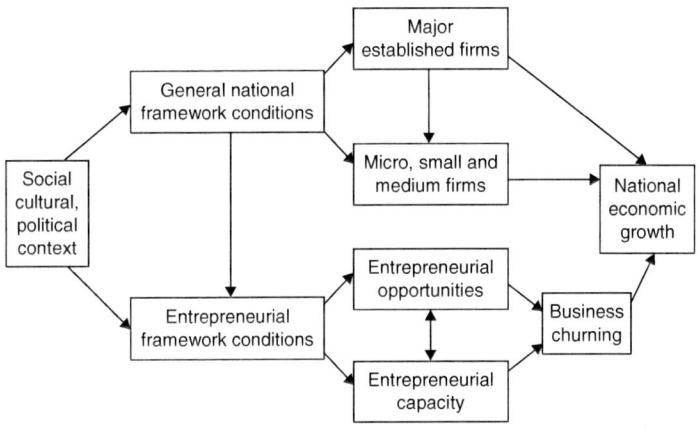

Figure 3.7 GEM conceptual model (the total process)
Source: A. L. Zacharakis, W. D. Bygrave and D. A. Shepherd, *Global Entrepreneurship Monitor National Entrepreneurship Assessment: United States of America, 2000 Executive Report* (Kansas City, MO: Kauffman Centre for Entrepreneurial Leadership, 2000), p. 6.
Permission to reproduce this diagram of the Global Entrepreneurship Monitor (GEM) conceptual model has been kindly granted by the copyright holders. My thanks go to the authors, national teams, researchers, funding bodies and other contributors who have made this possible.

Table 3.2 Interpretation of components of the GEM conceptual model

Variable	Interpretation
Social cultural and political context	Factors shown to play an important role in shaping a country's national framework conditions, such as demographics, investment in education, social norms and attitudes as they relate to, for example, independence and entrepreneurs
General national framework (GNF) conditions	Role of government institutions, R&D, physical infrastructure, labour market efficiency, legal and social institutions
Entrepreneurial framework (EF) conditions	Comprise factors believed to be more volatile than GNF conditions and reflect intermediate variables in the overall causal sequence. They include: • financial support: the availability of financial resources, equity and debt, for new and growing firms including grants and subsidies; • government policies: the extent to which government policies concerning taxes, regulations and their application are size neutral and/or whether these policies discourage or encourage new and growing firms;

(Continued)

Table 3.2 Continued

Variable	Interpretation
	• government programmes: the presence of direct programmes to assist new and growing firms at all levels of government – national, regional and municipal; • education and training: the extent to which training in starting or managing small, new or growing businesses features in the education and training system, and the quality, relevance and depth of such education and training in creating or managing small, new or growing businesses; • Research and development transfer: the extent to which national research and development leads to new commercial opportunities, and whether or not R&D is available for new, small and growing firms; • commercial and professional infrastructure: the influence of commercial, accounting and other legal services and institutions that allow or promote new, small or growing businesses; • market openness/barriers to entry: the extent to which commercial arrangements are prevented from undergoing constant change and redeployment, preventing new and growing firms from competing and replacing existing suppliers, subcontractors and consultants; • access to physical infrastructure: the access to physical resources – communication, utilities, transportation, land or space, at a price that does not discriminate against new, small or growing firms; • cultural and social norms: the extent to which existing social and cultural norms encourage, or do not discourage, individual actions that may lead to new ways of conducting business or economic activities and, in turn, lead to greater dispersion in wealth and income.
Entrepreneurial opportunities	The perception as well as the reality of market opportunities
Entrepreneurial capacity	Attitudes and resources of potential entrepreneurs
Business churning	The processes which lead to birth, death, expansion and contraction of businesses
National economic growth	Subsumes a variety of common economic measures such as growth in GDP, employment and per capita income

Source: S. Bridge, K. O'Neill and F. Martin, *Understanding Enterprise, Entrepreneurship and Small Business* (Basingstoke: Palgrave Macmillan, 2009), p. 134.

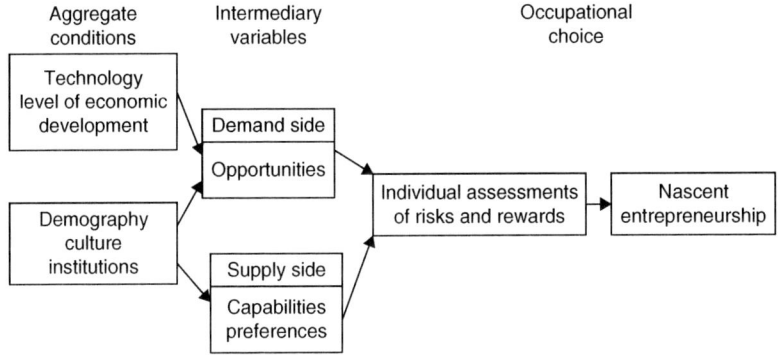

Figure 3.8 The determinants of nascent entrepreneurship
Figure Copyright Senate Hall Academic Journals
Source: S. Wennekers, L. Uhlaner and R. Thurik, 'Entrepreneurship and Its Conditions: A Macro Perspective', *International Journal of Entrepreneurship Education*, Vol. 1, Issue 1, 2002, p. 35.

curve for rather dispersed findings and GEM's own figures suggest that in practice the lowest and highest levels of entrepreneurship are to be found among countries with relatively low *per capita* GDP where, for instance, the level of entrepreneurship (as measured by GEM) can vary from 4 per cent to 27 per cent for the same level of GDP.

Thus such GEM findings are not helpful to countries trying to increase their level of entrepreneurship. GEM's individual country surveys do appear to provide other apparently helpful indicators such as whether people feel that they have the skills needed to run a business or whether fear of failure would discourage them. However such issues are not probed in the GEM work, which is based on a relatively simple survey, so it is not clear what fear of failure might mean. Also, instead of guiding policy, there is anecdotal evidence to suggest that such findings are used more to explain low levels of entrepreneurship than to suggest ways by which to increase them.

A model which is similar to the GEM model in that it does include aggregate conditions but which, unlike GEM, also includes the individual entrepreneur and his or her decision was suggested by Wennekers et al. It is shown in Figure 3.8 and it suggests that nascent entrepreneurship is the result of individual risk–reward assessments influenced by aggregate conditions and intermediate variables of supply and demand.

Another model which might indicate the factors which influence the level of entrepreneurship in a particular place is Stevenson's presentation of the entrepreneurial system. This is reproduced in Figure 3.9 and

52 *Rethinking Enterprise Policy*

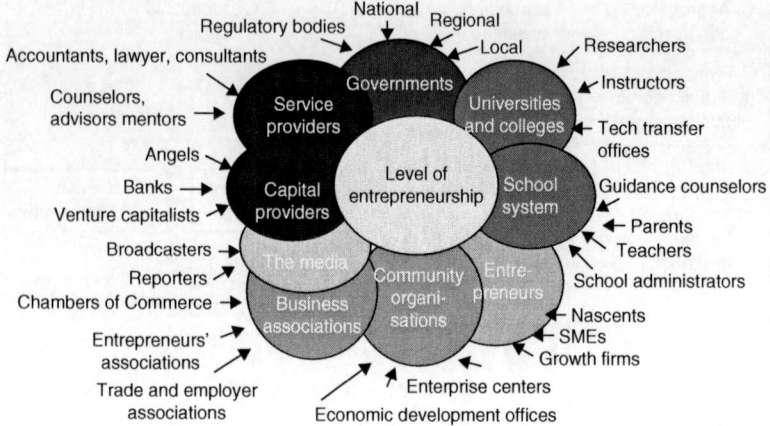

Figure 3.9 Stevenson's portrayal of the entrepreneurship system
Source: L. Stevenson, Presentation to 35th International Small Business Congress, Belfast, November 2008, with kind permission from Springer Science and Business Media.

appears to be an inclusive model which seeks to include all possible influences. While it might suggest to policymakers that any and all of these factors can have an influence, it does not indicate how they should be applied. For instance does it require changes in all the factors shown to have a significant impact on the level of entrepreneurship, or will any specific influence do it on its own? Can the model be used to guide policy, or just to illustrate it?

A somewhat more limited presentation than Stevenson's, but one which gives a rather starker presentation of the presumed influencing factors, is a model that has been prepared in an attempt to explain variations in global entrepreneurial activity and is summarised in Figure 3.10.

One attempt which has been made to give some structure and rigour to guide policymakers has been the general policy framework for entrepreneurship developed for the Danish government by the National Agency for Enterprise and Construction (FORA) working closely with the OECD. This framework is based on five factors, which 'according to both the theoretical and empirical literature constitute the five pillars of entrepreneurship. 1) entrepreneurship skills, 2) access to capital, 3) access to markets, 4) entrepreneurship incentives, and 5) entrepreneurship culture and motivation'. These factors are illustrated in Figure 3.11 and it is suggested that 'not all factors conducive to country entrepreneurial performances may be altered using policy instruments.

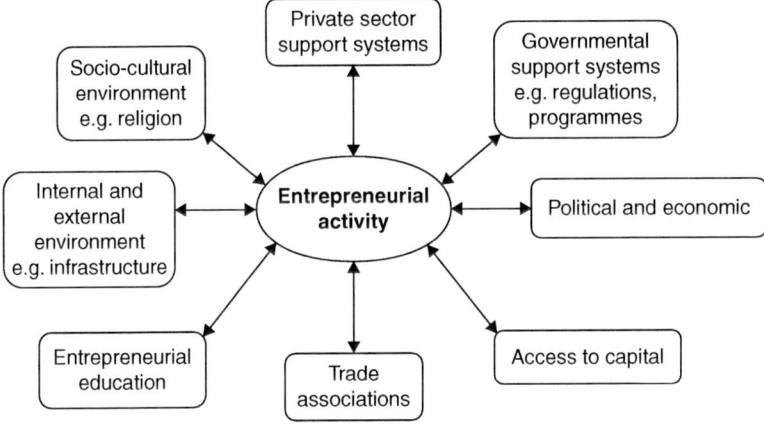

Figure 3.10 Comprehensive model of factors leading to entrepreneurial activity
Source: Based on J-H. Kim, A. Weinstein, S. Shirley and I. Melhem, 'Toward a Comprehensive Model of Global Entrepreneurship', a paper presented at the ICSB Conference at Seoul, Korea, in June 2009.

However, most factors can be influenced directly or indirectly by government policy'.[9]

The framework further suggests that 'each of the five factors is comprised of a number of policy areas believed to have an impact on these factors and therefore [on] entrepreneurship. A careful examination of entrepreneurial policies in the top performing countries combined with a theoretical run-down of the correlation between policy and entrepreneurship has materialised into 29 policy areas'[10] (see Table 3.3 and, also expanded by OECD, Figure 2.2). However, as noted in Chapter 2, the intention is that further analysis should be done 'to determine ... the significance of each supposed determinant in creating or hindering entrepreneurship and entrepreneurs and their relationship to the specific entrepreneurship performance indicators', and it is anticipated that this might lead to 'a reduction in the number of indicators included in the framework [if] some ... have no or very marginal impact on performance'.[11]

'Ideally', it is suggested, 'a perfect correlation between the indicators for entrepreneurial performance and impact would exist. Countries aiming at increasing GDP growth, for example, should be able to pick a few performance indicators and expect that an increase in those performance indicators will lead to higher GDP growth'.[12] The initiative has tried therefore to establish internationally comparable indicators

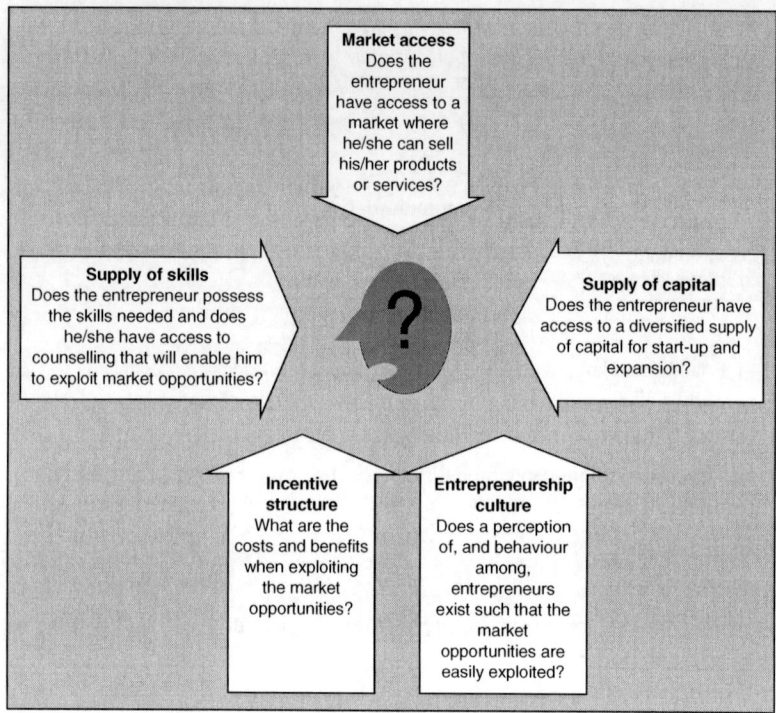

Figure 3.11 Factors impacting entrepreneurship
Source: National Agency for Enterprise and Construction, *Entrepreneurship Index 2006: Entrepreneurship Conditions in Denmark*, November 2006, at www.foranet.dk, accessed on 16 March 2009, p. 24.

for the policy areas so that, for instance, it should be possible for policy makers to establish both which policy areas score highly in countries with high levels of the outcome they want and how their own policy areas compare with those high scoring ones. Denmark, for instance, decided that it wanted more high-growth firms and therefore in the analysis for this initiative 'entrepreneurship is defined as the entry and creation of high growth firms'.[13]

Thus this initiative deliberately set out to guide policy. Ideally it should provide policy makers with an indication of the effectiveness of each policy area in its impact on entrepreneurship so that those responsible for policy can compare costs and effectiveness and select the best policy for their purposes. It does assume that the policy areas identified are the ones most likely to have an effect on entrepreneurship but it admits that 'the lack of time series for several indicators

Table 3.3 Policy areas with an impact on the five factors

	Factors				
	Market access	Supply of capital	Supply of skills	Incentives (motivation)	Culture
Policy areas					
	Access barriers	Loan capital	Traditional business education	Income tax	Cultural and social norms
	Access to international markets	Wealth and bequest tax	Entrepreneurship education	Corporate tax	Targeted initiatives
	New knowledge transfer	Venture capital	Restart possibilities	Administrative burdens – start-up	Introducing entrepreneurship in primary education
	Private demand	Stock markets	Entrepreneurship infrastructure (public)	Administrative burdens – operation	Communication on "heroes"/ "awards"
	Public demand	Capital tax	Entrepreneurship infrastructure (private)	Labour market regulation	
	Testing facilities	Business angels		Bankruptcy legislation	
				Financial incentives	
				Social and health insurance	

Source: Based on National Agency for Enterprise and Construction, *Entrepreneurship Index 2006 – Entrepreneurship Conditions in Denmark*, available on www.foranet.dk (accessed 2 July 2008), p. 25.

makes it impossible to show a causal connection between high quality framework conditions and a high level of entrepreneurial activity'.[14]

Other models

The models described above have been selected because they purport in some way to describe the process of entrepreneurship, in the sense of new venture formation or venture growth, and the factors which influence it. There are, of course, other models and diagrams which, if not indicative of the core process of developing entrepreneurship, do nevertheless illustrate some aspects of it. One of these is Casson's presentation of the supply and demand of entrepreneurship (see Figure 3.12) which suggests that if the expectation of reward for an entrepreneur is high then the supply of entrepreneurs will rise which will, in turn, reduce the reward available per entrepreneur, thus leading eventually to a supply/demand balance. This model therefore indicates that, in any particular situation, there will be an optimum number of entrepreneurs, and it implies that, in order for that balance to be achieved, individuals will be making conscious decisions about entrepreneurship based on their expectation of rewards.

A rather different presentation is that of Gibb (see Figure 3.13). As presented this has at its centre the small businesses rather than the entrepreneur, but the centre can be interpreted as the entrepreneur once

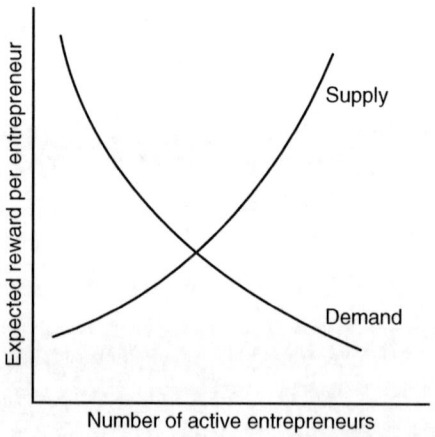

Figure 3.12 Casson's demand and supply of entrepreneurs
Source: Based on M. Casson, *The Entrepreneur: An Economic Theory* (Cheltenham: Edward Elgar, 2003), p. 196.

Figure 3.13 The layers of the small business support network
Source: A. A. Gibb, 'Towards the Building of Entrepreneurial Models of Support for Small Business', Paper presented at the 11th (UK) National Small Firms Policy and Research Conference, Cardiff, 1988, p. 17.

he or she is in business, and it suggests that the strongest network influence on such a person is the influence from family and friends which is a social influence rather than the more business-focussed influences from colleagues, customers and consultants.

Comparing the models

> What is interesting is that the attitudes of governments around the world to SME issues are so similar. Indeed, they seek inspiration from one another in devising assistance programmes.
>
> Graham Bannock[15]

The models considered above range from the earlier and generally relatively simple models to the later and generally relatively complex ones. Of the models described above only that presented in Figure 3.11 and Table 3.3 was specifically designed to influence policy; there seems to be little evidence that any of the others have done so directly. Nevertheless there does seem to be no inherent contradiction between most policies and most of these models. For instance many of the models include, or at least in some way allude to, many of the traditional components of enterprise, entrepreneurship and/or small business policy such as financial help (grants, loans, angels, and/or venture capital), market help (such as marketing courses, 'meet the buyer' events and/or trade missions), training and mentoring, and premises, together with supporting actions such as fiscal and regulatory support (reducing taxes and/or red tape) and enterprise education in schools, colleges and universities.

The rationale for policy based on these components seems to be an assumption that nascent entrepreneurship is the result of individually made, logical, risk–reward assessments, and therefore that the increased availability of things such as finance, marketing help, training and an absence of 'red tape' will in turn increase levels of entrepreneurship because by reducing the perceived risk and/or increasing the potential reward, they will have an impact on the risk–reward decisions that individuals are assumed to make. Of the models described, only that shown in Figure 3.8 explicitly includes individual risk–reward assessments and Wennekers et al. specifically state that 'central to their framework is the assumption that individuals choose between wage-employment and business ownership by assessing and weighing the potential financial and non-pecuniary rewards and risks'.[16] Also Casson, in developing the model which forms the basis of Figure 3.12, states that 'an individual's decision upon whether to become an entrepreneur will be based on a comparison of the expected reward to entrepreneurship and the reward for the best alternative use of his time'.[17]

Although they do not have such specific indications, the other models either appear to be based on, or are at least consistent with and do not deny, this assumption that entrepreneurial behaviour is the result of individual logical choice. They also suggest that that choice will be influenced by a number of relevant factors, expressed clearly, for instance, in the model in Figure 3.10. Further most of the models imply, and the explanation behind the depictions in Figure 3.11 and Table 3.3 specifically states, that increasing the amount of the identified factors associated with entrepreneurship will lead to an increase in the level of entrepreneurship. In this aspect it is as if each model subscribed to a 'default' assumption, illustrated in Figure 3.14, that if a factor is understood to have an influence on entrepreneurship, then increasing the amount of that factor will in turn increase the level of entrepreneurship. Possible exceptions to the logical choice assumption are Gibb's

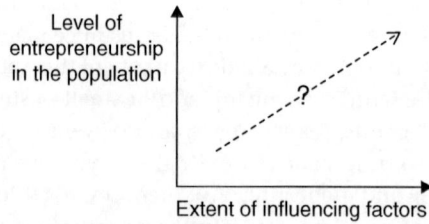

Figure 3.14 A default assumption about influences on entrepreneurship?

model in Figure 3.13 and Krueger's model in Figure 3.5. The latter, while suggesting individual actions, does include social acceptability as an influencing factor, and social acceptability may not itself necessarily be based on logic; however the rest of the model still seems to assume some sort of logical assessment process.

Market failure?

A further approach sometimes applied is based on the concept of 'market failure'. This concept is also mentioned in Chapter 2, and it is argued that it is only when markets are not operating as they should that government intervention can be justified and that intervention at other times will distort conditions and lead to other problems:

> It might be expected that attempts to promote enterprise and entrepreneurship would find favour in most quarters, but this is not necessarily the case. It is said that enterprise thrives in a free enterprise economy, and many advocates of this economic system caution against interference with market forces. These people argue that the laws of supply and demand, operating through the price system, send signals to interested parties, who respond to market opportunities and threats. Those persons who are able to interpret market forces accurately will reap economic rewards, and this pursuit of self-interest leads to the most efficient utilisation of economic resources. Enterprising individuals are inclined to be energetic, forward-looking people who take bold steps to realise opportunities, and it can be seen that free enterprise economic systems are an attractive milieu for enterprising individuals to display their skills. It is argued therefore that there is no point in promoting entrepreneurship and enterprise: the enterprising will avail themselves of opportunities, and the aggregate outcome of their decisions will produce greater welfare than decisions made by central authorities.[18]

Summary

Chapter 2 suggested that, on the whole, governments follow broadly similar enterprise and/or entrepreneurship policies. This chapter has looked at the evolution of those policies and at some of the models of enterprise which might, or might not, be behind them. This exploration suggests that most policies have been based on addressing perceived needs or on reported 'best practice'. That best practice has itself, however, probably been based on other best practice and ultimately on addressing perceived needs, which suggest that not a lot of new thought had gone into much enterprise policy.

A number of models have been proposed which might indicate what should influence the level of entrepreneurship, but there is not a lot of evidence that they have been consciously followed and, in any case, they themselves tend to suggest addressing more or less the same factors. Thus, if policy is not actually based on these models, it is at least consistent with them and, like them, it tends to assume that people make individual logical decisions to start businesses, based on some form of risk–reward assessment incorporating issues such as the perceived desirability of the goal, the ease of pursuing it, the help available and the perceived chances of success. Therefore it seems logical to assume that increasing one or more of these factors should lead to more people doing it.

For instance Figure 3.9 portrays what is probably the most recent, and most complex, model summarised in this chapter. It may look different from Figure 3.1 which is one of the earliest and simplest, but nevertheless they do have a lot in common. Two of the three components in Figure 3.1, Training and Finance, are broadly the same as the Supply of Skills and the Supply of Capital factors in Figure 3.9, and Networking is related to Entrepreneurship Culture. The other two factors in Figure 3.9 are Market Access and Incentive Structure and they are touched on in other models. The Danish and OECD initiatives, portrayed in Figures 2.2 and 3.11 and expounded further in Table 3.3, may be more comprehensive and more clearly structured than previous support models, but they do not add any new dimensions or factors which had not been considered before and do not suggest any new policy areas to try. What they do however do is to make explicit the promise that, once refined, the model should provide a good guide to effective policy.

The Danish model and its OECD derivation are based on the conceptual framework which is illustrated in its simplest form in Figure 3.15

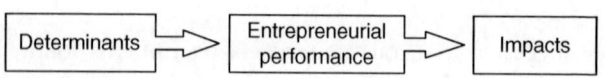

Figure 3.15 Simple form of the OECD/EUROSTAT framework for entrepreneurship indicators
Source: N. Ahmad and A. Hoffman, 'A Framework for Addressing and Measuring Entrepreneurship', *OECD Statistics Working Papers*, 2008/2, OECD Publishing, doi:10.1787/243160627270, p. 10.

(and in more detail in Figure 2.2). Its authors explain it with the following analogy:

> For simplicity however, and to assist interpretation, the basic idea behind the Conceptual Framework can be illustrated by means of an analogy. Passengers want to get from A to B by time t (reflecting the policy objective, *Impact*). There are various means of transport available, some more costly than others, with each means having many variants, (engine size, fuel consumption etc, which collectively form the *Determinants*). During the journey, passengers are informed whether they are heading in the right direction and on time via speedometers and GPS readings, (the *Performance* indicators). Different passengers (*policy makers*) will, of course, want to go to different places and get there at different times (different *Impacts*), using, whether by design or necessity, a mode of transport (*Determinant*) that reflects the price they're willing to pay for a certain level of comfort.[19]

The above quote overtly suggests that this model, once completed, could guide policy choice. The implication is that the model should both help policymakers to decide which determinants (policy areas) will best serve their purpose in achieving the impact they want at a price they are willing to pay and, through performance indicators, should provide them with feedback on how well their policies are doing. That assumes, however, that the determinants indicated are indeed capable of delivering the entrepreneurial performance sought and, through it, of achieving the desired impact. In other words it is testing the assumption that at least some current entrepreneurship policies both can and do work, and the validity of that assumption is the subject of the next chapter.

References

1. HM Treasury, *The Green Book: Appraisal and Evaluation in Central Government* (London: TSO, 2003).
2. R. Taylor, *Britain's World of Work – Myths and Realities* (Swindon: Economic and Social Research Council, 2002), p. 23.
3. Small Business Service (SBS), *A government action plan for small business: Making the UK best place in the world to start and grow a business – the evidence base*, (London: Department of Trade and Industry, HMSO, 2004).
4. S. Bridge, K. O'Neill and F. Martin, *Understanding Enterprise, Entrepreneurship and Small Business* (Basingstoke: Palgrave Macmillan, 2009), p. 380.
5. W. Bygrave, 'The Entrepreneurial Paradigm (I): A Philosophical Look at Its Research Methodologies', in *Entrepreneurship Theory & Practice*, Vol. 14, No. 1, 1989.

6. P. Armstrong, *Critique of Entrepreneurship* (Basingstoke: Palgrave Macmillan, 2005), p. 148.
7. Ibid., p. 137.
8. S. Shane, *A General Theory of Entrepreneurship: The Individual Opportunity Nexus* (Cheltenham: Edward Elgar, 2003), p. 10.
9. National Agency for Enterprise and Construction, *Entrepreneurship Index 2005: Entrepreneurship Conditions in Denmark*, October 2005, at www.foranet.dk, accessed 16 March 2009, p. 25.
10. National Agency for Enterprise and Construction, *Entrepreneurship Index 2006: Entrepreneurship Conditions in Denmark*, November 2006, at www.foranet.dk, accessed 16 March 2009, p. 24.
11. N. Ahmad and A. Hoffman, 'A Framework for Addressing and Measuring Entrepreneurship', *OECD Statistics Working Papers*, 2008/2, OECD Publishing. doi:10.1787/243160627270, p. 20.
12. Ibid., p. 17.
13. A. Hoffman and H. Gabr, *A General policy Framework for Entrepreneurship* (FORA, April 2006), at www.foranet.dk, accessed 16 March 2009, p. 5.
14. National Agency for Enterprise and Construction, op. cit., p. 27.
15. G. Bannock, *The Economics and Management of Small Business: An International Perspective* (London: Routledge, 2005), p. 134.
16. S. Wennekers, L. M. Uhlaner and R. Thurik, 'Entrepreneurship and Its Conditions: A Macro Perspective', in the *International Journal of Entrepreneurship Education*, Vol. 1, issue 1, 2002.
17. M. Casson, *The Entrepreneur: An Economic Theory* (Cheltenham: Edward Elgar, 2003), p. 195.
18. S. Bridge, K. O'Neill and F. Martin, op. cit., p. 352.
19. N. Ahmad and A. Hoffman (2008), op. cit., p. 10.

4
The Problem: The Facts Do Not Fit the Theory

Chapter 2 presented a summary of the rationale for, and the methods employed by, many government enterprise policies and showed that there is a lot in common between the methods employed by different governments. Chapter 3 then showed that in the main those policies are at least consistent with current theories and models of the influences on enterprise. But do those models work, is the policy 'based' on them effective, and are the facts of enterprise promotion consistent with the theory?

Evaluating policy initiatives

It is acknowledged, at least in some countries, that it is not enough just to implement policies well, but that it is also important then to evaluate those policies to see how well they worked and what lessons can be learnt from that experience. In the UK, for instance, the Government's *Green Book* on 'Appraisal and Evaluation in Central Government', defines an evaluation as a 'retrospective analysis of a project, programme or policy to assess how successful or otherwise it has been, and what lessons can be learnt for the future'.[1] This, according to the *Green Book*, involves comparing the results of the project both with what was targeted for the project and with what might have happened had the project not been implemented. It should then seek to draw lessons from this comparison and present, in its findings, the results and recommendations arising from this. In another instance the OECD Industry Committee's Working Party on Small and Medium-Sized Enterprises developed guidelines that would allow for the international comparability of SME programmes. According to the framework produced, programmes should be evaluated with regard to their efficiency in a number of areas, including:

- *Appropriateness*: Is the programme addressing an important objective and can this be related to a clearly identified market failure?
- *Superiority*: Is the programme more effective than other policies, programmes or instruments that would reach the same goals?
- *Systemic efficiency*: How does the programme interact with other programmes, and to what extent does its efficiency depend on conditions created by other government actions?
- *Own efficiency*: Is the programme cost-effective in achieving its particular objective?
- *Adaptive efficiency*: To what extent have results from evaluations been fed back into policy design and implementation, and does policy design ensure a degree of flexibility in responding to unpredictable changes?[2]

The rationale for, and principles of, programme evaluation are therefore clearly established, not least in the enterprise field. However, according to Curran, where there have been evaluations of small business policies in the UK, these have been of two main kinds:

- evaluations sponsored by government funding departments and/or agencies delivering the policy, conducted by private sector for-profit bodies. Most small business support evaluation in the UK is probably of this type and often the results never enter the public domain;

- evaluations by independent (usually academic) researchers on a not-for-profit basis, sponsored by others than those funding or delivering the initiative ... The results are normally made public with the aim of promoting constructive discussion.

'The distinction between the two', according to Curran,

> is important ... The first kind is much more likely to be favourable to the policy or programme than the second kind. Where those conducting the evaluation are dependent on the initiator or deliverer for their fees and future similar work, there will be pressures to be less critical, or at least not to publish any negative findings. This is less likely if evaluation is by researchers not reliant on policy-makers or policy-deliverers for their funding and the results are open to peer scrutiny. One result of such a poor record is that overall small

business initiatives receive more favourable recognition for promoting small businesses, employment and economic performance than they merit.[3]

Such observations led Bridge et al. to conclude that 'it is unusual to find evaluation studies that observe the principles of evaluation fully'.[4] There are, they and others suggest, a number of possible reasons for this:

- The cost of a rigorous study may be viewed as too expensive. To establish fully all the results might cost more than the original initiative. Also politicians tend to focus on their own input and on being seen to do something and on the possible impact of that on the next election and thus they may not be very interested in evaluating the policies of their predecessors or in the longer-term evaluation of their own policies. Therefore, for reasons such as these, policy evaluations may not be carried out.
- Evaluation studies may be deliberately circumscribed so as to 'prove' a desired outcome. This is, for instance, particularly possible when the researchers are reliant on the policymakers or deliverers for some or all of their funding.
- In some situations it is argued that there are so many variables at work that it is not possible in practice to isolate the effects of one or two.
- Even if a correlation can be demonstrated between inputs and outputs, it does not necessarily imply causation, or clarify its direction. Research is often supposed to be better if done impartially and so evaluators may be chosen for their non-involvement and therefore their apparent objectivity. However involvement in some form may be necessary if people are to gain some understanding of a process and the insight needed, for instance, to separate cause and effect.
- It is argued that many of the effects of an initiative can be intangible and therefore difficult or impossible to measure.
- It is not always easy to determine over what period results should be measured.

Another reason which might sometimes explain the lack of relevant evaluations is that the length of time over which a longitudinal study might need to be carried out in order to observe lasting effects is longer than the effective memory span of many organisations. Thus, for instance, when in the late 1980s the Local Enterprise Development Unit (LEDU) in Northern Ireland launched its 'Enterprising Northern Ireland' campaign to encourage more people to consider starting businesses (see Case 3.1), it recognised that this was a longer-term initiative which needed a longer-term assessment. Therefore, together with the Northern Ireland Small Business Institute (NISBI) at the University of Ulster, LEDU funded a survey of attitudes to enterprise in Northern Ireland. Its aim was to establish a baseline against which progress might be assessed and to establish a survey method which could be repeated at regular intervals (originally envisaged as every five or ten years) to see if attitudes were changing. (This is the initial survey work referred to in Case 2.2.) However, not long after the survey was completed, some of the key personnel involved moved, and eventually, at the instigation of different higher authorities, both LEDU and NISBI were merged with sister organisations or departments and ceased to exist as separate entities. As there was no real organisational memory for anything which was not regulatory and/or annual, the movement of people meant that the memory of the survey initiative quickly dissipated. Consequently the work was never repeated and the baseline never used. The overall effectiveness of 'Enterprising Northern Ireland' was thus never assessed.[5]

Whether for these reasons or for others, there does seem to be a dearth of publicly available, rigorous and impartial evaluations of programmes in the enterprise and small business field from which conclusions might be drawn on the effectiveness of such programmes. There is then also the difference between evaluations of a number of separate programmes and an overall view of the effectiveness of the policy of which the programmes may be a part. Thus, in considering the performance of the UK government's Small Business Service (SBS), the National Audit Office reported that 'government spends over £2.6 billion [in 2003–04] in providing support to small business. While SBS has evaluated a number of individual programmes it is not able to establish the overall impact of either its or wider Government activity on small businesses'[6] (but see also Case 4.2 for another estimate of UK annual expenditure).

Some evaluation evidence

Despite these issues there have been a few useful evaluations and recently the results of some longitudinal assessments and comparisons have also become available. One example of an evaluation which does appear to have looked beyond the apparent results of a programme to examine cause and effect in more detail was a study by Hart and Roper of the impact in the UK of Business Link (BL) assistance on the performance of small firms as measured by employment, turnover and productivity. Under this programme the main initial target of BLs was to be those firms which employed between 10 and 200 people and had growth potential, and they were to be helped by 'personal business advisors' (PBAs) who were capable of providing SMEs with holistic advice on business problems and signposting to the support services available to solve them. The study initially found that the businesses thus assisted had generally shown positive employment growth following that assistance. However after investigating further by comparing assisted firms with similar non-assisted firms, the researchers reported that

> in substantive terms we find little evidence that BL assistance was being targeted effectively at firms with a track record of rapid prior growth. Secondly, we find little evidence that after allowing for selection bias BL assistance over the 1996–98 period was having any significant effect on firms' sales, employment or productivity growth performance over the 1996–2000 period.[7]

Thus it appeared that while the businesses which received this assistance had subsequently grown, they probably would have grown anyway and the observed growth was not the result of the BL programme. The programme had not had the impact on businesses which it was supposed to have but Hart and Roper did argue that to rely solely upon an econometric approach to the evaluation of the economic impact of BL assistance is flawed as it provided no insights into the particular ways in which BL assistance interplays with the strategic management of the business concerned.

Another example of an independent study of small business support programmes is a study carried out by Roper and Hewitt-Dundas of grant assistance for small firm development in Northern Ireland and the Republic of Ireland. These are both areas where there have been high and sustained levels of public support for both start-ups and small business development. Nevertheless the researchers reported that their data suggested 'that assistance had no significant effect on either the turnover growth or profitability of assisted firms in either Northern Ireland or the Republic of Ireland over the period considered'.[8] This conclusion suggests that the relevant industrial development policy, which was largely justified by a market failure approach, was not being effective in this case. However it did not go further than this and it thus indicates the limitations of individual-programme evaluations, even when independently carried out, in looking more broadly at policy effectiveness.

Case 4.1 Accelerating Entrepreneurship: A case study in interpreting indicators

In June 2003 Invest Northern Ireland (Invest NI) launched its Accelerating Entrepreneurship Strategy followed in October 2003 by its key component, the 'Go For It' initiative. The impact of the strategy, the programme documentation indicated, was to be demonstrated by 'an enhanced level of entrepreneurial activity and achievement of a net increase in the volume and value of new business ventures in the Northern Ireland economy'.[9]

To measure the level of entrepreneurial activity Invest NI used the Global Entrepreneurship Monitor (GEM – see section on GEM in Chapter 3) and its Total Entrepreneurial Activity (TEA)* score for Northern Ireland. About three years after the launch of the Accelerating Entrepreneurship Strategy, Invest NI proudly announced that the evidence showed it was succeeding. To show this Invest NI presented the chart of GEM TEA measurements reproduced in Figure 4.1 which, it was suggested, showed that since the launch of the strategy, the level of entrepreneurship had risen from 60 per cent of the UK average to 80 per cent of the average and had then maintained that position. As late as 2008 Invest NI was still making reference to this evidence of 'success' stating that the GEM findings showed 'an increase in the Northern Ireland TEA rate of 1.6 percentage points since 2002 (3.3 per cent); resulting in a narrowing gap from 61.1 per cent of the UK average in 2002, to 87.1 per cent in 2007'.[10]

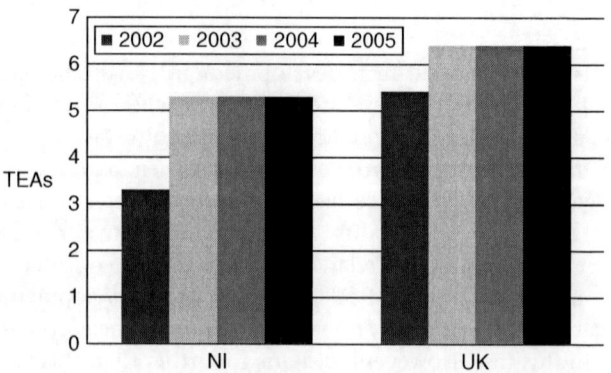

Figure 4.1 Invest NI presentation of GEM TEA measurements
Source: Based on Invest Northern Ireland, *Performance Report 2002/03–2004/05*, p. 89.

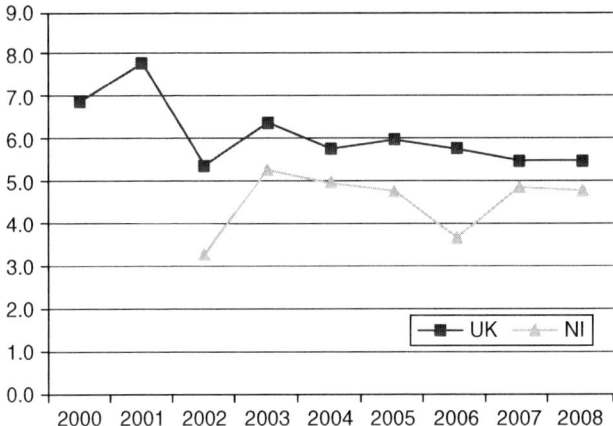

Figure 4.2 Plot of UK and Northern Ireland GEM TEA indicators 2000–8
Source: Based on figures given in UK and Northern Ireland GEM reports 2000–8.

An alternative view of the effectiveness of the initiative is reflected in the following analysis which looks at the GEM results plotted slightly more accurately in Figure 4.2.

The 2003 GEM figure for Northern Ireland was indeed published about nine months after the Accelerating Entrepreneurship Strategy was launched and this chart indicates that compared with the 2002 figure, it showed a substantial rise and that although the UK average figure had also risen, the Northern Ireland figure rose proportionally more. However the inclusion of the UK average figures for 2000 and 2001, which were the first years of GEM but for which separate Northern Ireland measurements were not made, indicates that, UK wide, the 2002 figure was out of line from the trend and was not therefore a good baseline indicator. Further, if the Accelerating Entrepreneurship Strategy was going to have an effect, it seems reasonable that its impact would not be immediate on the occasion of its launch in 2003 but would take time to develop and would not therefore be expected until 2004 at the earliest. Also, although the Northern Ireland result for 2003 was not released until sometime after the launch of the strategy, it was actually being measured at about the time of that launch and could not therefore have reflected the impact of that launch. These observations therefore suggest that the rise from 2002 to 2003 which Invest NI had claimed as an indicator of the success of its initiative was too early to be due to the initiative and was instead a UK-wide

> correction from an abnormal result the previous year. The best figures to show the impact of the Accelerating Entrepreneurship Strategy are therefore those from 2003 to 2008. These figures suggest that instead of a sustained relative rise in Northern Ireland due to the initiative, Northern Ireland appeared to have mirrored the UK trend which, over the period from 2000 to 2008 as a whole, had shown a steady decline. This interpretation suggests that there was no apparent significant impact from the Invest NI initiative.
>
> NB * The Total Entrepreneurial Activity (TEA) (now referred to as Early Stage Entrepreneurial Activity) rate for a country or region is the percentage of the adult population in the country who have taken some action towards creating a new business in the past year or who are the owner/managers of an active business less than 42 months old.

Some studies however have taken a broader view and looked at the cumulative effect of programmes. Huggins and Williams, for instance, produced a review of Labour government intervention in the UK over the ten-year period from 1997 to 2007. In their introduction they pointed out that 'despite the rapid growth of the SME sector since the 1970s, rates of entrepreneurial activity in the UK remain moderate by international standards' and that 'a priority for the UK government' has therefore been 'to create an environment conducive to stimulating entrepreneurship'. 'Since its arrival in 1997', they reported, 'the Labour government in the UK has taken steps to attempt to tackle barriers to enterprise and entrepreneurship by addressing economic, political, legal and cultural issues in order to boost rates of entrepreneurial activity'.[11] However the review concluded that despite these efforts, 'across the UK, as a whole, there has been little improvement in business start-up rates or other entrepreneurship indicators'.[12]

Besides national efforts in the UK, there have also been attempts 'to promote enterprise in more deprived areas and among the disadvantaged groups that are heavily represented there'[13] because it has been supposed that 'enterprise can be a route out of disadvantage and deprivation'.[14] Frankish et al. have pointed out that 'UK policy makers have observed that deprived areas exhibit lower levels of enterprise than more prosperous areas' and that 'considerable sums of public money have therefore been expended on seeking to raise "enterprise rates" in deprived areas on the grounds that enterprise constitutes an exit route from deprivation for those exhibiting such "enterprise"'.[15] Johnson, in looking at differences in UK regional firm formation rates, has also commented on the 'implicit or explicit commitment of a number of Regional Development Agencies to matching their region's formation rate to that of the county as a whole'. He added, though, that 'a policy aimed at raising a region's formation activity in relative terms faces a significant challenge' as it is clear from the data that 'no region was able to sustain a continuous year on year rise' in its actual number of new firm births relative to the national standard.[16]

Greene et al. looked at the changing nature of entrepreneurship over a 30-year period in the 'low' enterprise area of Teesside. 'Given the objective of policy in the 1980s and 1990s was to make Teesside more entrepreneurial', they asked, 'did it work?'[17] Their finding was that 'whilst Teesside has been a laboratory for enterprise culture experiments for thirty years, it has not resulted in any clear acceleration of entrepreneurial activity',[18] and that 'Teesside, along with almost every UK county and region remains in the same relative position as it did 10, 20 and probably 30 years ago'.[19]

Storey, in promoting the Greene et al. study, reported that

> the Tees Valley in North East England [is] pretty much the most consistently low enterprise area of England judging from official statistics. So what do we find? The answer is that despite this area being an enterprise laboratory with pretty much every imaginable potion being administered to promote enterprise, the new businesses and their performance looks remarkably similar over three decades.[20]

Green et al. therefore concluded that '[i]f there has been some form of enterprise/entrepreneurship policy over these decades it has clearly not resulted in any shift whatever in the relative position of the regions'.[21] 'The evidence that the provision of public support led to superior performance outcomes is', they suggest, 'weak at best'.[22]

Bannock, from an international perspective of small business economics, reported that 'our review of business policy instruments ... indicates that, with a few exceptions, results are unimpressive – and even for the exceptions, they are fairly marginal in their effects. There is no reason to suppose that if most subsidy and assistance programmes were abolished altogether, it would make a significant difference to the shape and prosperity of the SME sector anywhere'.[23] Although, he says, 'all governments recognise the importance of SMEs and wish to promote them', he concludes that 'most instruments used by governments to promote SMEs fail to achieve their objectives, or have only a very minor impact'.[24]

Such findings suggest that recent and current policies to raise the levels of enterprise and entrepreneurship have not worked. Although there are not many such findings which cast doubt on the effectiveness of these efforts, there nevertheless appears to be significantly more reliable evidence for such a conclusion than for the contrary view that intervention has worked. Although it can be, and often is, argued that individual programmes or projects might have had a positive effect, evaluations to show this are frequently conducted by, or for, the organisations responsible for implementing the programmes or projects and so their findings have to be discounted, unless they pass an open scrutiny. Instead it seems reasonable to conclude that what evaluation evidence there is indicates that traditional policies have not worked. As the previous chapter has indicated, those policies, if not directly based on current models of the enterprise/entrepreneurship process, have been influenced by or are at least consistent with those models and therefore the failure of those policies must call into question the validity of the models.

Case 4.2 Some findings from the Richard Report

> Douglas Richard was invited by the Conservative Party to convene a Small Business Task Force to consider the UK Government's role in supporting small business. The Task Force produced an interim report in 2007 and a final report in 2008. Although its primary focus was small business, the review did also consider entrepreneurship but found it hard to find sufficient evidence:
>
> > Genuine economic evidence of the impact (or otherwise) of assistance to small businesses is hard to find. The Government has been reluctant (or unable) to publish any and has restricted itself to anecdotal or survey-based data. These clearly *do* demonstrate that Government support does and can assist individual companies. But, given the scale of expenditure, does this add up to a real impact on regional economies?
>
> The Task Force also asked local authorities and Regional Development Agencies (RDAs) to provide their analyses of the effectiveness of the support schemes they operated, but again little relevant information was forthcoming. One RDA, for instance, replied that
>
> > you also asked for any evaluation material but unfortunately we do not have any information that we are able to provide at this time.

> In the absence of sufficient evaluation evidence from those who were responsible for the support, the Task Force commissioned its own analysis which, among its other findings, reported that
>
>> there is no positive correlation between increased government support and increased entrepreneurial activity.
>
> Overall, therefore, the Task Force concluded that
>
>> the current overall expenditure of over £12 billion per year cannot be justified in the absence of compelling evidence of effectiveness.

Source: *Richard Review on Small Business and Government*, Interim Report, March 2007, at www.conservatives.com/pdf/richardreport-interim-2007.pdf, accessed on 17 October 2009; and D. Richard, *Small Business and Government: The Richard Report* (London: NESTA, 2008).

Other findings about enterprise

The findings quoted above came from what might be classed as policy evaluations. However there are also other studies which, while they are not evaluations of policies or programmes based on the models in question, have produced findings which also raise doubts about the present approaches.

One such study is the Global Entrepreneurship Monitor (GEM) initiative. Although it was not designed to provide an evaluation of enterprise and SME policies, GEM did try to explore what makes a country more or less entrepreneurial, and it suggested a conceptual model, described in Chapter 3, which assumed that national conditions were a relevant factor. The GEM model thus assumed that it was relevant to look at national levels and tried to measure and compare national (and sometimes regional) levels of entrepreneurship.

However, as Chapter 3 also records, the only conclusion GEM now seems to present is that the rate of entrepreneurship in a country is related to that country's GDP *per capita*, although some would question even that finding. Despite its original aim, GEM has not provided support for models of entrepreneurship, even its own, which suggest relevant factors other than *per capita* GDP. However it has generally only looked at national factors and measures national, or sometimes regional, levels of entrepreneurship.

GEM's current model of the relationship between a country's level of entrepreneurship and its *per capita* GDP is a U-shaped curve suggesting that rates of entrepreneurship will be higher in countries with relatively low or relatively high *per capita* GDP. There is however considerable variance between the rates of entrepreneurship in countries with similar *per capita* GDP and this has been interpreted as deviations for various reasons from an 'equilibrium' or 'optimal' rate.[25]

Such studies and explanations, however, consider national, or at least regional, rates of entrepreneurship and seek to explain them by national, or regional, factors such as characteristics, conditions and/or equilibrium rates. They therefore offer no explanation for the significant variations in the levels of entrepreneurship within national or regional boundaries which other studies have found. For instance:

- Studies of VAT registrations in the UK show a level of new registrations (which is generally held to reflect the level of new business creation) in at least one London borough which is over six times the level in Durham (see Table 4.1). The reported rate in the City of London is almost 100 times the level in Durham but that is likely to be because the City of London actually has a very small resident population, and many businesses are registered in the City by people who live outside it. That is however less likely to be the reason for the high rate in the Borough of Camden, which is the example quoted in Table 4.1, as it could well be one of the places in which the people with businesses in the City live.
- Glaeser et al. looked at clusters of entrepreneurship in the US and found that 'semi-permanent differences in entrepreneurship supply

Table 4.1 Variations in business start-up rates across the UK (as indicated by VAT registrations per 10,000 resident adult population in 2007)

City of London	1692	Pembrokeshire	34
Borough of Camden, London	109	Cardiff	32
St Albans	73	Northern Ireland	32
Stratford-on Avon	61	Newcastle	30
Aberdeen	58	Liverpool	29
Bristol	42	Shetland Islands	28
Edinburgh	40	Oxford	25
Highland Scotland	39	South Tyneside	21
Cambridge	38	Durham	17
Glasgow	36	**UK overall**	**42**

Source: http://stats.berr.gov.uk, accessed on 3 January 2010 (2007 was the latest year for which figures were then available). Crown copyright material is reproduced with the permission of the Controller of HMSO.

exist spatially'. They tried to see if there could be explanations for this, exploring some possible reasons based on traditional economic assumptions, but concluded that their results were 'compatible with the Chinitz[26] view that some places just have a greater supply of entrepreneurs'.[27]

- Audretsch and Keilbach[28] reported on a study in which they looked at the capacity to create new firm start-ups (which they called entrepreneurship capital – see also Illustration 11.5) within different regions in Germany. They found that whether they were looking at knowledge-based entrepreneurial new ventures or low-tech entrepreneurial new ventures, 'entrepreneurship capital shows significant spatial autocorrelation and does not spill over into neighbouring regions'. They took that as 'evidence that entrepreneurship capital is indeed linked to cultural variables that are strongly spatially clustered', although it was not 'an analysis of the actual cultural variables involved'. They concluded that 'whilst entrepreneurship may in fact constitute the missing link for economic growth ... the capacity to generate entrepreneurship is in fact a local phenomenon'. It is relevant to note that, in finding this effect, Audretsch and Keilbach used data from the 440 German counties ('Kreise') which are much smaller units of population than those which GEM considers and the effect they observed is therefore likely to be missed by GEM's measurements of entrepreneurship. GEM produces figures for the level of entrepreneurship in countries or sometime regions, whereas the 'Kreise' or counties, on which the figures used by Audretsch and Keilbach were based, are much smaller than that.
- Stam, in looking at entrepreneurship in evolutionary economic geography, reports that 'there are pronounced differences within and between nations in rates of entrepreneurship ... and these differences tend to be persistent over time, reflecting path dependence in industry structure, institutions and culture'.[29]
- Parker, in a review of what economics adds to our understanding of entrepreneurship, states that 'it is now well established that white Britons and Americans have rates of participation in entrepreneurship that are between two and three times higher than their black compatriots. And a similar ratio applies to males' rate of participation in entrepreneurship relative to that of females in those countries. Furthermore, lower participation rates of blacks and females are not just a recent phenomenon'.[30]

Summary

Comparing what the models would predict, what the initiatives which were consistent with them had projected, and what the available evidence has indicated suggests that, in at least some cases, the facts do not fit the theory.

The scientific approach to establishing the validity of a theory is a process of continuous testing, until such time as the theory is disproved. Therefore many observations which are consistent with a theory are not taken as proof that it is correct, only that it has not yet been disproved and some aspects of it at least appear to work, whereas just a few reliable observations which are not consistent with it are generally held to have disproved it and to justify the need for a new theory. Thus a single observation, taken at a solar eclipse, which indicated that the path of light from the stars to the earth was bent if it passed close to the sun was enough to disprove Newton's theory and to support Einstein's, although Newton's 'law' of gravity was nevertheless still taken to be accurate enough to guide missions to the moon. Therefore, from a scientific viewpoint, it does not require 100 per cent contrary evidence to negate a theory. Even if only a small body of reliable findings are inconsistent with a theory, that is held to be enough to make a *prima facie* case against the theory, even if there also appear to be many observations supporting it.

This chapter has reported indications that there appears to have been little or no impact by entrepreneurship programmes on the relative levels of entrepreneurship which they were intended to raise. That in turn suggests that the programmes were based on the wrong form of intervention. That intervention was influenced by, or was at least consistent with, a number of theories and models purporting to explain the factors influencing the level of entrepreneurship. This, together with the indication that a number of other apparently independent findings are also inconsistent with the models, suggests that those models are themselves incorrect. Thus both aspects of this conclusion suggest that if our understanding of entrepreneurship is to be improved, and if efforts to raise levels of entrepreneurship are to succeed, then some new thinking is required.

Part I conclusions

Governments believe that enterprise/entrepreneurship can help their economies, and so they want to, and do, pursue enterprise and entrepreneurship policies. Those policies are informed by, or are at least consistent with, models of enterprise. However, it seems the models themselves are incorrect because the policies consistent with them do not work and because they do not explain other observations about levels of enterprise. In scientific terms it might be said that the models have been disproved, so there is a problem in our understanding of enterprise to be explored if new models are to be developed.

Using a medical analogy, it might be said that, following a diagnosis of low levels of enterprise, more enterprise has been prescribed in an attempt to improve the health of economies, but it appears that the prescription is not being effectively administered because more enterprise is not being delivered to the patient. Therefore, if the patient is not getting better, it is not appropriate to blame the medicine because that medicine is not being given to the patient and the effectiveness of the medicine cannot be tested until it is administered. More enterprise might help, but it is not being achieved, and its efficacy as a cure will not be tested until it is. In that situation the first step should be to find an alternative way of actually administering the medicine prescribed.

The problem seems to be that the models of how to deliver the medicine do not work and alternative methods of dispensation are required. Before they can be found, however, a better diagnosis of the dispensation issues will be required. Such a better understanding could be helped by exploring enterprise and entrepreneurship from different perspectives, and that is done in Part II.

References

1. HM Treasury, *The Green Book: Appraisal and Evaluation in Central Government*, London: TSO, 2003, p. 102.
2. OECD, *Small and Medium Enterprise Outlook*, 2000 edition, pp. 27–8.
3. J. Curran, 'What is Small Business Policy in the UK For? Evaluation and Assessing Small Business Policies', *International Small Business Journal* 2000, Vol. 18, No. 3, pp. 38–9.
4. S. Bridge, K. O'Neill and F. Martin, *Understanding Enterprise, Entrepreneurship and Small Business* (Basingstoke: Palgrave Macmillan, 2009), pp. 463–4.
5. Based on the author's personal experience and records.
6. National Audit Office, *Supporting Small Business* (London: The Stationery Office, ordered by the House of Commons to be printed on 23 May 2006), p. 5.
7. M. Hart and S. Roper, 'Small Firm Growth and Public Policy in the UK: What Exactly are the Connections?', paper presented at the *EISB Conference*, Turku, Finland, September 2004.
8. S. Roper and N. Hewitt-Dundas, 'Grant Assistance and Small Firm Development in Northern Ireland and the Republic of Ireland', *Scottish Journal of Political Economy*, Vol. 48, No. 1, February 2001.
9. Invest Northern Ireland, *Accelerating Entrepreneurship Strategy*, June 2003, p. 5.

10. Invest Northern Ireland, *Performance Information Report 2002/03–2006/07*, January 2008, p. 59.
11. R. Huggins and N. Williams, *Enterprise and Public Policy: A Review of Labour Government Intervention in the United Kingdom*, The University of Sheffield Management School Discussion Paper No. 2007.03, August 2007, p. 2.
12. R. Huggins and N. Williams, op. cit., p. 23.
13. BERR, *Enterprise: Unlocking the UK's Talent* (London: Department of Business Enterprise and Regulatory Reform, March 2008), p. 88.
14. Small Business Service, *A Government Action Plan for Small Business: The Evidence Base* (London: Department for Trade and Industry, 2004), p. 59.
15. J. Frankish, R. Roberts and D. Storey, 'Enterprise: A Route Out of Disadvantage and Deprivation?', paper presented at the 31st ISBE conference Belfast, November 2008.
16. P. Johnson, 'Differences in Regional Firm Formation Rates: A Decomposition Analysis', *Entrepreneurship Theory and Practice*, Vol. 28, No. 5, Fall 2004, p. 442.
17. F. J. Greene, K. F. Mole and D. J. Storey, *Three Decades of Enterprise Culture* (Basingstoke: Palgrave Macmillan, 2008), p. 233.
18. Ibid., p. 14.
19. Ibid., p. 245.
20. D. Storey, in an e-mail communication about Greene et al., 21 January 2008.
21. F. J. Greene et al., op. cit., p. 234.
22. Ibid., p. 245.
23. G Bannock, *The Economics and Management of Small Business* (London: Routledge, 2005), p. 133.
24. Ibid., p. 194.
25. See, for instance, R. Thurik, S. Wennekers and L. M. Uhlaner, 'Entrepreneurship and Economic Performance: A Macro Perspective', *International Journal of Entrepreneurship Education*, Vol. 1, Issue 2, 2002–3.
26. The reference quoted is B. Chinitz, 'Contrasts in agglomeration: New York and Pittsburgh, *American Economic Review*, Vol. 51, No. 2, 1961.
27. E. L. Glaeser, W. R. Kerr and G. A. M. Ponzetto, *Cluster of Enterprise* (US: Harvard Business School Working Paper 10-019, 2009), pp. 2 and 3.
28. D. Audretsch and M. Keilbach, 'The Localization of Entrepreneurial Capital – Evidence from Germany', Jena Economic Research Papers, at www.jenecom.de, 2007-029.
29. E. Stam, 'Entrepreneurship, Evolution and Geography', *Papers on Economics and Evolution*, edited by the Evolutionary Economics Group, Max Planck Institute, Jena, 2009, p. 1.
30. S. C. Parker, 'The Economics of Entrepreneurship: What We Know and What We Don't', *Foundations and Trends in Entrepreneurship*, Vol. 1, No.1, 2005, p. 29.

Part II
Exploring the Position

Introduction

Part I concluded that the current models of the factors influencing enterprise and entrepreneurship do not work. Therefore, if enterprise and entrepreneurship are to be promoted effectively, new models are needed. But new models do not appear ready formed just because they are needed: they have to be developed, and often such new approaches come from new ways of looking at things. Part II therefore looks at different aspects of enterprise and entrepreneurship to see if there are alternative ways of looking at the issues which, either separately or in combination, might suggest new approaches.

Chapter 5 first looks at enterprise from a number of difference perspectives. By exploring a multi-dimensional approach it seeks to highlight aspects which might be worth further consideration. These include the perspective of the individual and the social setting for enterprise and entrepreneurship, which might be relevant factors but which do not seem to feature in many models.

There are, however, two particular aspects of enterprise and entrepreneurship where there are differences of opinion and where misunderstandings might have arisen, so these are explored in Chapters 6 and 7. Chapter 6 focuses on the different perspectives on what constitutes enterprise and entrepreneurship. It looks at the evolving use of the words and the confusion that can now arise when different and conflicting meanings are used without adequate explanation. It therefore suggests a categorisation of enterprise to provide a common basis for discussion.

Chapter 7 looks at another area of contention and reviews arguments about whether entrepreneurs are born or made. It concludes that a review of the nature versus nurture argument does not indicate any very precise findings, but it does suggest that it would be reasonable to conclude that entrepreneurship is not exclusively genetically determined. That conclusion implies that nurture has a part to play and that a human tendency to entrepreneurial behaviour is open, to at least some extent, to environmental influences, although it does not indicate precisely what those influences might be.

Chapter 8 concludes this part by trying to see what pointers might be taken from this analysis for further development in Part III. It refers again to a medical analogy for enterprise and suggests that the different views of enterprise considered in Part II, while they do not directly lead to a new understanding, do nevertheless suggest some ideas to consider in the search for a better model. Chapter 8 also reflects on the gap that appears to exist between research and policy in this field.

5
Different Perspectives

Introduction

It is said that if three blindfolded people were each allowed to explore different parts of an elephant, without knowing what it was, then the person feeling the truck might suggest it was some sort of flexible hose, the person feeling a leg might suggest it was a tree and the person at the tail might suggest a brush. While that might be an oversimplification it does serve as a reminder that a single view of a complex subject is unlikely to reveal all its features. Engineers, for example, typically draw three different orthogonal views to portray an object and, if necessary, supplement that with other views to show obscure detail or hidden internal features.

So too is the case with issues such as enterprise and entrepreneurship. There are many aspects of these subjects but someone considering them from one viewpoint, especially if it is the same one that is often used by other people, may not be aware that there are other aspects that cannot be seen, or inferred, from that single perspective. This chapter therefore considers a variety of views on subjects related to enterprise and entrepreneurship, and in particular on the different views often obtained from business or individual people perspectives, in order to provide a more complete picture than is sometimes given. It suggests that there are different ways of looking at aspects of enterprise and entrepreneurship, each of which can provide different insights into their nature.

For instance communication is an example of one aspect of human interaction for which an appreciation of difference perspectives can be important. We accept that, when conversing with people who do not speak our language, we may need the services of an interpreter. What we sometimes fail to appreciate, however, is that we may need an interpreter even when conversing with someone who speaks the same language.

This is because what is important in understanding other people is not so much knowing what the words they are using are supposed to mean, but knowing what they mean by the words they are using. A straight dictionary definition of a word may not suffice to explain its import in every circumstance. For instance knowing that the word 'maybe' could mean neither yes nor no will not convey its meaning if it is used by someone who does not like to say no in polite communication. In such a situation knowing that it is the culture of the other person not to say no directly, and that saying 'maybe' is actually as negative as it is polite to be, can lead to a very different interpretation. Thus an appreciation of the different cultures of two people can help to avoid misunderstandings.

Perspectives on businesses

One example of the need to appreciate difference perspectives is to be found in the literature about small businesses. The author still has the first text book which he studied for a business course 40 years ago. It is an introduction to businesses and describes what they do and how they are formed and operate. One feature which, however, seems to be curious today is that, while the book indicates that some businesses are small, nowhere does it consider small businesses as a separate category within the business spectrum. In terms of their behaviour it treats all businesses as the same. Today, following the growth in interest in small businesses, most text books would indicate that small businesses have important distinctive features and do not behave just like small big businesses, but 40 years ago that distinction was missed by those who were not looking for it.

The different perspectives of the business professional and the business proprietor

In considering business success and failure, Bridge et al. suggest that there are (at least) two views on what constitutes small business success which they call the business professionals' model and the small business proprietors' model. They suggest that

> many business professionals (which term could include the professional managers of larger businesses, as well as business commentators, advisers, institutional shareholders and academics) look primarily at the business and have as their model of the successful,

or 'perfect', business one that is achieving its highest potential in terms of growth, market share, productivity, profitability, return on capital invested or other measures of the performance of the business itself. ... Many owner-managers of small businesses however do not have the same model as the one just described. Their main concern is whether the business is supplying the benefits they want from it. These benefits are often associated with a lifestyle and an income level to maintain it. If, as already noted, that is achieved satisfactorily then there is no need to grow the business further. Business success for them is being able to reach a level of comfort ('satisficing') rather than achieving the business's maximum potential.[1]

Thus Bridge et al. are suggesting that 'professionals' and 'proprietors' have different perspectives on business and, they suggest, the 'professionals' in particular may not be conscious that they are adopting a limited perspective because they may fail to see that there is an alternative. It is the professional view that often finds its way into text books, because academics also often use the professional model, which implies that the core aim of a business is, or should be, profit maximisation. Business proprietors often know differently, at least in their own case, but they may think that it is they who are deviating from the norm and are therefore just an exception to the general rule. Thus we get a common default view of a business as profit driven which may not accord with the view of the owners of many businesses who often seem to have a somewhat different set of requirements.

The perspective of the business or of its owner

As well as their comparison of 'professionals' and 'proprietors' models, Bridge et al. also report the observation that much analysis of small businesses has taken the firm, the enterprise or business created, as the primary unit of analysis:

It is easy to see why there should be such a focus. It is the business which can be seen to start or to end, it is the business which has the turnover or employment which can be measured, and it is the business which delivers things people want such as jobs and economic growth.

This existence of the business as a potential subject for consideration is clearest when the business is a separate legal entity, such as a limited company, and is least clear when the business is the activity of an individual operating as a 'sole trader'. The assumption may have been that the sole trader should be seen as an embryonic limited company which has not yet made it, but nevertheless the lack of a clear distinction between a sole trader and his or her business points to an important consideration. The business is not only the creation of the person but is also the expression of the person, even when the business is legally separate from that person. A person may start up and close down a business but the person will still continue to exist. The closure of the business is not therefore the end of the matter. It might, as in the case of a 'habitual entrepreneur' (see below), be followed by the start-up of another business and the reason for the closure may lie with the entrepreneur rather than with the business. To make sense of the totality of the entrepreneurial process it is therefore necessary to take the entrepreneur as the focus and unit of investigation, not the business.

Analysing the small business process from this different perspective also reveals another potentially useful focus: that of the group, or cluster, of businesses linked together in some way through common ownership and management by an entrepreneur or entrepreneurial team. Measured on the performance of their latest venture, habitual entrepreneurs may seem to perform no better than novice entrepreneurs, whereas if the performance is measured across the cluster it has been found to be considerably better. Indeed is it quite likely that new firm formation within a cluster is a growth mechanism and therefore that, while individual firms in a cluster may not grow, the cluster does. It may also be relevant to realise that the individual businesses in such a cluster may not, at least under the EU definition, be considered to be SMEs because they do not satisfy the ownership criterion.[2]

The comparison of views also suggests that at least in the case of many small businesses, whatever the theory might appear to say, the views, abilities and aspirations of the businesses owner(s) are crucial to understanding the business, and therefore a theory of business behaviour which ignores them is unlikely to be helpful.

The perspectives of the private sector or the third sector

The traditional view of the main sectors of an economy can be illustrated by the following statement from a recent book called *Modern Economics*:

> In examining how a mixed economy works, it is convenient to distinguish between the 'private sector' and the 'public sector'. The former consists of those firms which are privately owned. The latter includes

government departments, local authorities, and public bodies such as the Environment Agency. All are distinguished by the fact that their capital is publicly owned and their policies can be influenced through the ultimate supply of funds by the government.[3]

In this system businesses, not being public-sector bodies, must perforce be in the private sector. However closer observation indicates that there are many organisations (some of which are listed in Table 5.1) which are not public bodies and so do not belong in the public sector, but with capital which is not privately owned and which, although they may trade, exist for a social purpose rather than to make money for their owners, and so do not appear to fit with private-sector firms either. In the past it seems that the dilemma of where they belong in an economy may, to some extent, have been avoided by ignoring them.

These organisations may not be in either the public or the private sectors but, nevertheless, have an economic impact and are part of the economy because they spend money, because many of them employ people and, in some cases, because they generate income by trading. Some of these organisations, such as churches, have been around for a very long time, longer than any private-sector businesses, but they have

Table 5.1 Organisations and activities which are neither in the public nor the private sector

The following organisations and activities are all part of the economy because they trade, buy things and/or employ people. However, if the economy is thought only to consist of the private sector, in which organisations trade in order to make profits for their owners, and the public sector, in which organisations use public funding to deliver government services for the benefit of those who need them, then where do these organisations belong?

Amateur dramatic clubs	Mountain rescue services
Building preservation trusts	National Trust
Co-operatives	Oxfam
Donkey sanctuaries	Professional associations
Enterprise agencies	Quakers
Fair trade companies	Rotary clubs
Golf clubs	Scouts
Hospices	Trades unions
Independent schools	University colleges
St John Ambulance	Voluntary Service Overseas
Knights of St Columbanus	Women's Institute
Lifeboat service	Youth clubs

Source: S. Bridge, B. Murtagh and K. O'Neill, *Understanding the Social Economy and the Third Sector* (Basingstoke: Palgrave Macmillan, 2009), p. 12.

not been widely thought of as comprising a specific sector, possibly because we have lacked the language with which to make that distinction. Now the words needed are starting to appear and those organisations which belong in neither the public nor the private sectors of the economy are sometimes therefore said to belong in the 'third sector'.

The term 'sector' might be thought to indicate that there are clear divisions between these areas of economic activity but, in particular between the private and third sectors, the reality is more of a gradual progression like the changes in colour in a spectrum of light. Nevertheless there are organisations in the core area of the private sector which do have different outlooks from many organisations at the core of the third sector, and neither outlook can be held to be representative of all businesses.

It is the businesses in the private sector which are more likely to be focused exclusively on profit and on growth. Third-sector businesses, if they are to survive, cannot ignore the need for financial sustainability but have other aims beyond further financial return. As the concept of building on opportunity for financial return is behind many perceptions of entrepreneurship, it has lead to implications that third-sector businesses are by definition not entrepreneurial. Chell has picked up this point in an article looking at social enterprise and entrepreneurship,[4] in which she considered the nature of social enterprise and whether, indeed how, it might be considered to be a form of entrepreneurship. She suggests that 'the definition of entrepreneurship might be modified to include the creation of "social and economic value" and may thus be applied to private entrepreneurial ventures as well as social enterprises'. She concludes that[5] 'We examined critically a definition based on Hart et al. and Kwiatkowski that we believe, with a crucial modification, is applicable to both types of enterprise: it is that entrepreneurship is the process of "recognising and pursuing opportunities with regard to the alienable *and inalienable* resources currently controlled with a view to value creation"' (Chell's italics).

Thus comparing the perspectives of private and third-sector businesses suggests both that there are not clear boundaries between them but instead a gradual progression from one to the other, and that entrepreneurship can be exhibited in both contexts.

Perspectives of individuals

The different perspectives of government agencies and individuals

Another set of contrasting views on economic development, and on its potential components such as enterprise and entrepreneurship, is the potentially different perspectives of government economic development departments and agencies and the individual people they are trying to help and to encourage to participate in the desired economic development activity.

For instance development agencies may think that additional businesses in established sectors serving only local markets are unlikely to contribute to economic growth because, if they succeed, it will only be by displacing other already existing businesses. Therefore agencies may try to focus their efforts instead on high-technology businesses in new sectors with good export prospects. As a result, because they will not support them, they may discourage people who are thinking about starting businesses which are based on older technology and/or are locally focused. Nevertheless there are often opportunities in such areas which might be suitable for individuals who want an appropriate return from their businesses, whether or not it makes a new overall contribution to the economy (and see Case 5.1).

Because of the nature of their remit, government economic departments and economic development agencies tend to focus on those things which they think might help to grow an economy with the result that their world view might be summarised by the sketch in Figure 5.1. This, like all caricatures, is something of an oversimplification, but it might nevertheless help to suggest how such people, in their jobs, tend to see the world. If entrepreneurship were to be added to the sketch, it could be done as a series of arrows pointing to and along the new business start route because that is the direction in which such agencies would like entrepreneurship to lead. As individuals they might know that there is more to life than economic development but, as departmental and agency employees, that is the focus they are encouraged and required to have. In effect they have that view because their social setting requires it.

Individuals however, when contemplating their own lives, do not tend to see things the same way. Figure 5.2 is intended to suggest how someone might see the world ahead of them at the start of their working career, if they do see the further horizons at all clearly. It might be the world view, if they bothered to look, of someone about to leave school or university. For them entrepreneurship in the form of a sign saying 'this way to start a business' may not be very helpful but entrepreneurship as a possible means of getting from where they are to where they might want to be would be much more relevant.

On the assumption that to get what they want out of life, most individuals will have to work, presenting people with entrepreneurship as an option should increase the possibilities of selecting and doing

Case 5.1 The influence of agency agenda

> It was a policy of avoiding the potential displacement effects of new businesses entering apparently well-supplied local markets that led the Local Enterprise Development Agency (LEDU) in Northern Ireland not to support new restaurant businesses in the 1980s and 1990s. Nevertheless many new restaurants were started and the restaurant sector grew considerably. That was not on the basis of the tourist trade which was not then significant but it seems that instead people were encouraged to eat out more. It might therefore be said that the sector grew despite the lack of government grants for new restaurants.
>
> However it might also be argued that actually many restaurant businesses succeeded because of that lack of support. In other sectors when businesses knew grants were available they applied for them. Those applications were then followed by periods of negotiation, during which the applicant businesses were appraised by the agencies awarding the grants and this interchange often led to changes in the proposals at the suggestion of the agencies concerned. Also the eventual offers of grants might be tied into things like targets for additional employment in the businesses concerned. Thus applicants to those agencies often changed their plans, not for good business reasons, but to suit the agenda of the agencies concerned, which were often more focused on an official view of the wider economy than on a practical view of the individual business applications. However in the case of restaurateurs, because they knew that there were no grants for them, they just got on with it and made their own decisions without being diverted from their purpose by well-meaning agency staff who had other agenda.

appropriate work, whether that entrepreneurship is realised in new private-sector business formation, in social entrepreneurship or in being entrepreneurial while being employed by someone else. That therefore might be their perspective of entrepreneurship.

This comparison of perspectives thus raises the question of whether entrepreneurship is, or should be, defined solely in terms of new business creation and growth, or whether it is more relevantly seen as an approach to work which can variously be applied depending on the objectives and circumstances.

Figure 5.1 An economic development agency's world view?
Source: S. Bridge, 'Could a Comparison with Medicine Help Our Understanding of Entrepreneurship?', paper presented at the ISBE 28th National Conference, 2005.

The perspective of individual choice or of social context

Economic models are persistently incompetent, in the sense that they persistently fail to make the accurate predictions of which scientific models are routinely capable.[6]

90 Rethinking Enterprise Policy

Figure 5.2   An individual's world view at the start of working life?
Source: S. Bridge, 'Could a Comparison with Medicine Help Our Understanding of Entrepreneurship?', paper presented at the ISBE 28th National Conference, 2005.

Science likes to be accurate in its predictions, and it has found that the laws of physics can be used to make some acute predictions about human behaviour. Philip Ball, in his book, *Critical Mass*,[7] shows how human beings, when they act in groups, tend to behave as if they were conforming to physical laws, even though they make individual decisions about their behaviour. This, he suggests, is rather like gas particles which individually are free to go anywhere but together tend to conform to the movement of the other particles. We may think that we make separate choices but taken overall our behaviour can similarly conform to group patterns. By using the science of collective behaviour, Ball explains, it is possible to make some predictions about how people will behave collectively, even when they are subject to individual free will:

> The new physics of society: it seeks to find descriptions of observed social phenomena and to understand how they might arise from simple assumptions. Equipped with such models, one can then ask what we would need to do in order to obtain different results. ... What physicists are now trying to do is gain some understanding of how patterns of behaviour emerge – and patterns undoubtedly do emerge – from the statistical mêlée of many individuals doing their own idiosyncratic thing.[8]

'Collective actions and effects' Ball suggests, 'are inevitable. No matter how individualistic we think we are'.[9] But, he points out, 'there is nothing in these models ... that dictates what people *ought* to do. Rather, the aim is to find out what people *will* do, using some simple assumptions about what motivates them and allowing for the constraints they encounter'.[10] What Ball is suggesting is that human beings are affected by the behaviour of others and that, while we might each be free to make our own individual choice about what to do, nevertheless it can be observed that, taken overall, our behaviour is often influenced by that of the rest of society, even if we do not like to admit it. Therefore, as Ball states, 'individual tendencies do not necessarily extrapolate to group behaviour'.[11]

Logical choice or 'Fantasies, Feelings and Fun'

Studies of consumer behaviour, it has been said, used to be based on an information processing model which:

> regards the consumer as a logical thinker who solves problems to make purchasing decisions. The information processing perspective has become so ubiquitous in consumer research that, like fish in water, many researchers may be relatively unaware of its presence.[12]

However, although ubiquitous, that model has been found by some people to be an inadequate reflection of actual consumer behaviour:

> Researchers have begun to question the hegemony of the information processing perspective on the grounds that it may neglect important

> consumption phenomena. ... Ignored phenomena include various playful leisure activities, sensory pleasures, daydreams, esthetic enjoyment, and emotional responses. Consumption has begun to be seen as involving a steady flow of fantasies, feelings, and fun encompassed by what we call the 'experiential view.' This experiential perspective is phenomenological in spirit and regards consumption as a primarily subjective state of consciousness with a variety of symbolic meanings, hedonic responses, and esthetic criteria. Recognition of these important aspects of consumption is strengthened by contrasting the information processing and experiential views.[13]

Thus:

> a number of consumer researchers began to investigate the emotional aspects of advertising and the feelings derived from consumption. Increasingly, the contrast between cognitive and emotional factors – the respective roles of thoughts and feelings – became a theme of great urgency in consumer research.[14]

and:

> specifically, during the early 1980s, the conventional concern for decisions to buy, prevalent during the 1960s and 1970s, gradually gave way to an expanded interest in the consumption experience. In short, as the narrow decision-oriented view yielded in some circles to a broadened experiential perspective, many consumer researchers began to dwell on various aspects of consumer fantasies, feelings and fun.[15]

Consumer behaviour is believed to rest on value, but the value comes from the benefits provided by the goods or services purchased rather than from the goods or services themselves:

> The emphasis ... is upon the services of goods, not upon the goods themselves. Wants should be thought of not as desires for goods – but rather for the events which the possession of them makes possible ... Goods are wanted because they are capable of performing services – favorable events which occur at a point in time.[16]

The value sought is satisfying experiences and therefore:

> The thesis ... may be stated quite simply. What people really desire are not products but satisfying experiences. Experiences are attained

through activities. In order that activities may be carried out, physical objects or the services of human beings are usually needed. Here lies the connecting link between man's inner world and the outer world of economic activity. People want products because they want the experience – bringing services which they hope the products will render.[17]

This analysis suggests that instead of the more traditional view that consumption should be considered primarily as buying decisions made on the basis of some sort of logic and that consumers therefore seek information on which to base their analysis, it should be considered to be based on experience sought in which issues such as fantasies, feelings and fun are all relevant. It is not argued here that entrepreneurship is similar to this form of consumption, but if issues of fantasies, feeling and fun motivate one area of human activity in which a logical evaluation of benefits might have been expected, might they not apply in others? A logical evaluation of benefits does not explain the urge many people have to possess fashionable items of clothing or the desire of children to have the currently popular toy. Are they not instead being motivated by what their role-models have and their peers want and the satisfying experience they seek is to have the same thing for themselves and thus to feel part of the group?

The implications

This review of different aspects of business and individual aspects of enterprise and entrepreneurship suggests that these are not single-dimension issues which can be fully understood from just one perspective. Therefore, to appreciate what is going on, it is necessary to view issues from as many different angles as possible, and without the insight provided by such an overall perspective, it may not be possible to see how different aspects of enterprise and entrepreneurship might be influenced. This suggests that the sort of understanding that comes from multiple perspectives may be needed if useful new models of how actually to promote enterprise are to be developed.

Among the particular aspects that are suggested by such a multi-dimensional approach are the perspective of the individual and the social setting for enterprise and entrepreneurship. So they might be worth further consideration as the latter in particular does not currently seem to feature in many models.

References

1. S. Bridge, K. O'Neill and F. Martin, *Understanding Enterprise, Entrepreneurship and Small Business* (Basingstoke: Palgrave Macmillan, 2009), p. 245.
2. Ibid., pp. 179–80.
3. J. Harvey, *Modern Economics* (Basingstoke: Palgrave Macmillan, 1998), p. 22.
4. E. Chell, 'Towards a Convergent Theory of the Entrepreneurial Process', *International Small Business Journal*, Vol. 25, No. 1, February 2007, pp. 5–23.
5. Ibid., p. 18.
6. P. Ball, *Critical Mass: How One Thing Leads to Another* (London: Arrow Books, 2004), p. 224.
7. Ibid.
8. Ibid., pp. 35–6.
9. Ibid., p. 36.
10. Ibid., p. 182.
11. Ibid., p. 395.
12. M. Holbrook and E. Hirschman, 'The Experiential Aspects of Consumption: Consumer Fantasies, Feelings and Fun', *Journal of Consumer Research*, 9, September 1982, p. 132, © 1982 by the University of Chicago Press.
13. Ibid., p. 132, © 1982 by the University of Chicago Press.
14. M. Holbrook, *Consumer Research: Introspective Essays on the Study of Consumption* (Thousand Oaks, CA and London: Sage Publications, 1995), p. 13.
15. Ibid., pp. 107–8.
16. T. Morris, *The Theory of Consumer's Demand* (New Haven CT: Yale University Press, 1941), pp. 136–7.
17. L. Abbott, *Quality and Competition* (New York: Columbia University Press, 1955), p. 40.

6
Perspectives on Entrepreneurship and Enterprise

Chapter 5 explored different perspectives on some aspects of enterprise and entrepreneurship. This chapter follows that by examining different views on the meanings of the words enterprise and entrepreneurship themselves. It starts with an exploration of the different uses, meanings and dimensions of the words and, in an attempt to reduce some of the current confusion, suggests a way of categorising some of those differences. It then explores some of the issues that are revealed among the various interpretations and seeks to draw some conclusions.

Enterprise and entrepreneurship – the evolving use of the words

> Entrepreneurs are, like elephants, easier to recognise than to define.[1]
>
> While [a] generally accepted definition of entrepreneurship is lacking, there is agreement that the concept comprises numerous dimensions.[2]

The words entrepreneur, entrepreneurship and enterprise are related but trying to pin down their current multi-dimensional meanings of is not an easy task. In this respect Kilby[3] likened the entrepreneur, not to an elephant, but to a 'Heffalump': the much sought after, but never quite found, animal in *Winnie-the-Pooh*. Could an analogy for the search of entrepreneurship similarly be found in Lewis Carroll's *The Hunting of the Snark* because, in the cases of both the Snark and entrepreneurship, the quarry not only seems hard to find but might exist in multiple forms, at least one of which vanishes when cornered, unfortunately along with its pursuer?

> He had softly and suddenly vanished away –
> For the Snark *was* a Boojum, you see.
>
> Lewis Carroll, 'The Hunting of the Snark'
>
> The field of entrepreneurship is *'an intellectual onion. You peel it back layer by layer and when you get to the centre, there is nothing there, but you are crying'*.
>
> A senior faculty member at Harvard Business School[4]

The following is not in any way a complete history of the development and use of the words enterprise, entrepreneur and entrepreneurship but is instead an attempt to use some parts of that history to illustrate different approaches to their identification and the evolution of their various different definitions. It starts with the early history of the 'entrepreneur' in eighteenth- and nineteenth-century France.

The words enterprise, entrepreneur and entrepreneurship are all believed to be derived from the same root which was the French word *entreprendre* meaning 'to take between' (also sometimes given as 'to undertake') and *entrepreneur* referred originally to a 'go-between' or broker. Many commentators[5] have credited the evolution of the concept of the entrepreneur to an Irish economist living in France called Richard Cantillon, who introduced the word into economic literature in his *'Essai sur la nature de commerce en général'*, which is said to have been written in 1734 but was not published until 1755, 21 years after his death. However the *Oxford English Dictionary* records the use of the word entreprennoure in 1475 in the description: 'That most noble centoure Publius Decius so hardie an entreprennoure in the bataile'.[6]

Cantillon suggested that the entrepreneur engages in exchanges for profit and that he is someone who exercises business judgement in the face of uncertainty. This concept of the entrepreneur is a broad one, but it is based on the entrepreneur as a person, an arbitrageur, with the foresight and confidence to operate in conditions when costs may be known but rewards are uncertain. Later other French economists further developed the concept. Nicholas Baudeau (1730–92) saw the entrepreneur as an innovator and Jean-Baptiste Say (1767–1832), the first professor of economics in Europe, produced a definition of the entrepreneur that involved the combination and coordination of the factors of production to accommodate and overcome the unexpected problems. Say helped to popularise Cantillon's theory but tended to see the entrepreneur, at least in part, as a manager. However all these commentators could be described as looking at what existed and trying to put a label on what they saw. They observed the process of applying technology, capital, material and/or labour to deliver a (successful) business outcome and identified the entrepreneur as a distinct and essential agent in that system.

In contrast the recent interest in enterprise and entrepreneurship arose in the late twentieth century, not least in the US and the UK. This interest has been identified as starting with, or at least as being significantly encouraged by, the identification in the 1970s and 1980s of small businesses as an important source of new jobs. As indicated in Chapter 1, after the Second World War economic prospects seemed to be relatively good and Keynesian economic theory seemed to be working: the experiences in the 1930s of practical employment creation seemed still to be valid, sustained full employment seemed to be a possibility and, in Britain, in the 1950s and 1960s unemployment had seemed to be relatively steady at about a quarter to half a million. During the 1970s this figure grew to one-and-a-half million, and in the 1980s it rose again to three million. That shattered notions about the practicality of achieving sustained full employment using the then current models, and governments were urgently seeking new ways to stimulate employment creation.

It was David Birch in particular who has been credited with indicating small businesses as such a new approach. It was in 1979 that he published the results of his research into employment in the US from which he concluded that it was small firms, defined as those with 100 employees or fewer, which had in the early 1970s created over 80 per cent of net new jobs. The implication was that, at least in the US, it was small firms which were responsible for much of the economic growth and were the prime source of employment creation. Although many people discounted Birch's work when it was first published, further work seem to uphold his main conclusion and governments started to focus on small businesses as an important source of the economic benefits they wanted. While not all small businesses create additional jobs and many small businesses are in the service sector where work is generally more labour intensive than in the manufacturing sector, it does not detract from the perceived value of the small business sector as an important source of employment. It has also been shown that small businesses can provide other economic benefits, such as a relatively greater rate of innovation.[7]

As a result governments wanted to encourage the creation and growth of more small businesses. Because it was entrepreneurs who were understood to be the people who created and grew small businesses, and because that process had been labelled entrepreneurship, many government initiatives sought to promote more entrepreneurship through a process which was often labelled enterprise. Thus pronouncements were made such as, 'We must have an enterprise culture, not a dependency culture'[8] and 'Working together we can do more to enhance Britain's great entrepreneurial culture – ensuring that there is no no-go area for enterprise in any part of Britain'.[9]

Consequently governments funded programmes to encourage more enterprise and entrepreneurship but they did so, not because they wanted enterprise and/or entrepreneurship for themselves, but because they wanted the economic benefits which were expected from the businesses which they supposed entrepreneurs would create and/or grow. Thus, where enterprise and entrepreneurship had to be defined, it tended to be in terms of businesses creation, which was the entrepreneurial output which was supposed to lead to the desired economic outcome.

A further difference of perspectives, it is suggested, can be found when entrepreneurship is considered from occupational and behavioural viewpoints. The occupational notion, it has been suggested, refers to individuals owning and managing a business for their own account and risk and is usually denoted as self-employment, independent entrepreneurship or business ownership. The behavioural notion focuses on entrepreneurial behaviour in the sense of pursuing an economic opportunity and is generally denoted as entrepreneurship. Obviously these two notions are not mutually exclusive.[10]

Although the association of entrepreneurship primarily with private-sector business has not been universal, the lure of the supposed needs of economic development have proved to be hard to resist. That drive has led in some areas to a focus in particular on those new businesses which are emerging-technology-based, high-value-added and export-focussed, as they are thought to contribute most to economic growth. Sometimes such businesses are classed as HPSUs: high potential start-ups, and they can be a key component in policies to encourage the provision of jobs in high-value-added sectors in the hope that they will deliver high labour productivity growth. Although the search for such 'high-end jobs' has been likened to that for the holy grail, they nevertheless often appear to be 'the preferred route to regional prosperity'.[11] Thus there is an evolving use of the term entrepreneurship which seems to produce ever narrower definitions, driven, it appears, by such economic development considerations. For example the Danish entrepreneurship initiative summarised in Chapter 3 was designed to help the Danish Government to achieve its goal that 'by 2015 Denmark [would be] among the countries with the highest start up rates of high-growth enterprises'.[12] It thus defined entrepreneurship specifically as 'the entry and creation of high-growth firms'.[13] Similarly Invest Northern Ireland, in its Corporate Plan for 2008–11, declared that its Accelerating Entrepreneurship Strategy 'will increasingly emphasise the acceleration of high-potential existing and start-up companies ... (to) provide the supply line for future exports based on new product and process innovation'.[14] This aspect of entrepreneurship has even been acknowledged by GEM in its reporting on 'High (Job) Expectation Entrepreneurship'.

In many countries this desire to promote more entrepreneurship has also led to funding being made available for 'entrepreneurship (or enterprise) education' in which entrepreneurship is to be taught, or otherwise introduced, to students at all levels in the education system. This has also led to different interpretations of entrepreneurship, connected to whether this education should teach 'about, through, or for' entrepreneurship. For instance those funding or otherwise promoting entrepreneurship education have not always clearly specified what entrepreneurship meant to them in this context. They have tended to assume a business start-up 'default' definition based on economic development considerations, while those charged with running the courses have sometimes wanted to use an 'enterprise for life' definition which was more appropriate for their students.[15] The result has been a number of different approaches. One American commentator, for instance, asserted that 'one of the major objectives of entrepreneurship education is to provide students with the necessary skills to design, create, launch and effectively manage a business',[16] while, on the other hand, at least one UK university linked its approach instead to 'employability' which it defines as 'enabling students to acquire the knowledge, personal and professional skills and encouraging the attitudes that will support their future development.[17] A paper on evaluating entrepreneurship education by Hytti and Kuopusjärvi[18] suggested that there are three different roles which might be assigned to enterprise and/ or entrepreneurship education programmes depending on which of the following aims was being pursued (Incidentally this paper followed the practice of others in not distinguishing between the words 'enterprise' and 'entrepreneurship', often using them jointly and treating them more or less as one concept.):

- to learn to understand entrepreneurship (What do entrepreneurs do? What is entrepreneurship? Why are entrepreneurs needed?), or
- to learn to become entrepreneurial (I need to take responsibility for my learning, career and life. How to do it.), or

- to learn to become an entrepreneur (Can I become an entrepreneur? How to become an entrepreneur? Managing the business.)

The second of these aims thus reflects the approach of those who seek to teach what they believe will be useful for the majority of students and the third aim reflects the definitions advanced by those who seek what they suppose to be direct economic development outcomes of entrepreneurship. An example of a definition which takes the latter approach is that of the Global Entrepreneurship Monitor (GEM), the aims of which have included assessing the extent to which the level of entrepreneurial activity affects a country's rate of economic growth and prosperity. GEM, in its efforts to compare the rates of entrepreneurship in different countries, defined entrepreneurship as 'any attempt to create a new business enterprise or to expand an existing business by an individual, a team of individuals or an established business'.[19] Contrasting examples of the 'entrepreneurial' approach can be found in a Scottish Enterprise paper on enterprise and economic growth which states that 'entrepreneurial and enterprising behaviour is not confined to the creation of new businesses ... and can also be found in organisations of all sizes in both private and public sectors',[20] and in the Northern Ireland government's Entrepreneurship and Education Action Plan, published in 2003, which indicated that, for the purposes of the Action Plan, entrepreneurship was considered to be 'the ability of an individual, possessing a range of essential skills and attributes, to make a unique, innovative and creative contribution in the world of work, whether in employment or self-employment'.[21] In this sense, as Gibb recognises,

> Entrepreneurship relates to ways in which people, in all kinds of organisations behave in order to cope with and take advantage of uncertainty and complexity and how in turn this becomes embodied in: ways of doing things; ways of seeing things; ways of feeling things; ways of communicating things; and ways of learning things.[22]

A somewhat different definition of entrepreneurship is that used in Harvard University which is that 'entrepreneurship is the pursuit of opportunity beyond the resources you currently control'.[23] This definition differs from many others in that it does not specifically limit entrepreneurship to a business application, whereas, according to a special report on entrepreneurship in the Economist, 'for most people the term "entrepreneur" simply means anybody who starts a business, be it a corner shop or a high-tech start up'. The Economist did add however that the special report would 'use the word in a narrower sense to mean somebody who offers an innovative solution to a (frequently unrecognised) problem'. Thus, it suggested 'the defining characteristic of entrepreneurship, then, is not the size of the company but the act of innovation'.[24]

Different dimensions and categories

As in many examples of evolution, the words enterprise, entrepreneur and entrepreneurship may have had a common source, but their developing use has produced several different branches, so that in modern usage the words are no longer confined to a single common meaning. Several attempts have been made to categorise some of these uses, or at least to highlight some of the different aspects of entrepreneurship they might reveal. For instance Hytti's and Kuopusjärvi's categorisation of the various approaches taken in entrepreneurship education is given above. Naudé, in looking at that role of entrepreneurship in economic development, reported that Wennekers and Thurik had identified 13 distinct roles of an entrepreneur and suggested that one reason for this multiplicity of definitions/roles is the fact that entrepreneurship is studied in so many different disciplines. He also suggested that, within economics, the entrepreneur is most often approached from an occupational definition, a behavioural definition or an outcomes definition. On the basis that a person can be either unemployed, self-employed or in waged employment, the occupational definition sees entrepreneurs as the self-employed. The behavioural view includes Schumpeter's view of the entrepreneur as the agent of creative destruction and, as such, the entrepreneur is an innovator and/or someone who starts or expands new businesses. The outcomes of entrepreneurship are often seen to be the creation of new firms but can include other results such as corporate entrepreneurship.[25]

Baumol looked at entrepreneurship from a different angle and highlighted its potential to be productive, unproductive or destructive. His basic hypothesis is that the productive contribution of entrepreneurs to society varies less because of the total supply of entrepreneurs than it does from the way that the available entrepreneurship is applied to productive, unproductive or destructive applications. By looking at historical evidence from ancient Rome, early China, the Middle Ages and Renaissance Europe, he shows that the role entrepreneurs play is influenced by the rules of the society in which they operate. In ancient Rome, he suggests, 'people of honourable status had three primary and acceptable sources of income: landholding, usury and political payments'.

Productive commerce and industry could generate wealth but not prestige, so those who wanted prestige directed their entrepreneurship to the acceptable applications which helped the individual concerned but were unproductive for society as a whole. In Medieval China also the rules did not favour productive entrepreneurship and instead accorded supreme prestige to high positions in the state bureaucracy, thus again encouraging the application of entrepreneurship to unproductive activity. In England in the early Middle Ages, the institution of primogeniture meant that often the only opportunity for the younger sons of barons lay in warfare, with the result that their entrepreneurship became destructive. (Is that therefore the meaning implied in the 1475 usage quoted earlier?) Thus, under all these systems entrepreneurship was not necessarily lacking but was directed by society's rules to unproductive or destructive applications. However, in situations like that in England at the time of the Industrial Revolution, when the rules had changed to allow those who engaged productively in industry to accumulate, not just wealth, but also respect and influence, the application of entrepreneurship to productive purposes was encouraged and the economy benefitted.[26]

Another way of looking at entrepreneurship is that of Acs and Szerb who, in constructing a Global Entrepreneurship Index, use as their definition of entrepreneurship: 'a dynamic interaction of entrepreneurial attitudes, entrepreneurial activity, and entrepreneurial aspiration that vary across stages of economic development'.[27] Entrepreneurial attitudes they consider to be 'the general attitude of a country's population toward opportunity recognition, knowing entrepreneurs personally, attaching high status to entrepreneurs, accepting the risk associated with business start-up, and possessing the skills required successfully to launch businesses'.[28] Entrepreneurial activity they define as 'the startup activity in the medium or high technology sector, initiated by educated entrepreneurs and launched because of opportunity motivations in a not too highly competitive environment'[29] and entrepreneurial aspiration recognises 'the effort of the early-stage entrepreneur to introduce new products or services and/or new production processes, to penetrate new markets, to increase employment and to finance the business with formal or informal venture capital'.[30] This definition of entrepreneurship may have been designed to facilitate the construction of an index by listing more or less measurable components, but it does present different facets of entrepreneurship thus indicating that it is multi-dimensional. However, in its definition of entrepreneurial activity, it does limit it to the narrow field of medium- to high-technology businesses.

Categorising the uses

Three phases have been discerned in this process of the evolution of the current variety of meanings of the words enterprise and entrepreneurship:

1. The first phase was a single meaning phase in which it was at least assumed that the words meant the same things to everyone. Entrepreneurship appeared to refer to the process of starting and growing businesses whereas enterprise appeared to have a wider connotation. Therefore, although each word might sometimes have been used in different ways, those differences were often not perceived and, as a result, little need was seen for more careful definitions.
2. The second phase could be said to be a multiple meaning phase. In this phase it became apparent that the meanings of the words had widened and/or changed, that there were different interpretations of them, and they were not being used in the same way by everyone. Sometimes both enterprise and entrepreneurship were used with quite broad meanings but not always, and it wasn't always clear which meanings were being assumed.
3. The third phase might be described as the competing meanings phase. Whereas in the multiple meanings phase it was generally possible to place meanings in a progression model in which narrower definitions could be seen to be refinements of, or possible developments from, the broader definitions; in this phase some uses seem to be opposed to others. Thus attempts to present entrepreneurship as only encompassing high-tech, high-growth businesses and to focus on them alone, seem to suggest that these businesses, the HPSUs, have separate roots from other businesses the formation of which therefore could no longer be classed as entrepreneurship, or supported through entrepreneurship policy.[31]

The result of this proliferation of uses, interpretations, dimensions and meanings of both enterprise and entrepreneurship is that the current state might be described as one of multiplicity, contradiction and confusion. Both the words now have a range of meanings and those ranges overlap. Thus the words can be, and sometimes are, used interchangeably (for instance in the paper by Hytti and Kuopusjärvi, 2004) but they can also be used with different and sometimes contradictory meanings.

The result is that it is often not clear which meaning is intended at any particular time and that leads to failures of communication when people are referring to different things without realising it. It is therefore hard to discuss all this without some means of categorising the different meanings of both enterprise and entrepreneurship so that those meanings can be referred to simply and unambiguously.

That is not, however, a simple task. The variety of definitions of entrepreneurship, and the different categorisations of it given above, indicate that in common usage it does now have a number of different perspectives or dimensions. Three of these might be:[32]

The type of entrepreneurship. Some people refer to different types of entrepreneurship. Baumol for instance, as indicated above, highlighted the potential of entrepreneurship to be productive, unproductive or destructive. He has also suggested that an obvious subdivision is that between 'innovative' and 'replicative' entrepreneurs, with the former being people who do something that has not been done before and the latter being people who organise 'an enterprise of a variety that has been launched many times before'.[33]

The stage of entrepreneurship. Another dimension of entrepreneurship is its stage of development. Some definitions, such as GEM's, apply the label entrepreneurship only to the stages around actually founding or growing a venture. Others, such as Gibb, have extended entrepreneurship further back to include acting entrepreneurially, aided by the possession of essential skills and attributes, and even to having appropriate entrepreneurial attitudes and aspirations.

The focus of entrepreneurship. Another key dimension is what might be termed the focus of entrepreneurship. Some definitions of entrepreneurship are narrow, applying only to private-sector businesses or, as described above, even more narrowly to high-technology high-growth businesses. Then there are relatively broad definitions of entrepreneurship encompassing its realisation in many fields of human activity. In between the possible extremes of the destructive and the high-tech productive business there are then other manifestations such as:

- *Social entrepreneurship.* As Chell has pointed out, social entrepreneurship is increasingly being recognised as a branch of entrepreneurship which is often realised in the founding and growth of social enterprises.

- *Various forms of self-employment.* The self-employed include sole owners, lifestyle 'entrepreneurs', tradespeople and small business owners and only a minority of people will found high-growth sustainable businesses.[34] To this can also be added free-lancing.
- *Women's enterprise.* Many countries have programmes specifically designed to encourage and support more entrepreneurship by women.
- *Employability.* The Entrepreneurship and Education Action Plan quoted earlier is one example of an initiative for which entrepreneurship is defined in a way which includes its application in employment, thus implying that one manifestation of it can be to make people more employable.
- *Non-business ventures.* It can also be argued that the launch of a new theatrical production or other artistic venture, a new scientific initiative or a new geographic exploration are all ventures which require a considerable degree of entrepreneurship, even if they are not business ventures.

Thus the stage and type of entrepreneurship between them can cover quite a range of human endeavour. Figure 6.1 attempts to use these two dimensions to show all the areas which might thus be classified as entrepreneurship and to provide a plot on which the different possible areas of entrepreneurial activity might be positioned. Few people are likely to want to promote entrepreneurship across all of its possible range, as that includes destructive entrepreneurship. However this plot

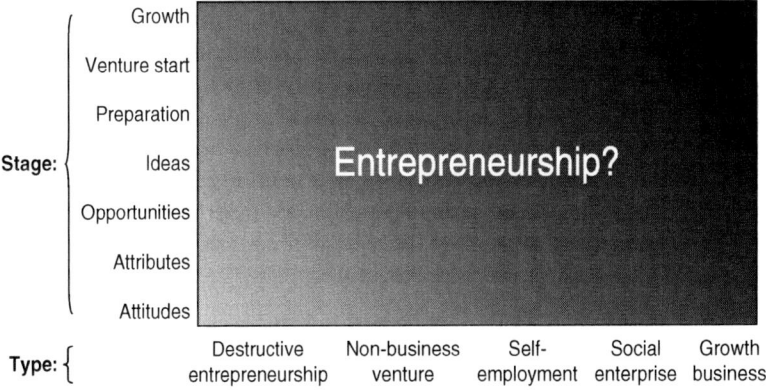

Figure 6.1 Two dimensions of entrepreneurship: Stage and type

does indicate that it might have a much greater range than is indicated by attempts to define it in terms of the high-tech high-growth businesses and thus limit it only to the area at the top right.

Another way of categorising enterprise and entrepreneurship might be the focus of the words in their different applications. This might be considered to be a third dimension, different from the two dimensions in Figure 6.1 and this aspect often seems to be the most contentious. Should the focus of enterprise and entrepreneurship be wide enough to encompass all forms of enterprising activity shown along the x-axis or be narrowed only to those new high-tech, high-growth businesses upon which some policymakers would like to concentrate? Thus, instead of the type dimension of entrepreneurship used above, which is not a progression as such but more a list of the different forms entrepreneurship might be considered to take, the focus can go from very broad to very narrow with the broader always including the narrower.

In an attempt to provide a possible means of categorising this focus of entrepreneurship, a system of 'E-numbers' is proposed and used here. It is based on the system used by economists when referring to different measures of the money supply. In this system the base and narrowest measure is called M0 and is the notes and coins in circulation and in bank vaults plus the reserves commercial banks hold with the central bank. The next is M1, which is the funds that are readily available for spending, and then there is M2, which is M1 plus savings and small time deposits. The broadest is M3, which is M2 plus large time deposits, institutional money-market funds, short-term repurchase agreements and other larger liquid assets. On the assumption that it would be helpful to apply a similar system to enterprise and entrepreneurship, the 'E-number' system uses E0 to indicate the base (broadest possible) definition and then higher numbers to indicate narrower interpretations which are each subsets of those E-numbers lower than it. (This is the other way around from the M numbers for money because the interpretation of the money supply starts from the base and then gets broader, whereas in the case of enterprise there has been a tendency to establish a base and then to narrow the definitions.) Descriptions of the possible E-numbers, and possible comparisons with a number of definitions and usages quoted above, are given in Table 6.1 and the system is portrayed diagrammatically in Figure 6.2.

Table 6.1 E-numbers: Interpretation and some comparable uses

E-number	Interpretation	Comparable uses?
E0	The application of enterprise attributes in any context, for instance in sport, exploration or art.	Broader definitions of enterprise
E1	The application of enterprising attributes for the economic advancement of self and/or others, but not necessarily as a business (for instance in employment or in unproductive or even destructive entrepreneurship).	Baumol NI Entrepreneurship and Education Action Plan Social enterprise
E2	The formation of any new economic venture (or its subsequent growth), including self-employment and me-too businesses.	Birch GEM (but with time limits) Social entrepreneurship
E3	The formation and/or growth of novel private-sector business ventures, i.e. ventures which are a distinct development from what already exists.	The target of much entrepreneurship policy?
E4	The formation and/or growth of new, innovative, high-tech, fast-growth, high-added value, knowledge-intensive, exporting business ventures.	Gazelles, HPSUs Recent Invest NI and Danish uses
E5	Could there be narrower definitions – for instance with the same focus as E4 but limited only to certain targeted sectors?	

Some issues

It is hoped that by separating out the different aspect of enterprise and entrepreneurship in the way that has been tried above, it will be easier to identify some of the relevant issues for this book, issues which might otherwise have been hidden in the confusion of the jumbled terminology.

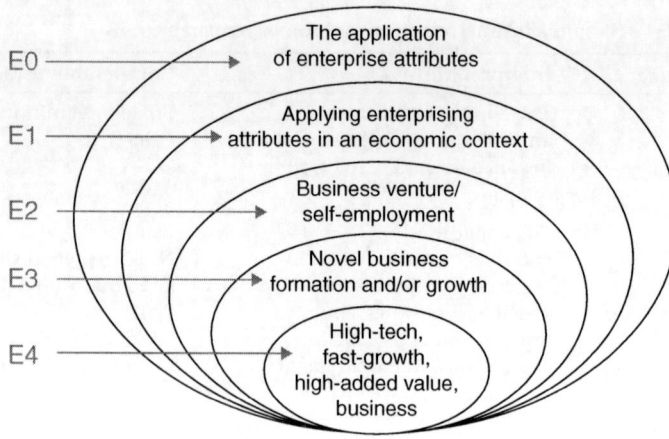

Figure 6.2 E-numbers: A categorisation of enterprise and entrepreneurship

Are some definitions based on observation and some on wishful thinking?

Casson has suggested that 'by and large, economic theorists have adopted a functional approach [to entrepreneurship] and economic historians an indicative one'.[35] Could it be that some agencies are now adopting an aspirational approach? It seems clear that the early use of the word entrepreneur was as a term to identify an observed component of the venture creation process. However one branch of the subsequent evolution of its meaning has focused instead on the results of entrepreneurship and has tried to define entrepreneurship in terms of the sort of businesses which it is hoped entrepreneurship will produce. For example those definitions which equate entrepreneurship only to high-tech high-growth business outcomes (i.e. E4) are clearly associated with strategies designed to achieve just those outcomes Thus, instead of identifying entrepreneurship because it could be shown to exist, as the eighteenth- and nineteenth-century French school did earlier, it appears that the motivation for defining entrepreneurship sometimes now seems to be the particular outcome that is desired. For instance are those definitions which fall into the E4 category based more on wish than experience? Gazelles are not common and it has been observed that 'many countries lack a sufficient portion of gazelles',[36] so therefore the motivation for E4 definitions seems to be based more on a wish for more gazelles than on an observation that they are a relatively common form of entrepreneurship.

Are there common roots?

Some definitions of entrepreneurship focus on its outcomes, such as those approaches which see it as being realised only in high-tech businesses. However, as indicated above, others consider almost any act of individual endeavour which results in a new venture to be entrepreneurial. This leads to the issue of what might be termed the degree of separation of entrepreneurship.

It is understandable that governments would like to see the emergence of more gazelles (E4 entrepreneurship) but to what extent can gazelles alone be encouraged? Is there a specific stream of business-creation activity which leads exclusively to the creation of innovative new-technology-based, high-value-added, export-focused E4 businesses? Or is there instead a wider stream from E0 leading to several possible outcomes including E2 and E3, only one of which is new-technology based, high-value-added, export-focused businesses of E4? Assuming that there is an exclusive stream is fine if reality accords with that assumption, but is it actually a case of trying to apply definitions based on a narrow desired outcome to a reality which is much broader?

We can, of course, apply the term entrepreneurship to whatever part of the process we choose but, in doing so, are we using it to label an observably distinct area of activity? Is there a general concept, whatever it is called, which, if it is to be promoted, has to be done all together or not at all, or can parts of it be isolated for separate promotion? To what extent can the promotion of entrepreneurship be focused only on E4, if E4 is just one of the shoots or branches growing from roots which are also common to E2, E1 and even E0? Is it therefore legitimate to define entrepreneurship in terms only of the formation and growth of high-growth businesses, if its antecedent stages are not exclusive to that outcome? This may seem like semantics, but if we want to promote entrepreneurship, we need to understand the real nature of the phenomenon we are trying to promote.

At what stage is it possible to distinguishing E4?

If all forms of entrepreneurship do indeed have common roots, then at what stage is it possible to distinguish E4 entrepreneurship as a separate strand? Businesses have been likened to bamboo in that, once established, they can lie dormant for several years before showing any signs of growth.[37] Therefore, if all entrepreneurship, even that which gets no further than E0, grows from the same seed, then should the growth of all green shoots be encouraged? This raises the question of when (at what stage) E4 becomes a discernable area of activity which can be separately supported, or is there instead a spectrum of varying non-discrete positions, different parts of which can be indicated broadly or narrowly? Are parts of entrepreneurship discrete areas of activity, separate from other activities as, for instance, playing football is different from shopping, whatever either of them is called, or is it like locating the colour orange on a spectrum of light which tends to red on one side and to yellow on the other and has no discrete boundaries between any of them; thus rendering any definition, broad or narrow, equally valid?

It is clear that most new ventures, when realised, are separate legal entities, but it has been said that the only way to identify growth businesses is to wait and see which ones grow. Therefore, if the label entrepreneurship is limited only to E4, are earlier stages in the development of a venture not to be considered to be entrepreneurship because they might not lead to such growth businesses, or are earlier stages to be included in the term entrepreneurship in the hope that they are distinguishable? If it is only possible to identify E4 gazelles when they have grown and not when they are formed as businesses, it is reasonable to try to target them at an even earlier stage? Are there, for instance, separate E0 attributes and attitudes for each different sort of new venture, or should entrepreneurial attributes and attitudes be seen just as general ground from which the full range of different ventures can grow or, to use another analogy, a general foundation upon which a wide range of different entrepreneurial edifices might be constructed? Is it the case that separate foundations could be distinguished for each outcome, or is it the case that the foundations are homogeneous and that to try to split them up would be artificial? To revert to the ecological analogy, are the different possible outcomes:

- like different mushrooms which, although they appear apparently separately above ground, are in reality just different fruiting bodies put out by the same underground organism;
- like different breeds of dog which are all members of the same species even if they are as different as Yorkshire Terriers and St Bernards; or
- like a range of different species of trees, each of which is genetically distinguishable from the others and has its own separate roots although they are all growing in common ground?

What are the implications for entrepreneurship policy?

The answers to questions such as those posed above will be important to policymakers, especially those who want to encourage more E4 entrepreneurship. The creation of more E4 businesses may be a legitimate aim, but just narrowing the policy definition of entrepreneurship to E4 does not mean that it is necessarily possible to identify E4 early on as a discrete activity, and if that is not possible and it cannot in practice be identified until it actually happens, how can its early stages be targeted exclusively? There may be evidence that growing more new E2 or even E3 firms may not necessarily produce more E4 gazelles[38] but that does not mean that E4 can be grown separately by effectively targeting at an early stage. So which E-numbers should be targeted by government policy?

Which E-numbers should be measured?

Another implication of such considerations relates to which aspect or aspects of entrepreneurship should be measured. If Baumol is correct and the overall supply of entrepreneurship is relatively constant, but can be applied as productive, unproductive or destructive entrepreneurship, then how helpful is it to our understanding of entrepreneurship to measure only productive entrepreneurship, and only those parts of productive entrepreneurship which are usually measured, such as E2 (which is essentially what GEM measures but with the addition of time limits)? If foundations such as attitudes and attributes which are precursors even to E0 and E1 are helpful to a wide range of entrepreneurial outcomes, then would it be helpful in guiding policy to measure them also, instead of just the specific outcomes which are usually measured? That however assumes that the relevant foundations are known and that is what this book is considering.

Conclusions

Is it realistic to define entrepreneurship narrowly?

If the early use of the word entrepreneur was as a term to identify an observed component of the venture-creation process, one branch of its subsequent evolution has focused instead on the results of entrepreneurship and has tried to define it in terms of the sort of businesses which it is hoped it will produce. Thus, instead of identifying entrepreneurship because it could be shown to exist, as the eighteenth- and nineteenth-century French school had earlier applied the label entrepreneur to a component in an observed process, the motivation for defining entrepreneurship sometimes now seems to be the particular outcome it is hoped it will produce. Thus the definitions, in that branch, become based, not on observation, but on desire.

Then there are other branches of the use of the term, such as those indicated by Baumol's inclusion of unproductive and destructive entrepreneurship and Hytti's and Kuopusjärvi's distinction between being an entrepreneur and being entrepreneurial. However the shift from an observation base to a results base for definitions does raise the issue of whether the phenomenon which is entrepreneurship can be constrained only to the production of a narrow set of outcomes. Davidsson, for instance, in discussing entrepreneurial research, points out that entrepreneurship research cannot be limited to retrospective accounts of economic outcomes. He therefore proposes that entrepreneurship should be taken as 'the behaviours undertaken in the process of discovery and exploitation of ideas for new business ventures'.[39]

Is entrepreneurship a specific stream of activity which leads exclusively, not just to business creation, but to new-technology-based, high-value-added, export-focused businesses creation? Or is it instead a wider stream leading to several possible outcomes only one of which is new-technology based, high-value-added, export-focused businesses? Assuming the first is fine if reality really does accord with what we wish it to be, but is the second, broader approach more realistic and therefore are narrow definitions based on at least an element of wishful thinking?

If entrepreneurship is a discrete area of activity then it can be observed and its defining characteristics agreed upon, but the area of distinct activity cannot suddenly be changed because someone wants it to be different or more focused. In football there can be different positions on the team, and different moves on the pitch, but they are all football and defining only goal-scoring as football is not helpful, however much goals are desired. Someone might indeed wish to encourage more goal-scoring, but to exclude general football training, on the grounds that it might lead to activities other than goal-scoring, may not be a very productive way of doing it. If however, instead of being a discrete area of activity like football, entrepreneurship is more like an area of colour on the whole spectrum of colours, then it is quite legitimate to define a very limited wave-band as the colour specified if that is the precise shade required. (And see Illustration 6.1.)

Cantillon observed a phenomenon and gave it a name, and what he observed might be classed as E2. Subsequently some of those examining the observed phenomenon of entrepreneurship have suggested that the same approach that Cantillon observed in private-sector business might have a wider application, such as in social enterprise, which implies that what Cantillon observed in E2 is actually only a part of a broader phenomenon which is E1 or even E0. Others, though, because they want to see more E3 and especially E4, have suggested that the label entrepreneurship should be applied only to those areas of activity. Crucially, in seeking

Illustration 6.1 Recognising the process for what it is, rather than what we would like it to be

The different possibilities for the nature of entrepreneurship might be likened to the trees needed to make wooden ships. If shipbuilders prefer the wood of oak trees, then it is relevant to try to grow trees only from oak seedlings as oak seedlings are genetically and visually different from the seedlings of other trees. If however, for certain key parts of their ships, the shipbuilders want curved timber, then trying to separate those seedlings which will grow into curved trees is a pointless activity because the curvature is a result of the way in which the trees are grown and is not a function of which trees are grown in the first place.

In this analogy is the definition of entrepreneurship as referring only to high-growth businesses like specifying oak wood or like specifying curved wood? Is the strand of development which leads to high-growth businesses distinguishable early in the lives of people and/or their businesses, in which case it can be encouraged and promoted from an early stage, or are high-growth businesses the chance result of later factors applied to receptive (i.e. entrepreneurial) people?

Another analogy for trying to promote more enterprise is trying to supercharge an engine. In theory if we can connect a supercharger to the air intake of an engine, we can force more air into it and as a result get more power out. However to do that we need a model: an understanding of how the components of the engine are connected together and how the whole assembly then works, so that we can 'blow' air in the right place to lead to the desired outcome. This requires that there is a unique exclusive path from the air intake to the cylinder block so that extra air introduced will lead to more mixture in and more power out. If we specifically want more high-tech high-growth businesses, is there a particular stage at which we can apply influence which will lead exclusively to that outcome? Can we identify a particular process which creates, nurtures and develops exclusively the specific sorts of entrepreneurs we want, so that we can stimulate it to do more?

Water flowing down a river can drive a mill, cool an engine, or irrigate a field, but those different applications of the water do not require water from different sources. A coin, when tossed, can land heads or tails, but a coin which lands tails, when heads are sought, is not necessarily a different coin, which should thus be excluded from the definition of a coin.

to limit entrepreneurship only to those activities which they want to see, they do not yet appear to have shown that there is a discrete process which leads only to the output they want. Also, in seeking to define entrepreneurship their way, they have tended to concentrate on the business, yet it is people who start businesses and, as Chapter 5 observes, those people often have different perspectives from that of the 'professionals' observing a situation from a business standpoint. Thus there is a difference between the role that people might play in business entrepreneurship and the role that entrepreneurship might play in people's lives. As ultimately entrepreneurship has to come from people, the role that entrepreneurship might play in their lives is explored further in Chapter 9.

Comments and implications

This chapter has examined entrepreneurship, and its associated concept of enterprise, because of the desire by governments, and others, to promote one or both of them. It might have been thought that, in seeking to promote them, governments would be clear what they were, but this does not necessarily appear to be the case and often initiatives seem to have targeted enterprise and/or entrepreneurship without clearly indicating what they are. That makes it hard to determine what might have gone wrong if, as often seems to be the case, such initiatives do not deliver the hoped-for results.

Governments, it would seem, initially wanted more enterprise and/or entrepreneurship because they had been told that enterprise/entrepreneurship created small businesses and that small businesses created jobs. Then they gathered that enterprise and small businesses provided other economic benefits as well as jobs and that social enterprises were beneficial as well as private-sector ones. Now some of them feel that the major economic benefits come particularly from high-tech high-growth businesses and so they want to focus on them. Thus some governments appear to have changed their definitions of entrepreneurship to reflect that desire.

However not all definitions of entrepreneurship have shifted, so there is now a range of ways in which the word is used, for instance between broad uses covering all the area indicated in Figure 6.1 to very narrow uses referring only to a very small portion at the top right. Thus it might be broad or narrow, but it cannot simultaneously be both, it has to be one or the other. For instance if Baumol is right, and entrepreneurship can be unproductive sometimes because it is applied in usury, or destructive because it is applied in warfare, then it cannot be limited only to high-technology business and it is potentially very misleading to use the same word in both contexts. Also, if that branch of entrepreneurship which does lead to high-tech businesses is not a distinguishable separate activity at an earlier stage, attempts to exclude activity with a different outcome are likely to be frustrated.

Should entrepreneurship therefore be considered to be a journey or a destination? Journeys can change as they progress because priorities change, and thus they can end in different destinations from those originally envisaged. Or maybe they are not undertaken with specific destinations in mind but are instead journeys of discovery undertaken to find where paths might lead. Trying to constrain such journeys to one specific end, or defining as acceptable journeys those which are the means to only one such end, could be very limiting.

It is understandable that economic development agencies might want a process that produces mainly, or even only, high-tech businesses (although it might be argued that such a strategy is misguided) but does that mean that entrepreneurship can be shaped to fit their requirement? If there is to be government intervention to encourage and support the process, can it grow only that output which governments want, or do they have to grow more generally and provide more specific support at later stages? However it might also be presumed that governments will not want to promote destructive and unproductive forms of entrepreneurship, so if Baumol's analysis is accepted, it means that along with very general entrepreneurship promotion, there should also be some means of focussing at least part of it in the desired direction for the prevailing policy objectives. All that assumes that governments can promote more entrepreneurship, whether defined broadly or narrowly. (And see Illustration 6.1.)

References

1. G. Bannock, *The Economics and Management of Small Business* (London: Routledge, 2005), p. 89.
2. Z. J. Ács and L. Szerb, 'The Global Entrepreneurship Index (GEINDEX)', Jena Economic Research Papers 2009-028, p. 14.
3. P. M. Kilby, *Entrepreneurship and Economic Development* (New York: Macmillan, 1971), p. 1.
4. Reported in H. H. Stevenson, 'Intellectual Foundations of Entrepreneurship', in *Entrepreneurship: The Way Ahead*, edited by H. P. Welsch (New York and London: Routledge, 2004), p. 3.
5. For instance S. Bridge, K. O'Neill and F. Martin, *Understanding Enterprise, Entrepreneurship and Small Business* (Basingstoke: Palgrave Macmillan, 2009), Ch. 2; and E. Chell, *The Entrepreneurial Personality: A Social Construction* (Hove: Routledge, 2008), Ch. 2.
6. The Compact Edition of the *Oxford English Dictionary* (London: Book Club Associates, 1979), p. 879.

7. For instance see in Z. J. Ács and D. B. Audretsch, *Innovation and Small Firms* (Cambridge: MIT Press, 1990).
8. Lord Young, one time UK Secretary of State for Employment, in answer to questions during a celebrity lecture in Northern Ireland (May 1993).
9. Gordon Brown, as Chancellor of the Exchequer, launching 'Enterprising Britain' in 2004.
10. See S. Wennekers, A. Van Stel, M. Carree and R. Thurik, *The Relationship between Entrepreneurship and Economic Development: Is It U-shaped?*, (Netherlands, Zoetermeer: EIM Research Report No. H200824, December 2008), p. 6.
11. See T. Jackson, 'Beyond Rhetoric', *RSA Journal*, Winter issue 2009.
12. National Agency for Enterprise and Construction, *Entrepreneurship Index 2006: Entrepreneurship Conditions in Denmark*, November 2006, at www.foranet.dk, accessed 16 March 2009, p. 5.
13. H. M. Gabr and A. Hoffmann, *A General Policy Framework for Entrepreneurship*, FORA (Ministry of Economic and Business Affairs' Division for Research and Analysis) Copenhagen, Denmark, April 2006.
14. Invest Northern Ireland, *Corporate Plan 2008–2011*, at www.investmi.com, accessed 11 February 2009, p. 5.
15. See for instance S. Bridge, C. Hegarty and S. Porter, 'Rediscovering Enterprise: Exploring Entrepreneurship for Undergraduates', a paper presented at the Institute for Small Business and Entrepreneurship 31st National Conference, Belfast 2008.
16. D. Jasinski, 'A New Approach to Integrated Entrepreneurship Education', paper presented at the ICSB 48th World Conference, Belfast 2003.
17. S. Brown, 'Enterprise in the Curriculum at Sheffield Hallam University', paper presented at Institute for Small Business Affairs 27th National Conference, Newcastle 2004.
18. U. Hytti and P. Kuopusjärvi, 'Three Perspectives to Evaluating Entrepreneurship Education: Evaluators, Programme Promoters and Policy Makers', paper presented at the EFMD 34th EISB Conference, Turku 2004, based on *Evaluating and Measuring Entrepreneurship and Enterprise Education*, Small Business Institute, Turku, Finland, 2004 – from a Leonardo funded project.
19. A. L. Zacharakis, W. D. Bygrave and D. A. Shepherd, *Global Entrepreneurship Monitor United States of America 2000 Executive Report* (Kansas City, MO: Kauffman Centre for Entrepreneurial Leadership at the Ewing Marion Kauffmann Foundation, 2000), p. 5.
20. Scottish Enterprise, *Enterprise and Economic Growth*, SEBPC(08)01, at www.scottish-enterprise.com, accessed 15 February 2009.
21. The *Entrepreneurship and Education Action Plan*, published in March 2003, a joint plan developed by the Department of Enterprise Trade, and Investment (DETI, the Department of Education (DE) and the Department for Employment and Learning (DEL)).
22. A. A. Gibb, 'SME Policy, Academic Research and the Growth of Ignorance, Mythical Concepts, Myths, Assumptions, Rituals and Confusions', *International Small Business Journal*, Vol. 18, No. 3, 2000, pp. 13–35.
23. 'What Do We Mean by Enterprise?', *Employment Initiatives*, February 1990, pp. 3–4.
24. A. Wooldridge, 'Special Report on Entrepreneurship', *The Economist*, 14 March 2009.

Perspectives on Entrepreneurship and Enterprise 117

25. Based on W. Naudé, *Entrepreneurship in Economic Development*, United Nations University – World Institute for Development Economics research (UNU-WIDER) Research Paper No. 2008/20, March 2008.
26. Based on W. J. Baumol, 'Entrepreneurship: Productive, Unproductive, and Destructive', *Journal of Political Economy*, Vol. 98, No. 5, 1990, pt. 1.
27. Z. J. Ács and L. Szerb, op. cit., p. 17, at www.jenecon.de, accessed 23 April 2009.
28. Ibid, p. 17.
29. Ibid, p. 18.
30. Ibid, p. 18.
31. Based on S. Bridge, C. Hegarty and S. Porter, 'Clarifying Entrepreneurship: Gazelles or Green Shoots', paper presented at 32nd ISBE Conference, Liverpool, November 2009.
32. Ibid.
33. W. Baumol, 'Entrepreneurs, Inventors and the Growth of the Economy', *Economics Program Working Paper Series* (New York: The Conference Board, 2008), pp. 2/3.
34. E. Chell, op. cit., Ch. 2.
35. M. Casson, *The Entrepreneur: An Economic Theory* (Cheltenham: Edward Elgar, 2003), p. 19.
36. A. Hoffmann, presentation to the pre-conference policy forum, ICSB Conference, Halifax, Nova Scotia, June 2008.
37. S. Bridge, C. Hegarty and S. Porter, op. cit.
38. A. Hoffmann, op. cit.
39. P. Davidsson, *The Entrepreneurship Research Challenge* (Cheltenham: Edward Elgar, 2008), p. 45.

7
Nature or Nurture?

Chapter 6 explored the different meanings sometimes assigned to the words enterprise, entrepreneur and entrepreneurship and suggested a way of categorising some different definitions of enterprise and entrepreneurship to make it possible to indicate which meaning is being considered at any particular time. Thus the E-numbers this suggested will be used where that might be helpful.

Chapter 6 also looked at some of the implications the different interpretations of entrepreneurship might have. Whether entrepreneurship is defined broadly or narrowly, those implications are only relevant to government efforts to promote more entrepreneurship if such promotion is, indeed, possible. If, for instance, entrepreneurship is entirely inherited, then there is going to be little in practice that governments can do to create more of it, although they might try to release more of it if it is latent or to support it when it is released. This chapter therefore looks at the associated issue of whether entrepreneurs are born that way, or whether it is their upbringing, environment and experience that make them entrepreneurs. Anyone studying the literature on entrepreneurship, sooner or later, will find references to this nature or nurture debate, but identifying what its conclusions might be seems to be a different matter.

Although there are references to a nature or nurture debate, it is hard to find clear indications of when the debate took place, or what the arguments were on either side, or even what the result might have been. While some sources seem to suggest that entrepreneurship is primarily due to nurture, there are still those who insist that entrepreneurs are born, not made, which suggests that, if there was a conclusion to the debate, it was not universally promulgated or accepted.

In some respects researching the debate is like trying to carry out an archaeological examination of a building which is no longer standing and even the exact location of which is no longer clear. Any surviving pictures of the building are more likely to be single-view artists' impressions rather than accurate multi-faceted architects' drawings, and the surviving accounts of it differ, so it is hard to determine whether such records are based on accurate reminiscences or just on distorted folk memory. If the material of the building was perishable then digging may not even find any actual remains, just traces from which the former presence of the building might be inferred.

However, for this chapter, it is not necessary to attempt to dig up and reconstruct any historic debate but instead to consider the arguments that might now be advanced for or about nature and nurture as influences on entrepreneurship. It therefore considers the basis of the views that appear to have been at the heart of the debate together with some recent suggestions that are still being advanced about the possible interplay between genes (nature) and conditioning (nurture). It does this, not to pick a winner between the various views offered, but to try to establish how entrepreneurship should be viewed by those who want to influence it. It seeks to indicate the relevant factors that studies of the development of entrepreneurship in people suggest should be taken into account in enterprise and entrepreneurship theory and policy.

One final bit of introduction may however be helpful. Following the previous chapter it is relevant to ask which sort of entrepreneurship (which E-number) is being discussed in the nature versus nurture debate. Unfortunately, like a number of other aspects of the debate, this is rarely made clear, possibly because the debate started during a phase when the possibility of different usages of the word entrepreneurship was often not perceived. In retrospect, however, it would seem that, if the question had been asked, it would probably have appeared that a major portion of the debate was about E2 entrepreneurship (which therefore included E3 and E4) but could equally well have applied to E1 or even E0.

The start of the debate

A starting point for the nature or nurture debate may have been personality traits and the consideration of their possible relevance to entrepreneurship and of the extent to which they were genetically determined. Chell, in discussing the relevance of personality theory, refers to 'the belief that there is a set of traits that characterise an entrepreneur and are predictive of entrepreneurial behaviour',[1] and, in introducing the subject of entrepreneurship, Deakins suggests that

> literature concerning entrepreneurship can sometimes be seen as stemming from three sources: firstly, from the contributions of economic writers and thinkers on the role of the entrepreneur in economic development and the application of economic theory; secondly, from the psychological trait approach on personality characteristics of the entrepreneur ...; thirdly, a social behavioural approach which stresses the influence of the social environment as well as personality traits.[2]

It is the second and third of those sources which can be aligned with the two sides of the debate. If entrepreneurs are born, then it is suggested that they should have observable traits which predispose them to entrepreneurial behaviour. If, however, they are made, then there should be indications that their behaviour has been influenced by their social environment.

The case for nature

> No real entrepreneur actually believes entrepreneurial skills are learnable or transferable. You're either an entrepreneur or you're not. It's a state of being, not a trade or a vocation.[3]
>
> Young entrepreneurs are often born, rather than bred.[4]
>
> The study found that almost half a person's propensity to be self-employed was due to genetic factors. Family environment and upbringing had little bearing, it said.[5]

After considering the role of the entrepreneur, Deakins suggests:

> The second approach to entrepreneurship is to identify certain personality characteristics or 'traits' in individuals that appear to be possessed by successful entrepreneurs. The characteristics literature has been concerned with testing and applying some perceived characteristics in individuals. From this approach it is possible to argue that the supply of potential entrepreneurs is limited to a finite number of people with innate abilities, that they have a set of characteristics that mark them out as different, and have particular insights not possessed by others. This has led to some controversy and, in terms of policy, has significant implications. Obviously, if entrepreneurial characteristics

are inherent, then there is little to be gained from direct interventions to encourage new entrepreneurs to start new businesses, although interventions to improve the infrastructure or environment may still have an effect. Whether an 'entrepreneurial personality' exists, however, is the subject of controversy and, despite attempts to provide prototypical 'lists' of characteristics of the entrepreneurial personality, this author remains sceptical of such approaches.[6]

One of the problems with a traits approach is that, if it did explain what makes people become entrepreneurs, then it might be expected that all entrepreneurs would share the same traits and that everyone with those traits would be an entrepreneur. Neither part of that assumption seems, however, to be the case which suggests that traits are, at best, only a partial explanation.

Shane also distrusts the trait approach:

> A large number of entrepreneurship researchers have sought to explain the entrepreneurial phenomenon by identifying those members of society who could be considered 'entrepreneurial individuals'. In general, this school of thought has focused on explaining entrepreneurship as a function of core human attributes, such as willingness to bear uncertainty, tolerance for ambiguity, or need for achievement which differentiate entrepreneurs from the rest of society. Unfortunately, this approach has proved largely unsuccessful, perhaps because entrepreneurial activity is episodic. Because people engage in entrepreneurial behavior only at particular points in time, and in response to specific situations, it is impossible to account for entrepreneurship solely by examining factors that should influence all human action in the same way all of the time.[7]

Chell has explored this approach in some detail, for instance in her book on the entrepreneurial personality.[8] A fundamental problem, she explains,

> is to arrive at an understanding of the nature of personality in general, given the considerable revisions in thinking that have taken place in recent years. ... The question of what is 'personality' and what is the basis of the trait construct are fundamental to such concerns. The lay person uses the term 'personality' in a very different way to that of the psychologist. ... Thus, when the lay person uses the term 'entrepreneur' they are referring to a type; they can 'recognise one when they see one' because they believe that they have sufficient public information to

label that individual as an entrepreneur: This is not the same, clearly, as the scientific process that a psychologist engages in – the ability to isolate traits that are predictive of specific behaviours; in this case it is the belief that there is a trait or set of traits that characterise an entrepreneur and are predictive of entrepreneurial behaviour.[9]

The trait argument, she suggests, has, to some extent, swayed to and fro. In this context a trait is a single dimension of personality, which is made up of a number of components of behaviour and cognition. However a question which still needs to be addressed is whether, if it is trait based, there a single trait of 'entrepreneurialism' or there is instead a relevant profile or constellation of traits. Also do all entrepreneurs have the same trait or traits, and is everyone with those traits an entrepreneur?

For the trait approach to demonstrate that entrepreneurs are born, not made, it is necessary to show both that traits do determine the entrepreneurial personality and that they are genetically determined presumably because the relevant traits can be linked to specific genes. However neither of these conditions appears yet to have been established conclusively, and even if both assertions were true, which appears at best to be doubtful, can the relevant traits be identified and measured? Chell concludes that more sophisticated research is required to provide more convincing evidence that any traits are prototypical of entrepreneurs and predictors of entrepreneurial behaviour and that, while entrepreneurs may be born with the psychological apparatus to behave entrepreneurially in later life, the strong social component suggests that there is a role for social learning and personal development.[10] (And see also Illustration 12.3 for a further reference to the inadequacy of trait approach.)

The case for nurture

> At the heart of the matter is whether the psychological and social traits are either necessary or sufficient for the development of entrepreneurship. ... While many authors have purported to find statistically common characters of [the] entrepreneur, the ability to attribute causality to these factors is seriously in doubt.[11]
>
> Social psychologists have claimed that an individual's attitudes and traits are not inherited but are developed in interaction with the social environment.[12]
>
> There is clear evidence that entrepreneurship can be learned.[13]

A counter argument that has been expressed to the trait approach is that entrepreneurship is about 'doing' (i.e. behaviour) and not 'being' (trait characteristics). 'Such a line of argument does not itself negate the possible influence of personality, as behaviour and personality are related. However, the theoretical position that behaviour is solely a function of personality may not hold up in the case of the expression of entrepreneurship. Rather, it could be argued that behaviour is a function of personality and situation, and their interaction.'[14]

However if doubts about the case for nature might be seen to support a nurture or environmental approach, Shane does not think that works either.

> Another group of researchers has sought to explain entrepreneurship by reference to the environment in which entrepreneurs have been found. In general, this school of thought has sought to identify situations in which entrepreneurial activity, often measured as new firm formation, is more likely to occur. Key situational factors that have been argued to lead to entrepreneurial activity have included competence-destroying technological change, industry dynamics, and market structure. Unfortunately, this approach, too, has failed to provide an adequate explanation for entrepreneurship, largely because it does not consider the human agency. Entrepreneurship is a self-directed activity that does not occur spontaneously from the presence of technological or industrial change. Rather, it requires the action of individuals who identify and pursue opportunities. No amount of investigation of the environment alone can provide a complete explanation for entrepreneurship.[15]

The nurture argument does not necessarily deny personality traits but stresses the influence of the social environment, for instance in forming or developing those traits. Nevertheless sometimes the case for nurture seems to be based more on the failure of, or lack of proof for, the case for nature than on any hard evidence in favour of nurture. That sort of reasoning however presupposes that if it is not one then it must be the other, and some commentators, such as Shane in the quotes above, seem to suggest that neither side has convincing arguments on its own.

Some other suggestions

The nature–nurture debate has not only taken place in respect of entrepreneurship, but also in other aspects of human behaviour and what has been described as the 'gold standard' for nature versus nurture studies has been to compare the development of adopted identical twins raised by different parents. In this way, it is supposed, it should be possible to assess the extent to which a trait such as aggression seems to be due to influences from the family, and how much to biology alone.

Initially such studies seemed to indicate that certain traits were largely due to genes, but it now appears on closer examination of more carefully collected data that the situation could be more complicated. One example given is that,

> while parents naturally cuddle babies who flirt and hug back, testy and indifferent babies get less cuddling. In the worst case, when a child's genetics lead him to be irritable, aggressive and difficult, parents tend to respond in kind, with harsh discipline, tough talk and their own criticism and anger. That route worsens the child's difficult side, which in turn provokes more of the parents' negativity in a vicious spiral.[16]

Thus the child's behaviour is mainly the result of nurture, although that nurture may initially have been provoked by something in the child's nature.

One example of the apparent impact of training on what might be thought to have been a genetic predisposition might be found in ice hockey players. In his book *Outliers*[17] Malcolm Gladwell reports that in Canada a very high proportion of professional hockey players are born in January, February or March. This, Gladwell suggests, is not because people born in those months are naturally better ice hockey players, but because ice hockey is a prestige sport for which children are selected to play at an early age. Thus, each January, a new cohort is available for selection for the youngest teams but, at the age of seven or eight, those in the cohort who were born at the start of the year have a very significant age advantage over those who were born at the end of the year. Then, having been selected, they get additional training so that they continue to improve, and so are likely to be reselected the following year, whereas those who were not selected, do not get the training and do not therefore improve to the same extent. Thus the eventual composition of the professional teams is based, not on those who initially had the most ability, but on those who had the advantage of being born early in the year and who had some ability, which was then improved by a lot of training. Some of those born at the end of the year might have had more initial ability but did not get the training to develop that ability.

Such evidence does not suggest that there is no genetic basis to behaviour, but that nurture can often change habitual behaviour because it would seem that the human brain can be 're-wired' by appropriate conditioning. For instance a baby's reaction to novelty has been shown to be a reliable predictor of whether it will grow up to be particularly timid and shy. If, however, children thus shown to have a tendency to timidity are encouraged, and even pressured, to spend time with other outgoing children who they might normally have avoided, the timid children can often overcome their genetic predisposition towards shyness.[18]

Such studies suggest that debating nature against nurture is the wrong approach because it is not one or the other but a combination of both. Sometimes it seems that nature can be reinforced by nurture, sometimes it can trigger certain aspects of nurture, and sometimes it can be countered by nurture. It may therefore wrong to ignore nature in seeking the source of entrepreneurial traits, but it would also be wrong to ignore nurture. It may not be either one or the other, but both.

Recently, Nicolaou and Shane have suggested some arguments specifically for the possible influence of genetic factors on entrepreneurship:

> We propose that genetic factors may influence the tendency of people to engage in entrepreneurial activity in four complementary ways. First, genes may affect chemical mechanisms in the brain to increase the likelihood that people will engage in entrepreneurial activity. Second, genes may influence individual differences, such as extraversion and internal locus of control, that predispose people to engage in entrepreneurial activity. Third, genes may make some people more sensitive than others to environmental stimuli that increase the likelihood of engaging in entrepreneurial activity. Fourth, genes may affect the tendency of people to select into environments that are more favorable to entrepreneurship.[19]

Nicolaou and Shane illustrate this with a diagram like that in Figure 7.1, which includes not genes *or* environment, but both genes *and* environment. They also explain that they are not proposing that individuals are born with a gene or genes for entrepreneurship, but rather that there are four complementary mechanisms through which genetic factors might affect the tendency of people to engage in entrepreneurial activity, and point out that, at present, their proposals have yet to be tested so there is no direct empirical evidence that genetic factors affect people's propensity to engage in entrepreneurial activity in the ways they suggest.[20] Thus, even though entrepreneurs may not be born with

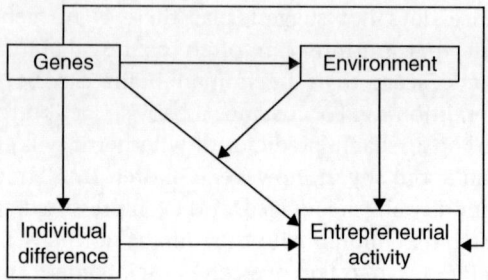

Figure 7.1 Mechanisms through which genetic factors might influence entrepreneurship
Source: Reprinted from N. Nicolaou and S. Shane, 'Can Genetic Factors Influence the Likelihood of Engaging in Entrepreneurial Activity?', *Journal of Business Venturing*, Vol. 24, Issue 1, p. 2. Copyright 2009, with permission from Elsevier.

traits that lead them to behave entrepreneurially whatever the other factors, nevertheless their genes might predispose them to develop entrepreneurial characteristics, given a suitable environment.

A further issue within the case for nurture is the possible difference between the impact of early stage upbringing and later environmental influences. The saying 'give me the child until he is seven and I will show you the man' is attributed to the Jesuits and it highlights the importance of childhood influences and suggests that they can be more important than any later instruction. The implication might therefore be that, if some aspects of behaviour are due to nurture, the timing of that nurture may be crucial. Thus promoting some aspects of behaviour may be much more effectively done when people are young and much harder to do when they are adults.

In the debate on entrepreneurial influences, Drakopoulou Dodd and Anderson also raise what they describe as the agency or structure issue: is it the entrepreneur or entrepreneurship which is being considered? Much of the early entrepreneurial literature, they report, included individualistic explanations that were seen as *a priori* true; 'entrepreneurs were different from other people so that difference must explain what they do'.[21] The same sort of argument, they indicate, has been applied to unemployment. If it is viewed through an individualistic lens, then it might appear that only some people cannot get jobs so unemployment must be caused by individuals' lack of skills or of application. However unemployment can also reasonably be explained by structural changes, industrial developments and even political considerations. The problem is to try to achieve a balanced explanation involving the action of individual agents in the context of the social environment.

Illustration 7.1 Can the supply of entrepreneurs be increased?

The case for nature, and/or for early nurture, suggests that, once people are adults, their entrepreneurial leanings are fixed and therefore, if they are not entrepreneurial by then, no further encouragement or promotion will change that. The wider case for nurture however suggests that environmental factors are important and that, even when they are adults, many people can still be influenced to be more entrepreneurial. Thus there are two schools of thought on the issue of whether and how the supply of entrepreneurs can be increased and these are illustrated by the following summaries of the views of some proponents.

Jovanovic[22] argues that the supply of entrepreneurs can be increased, believing that new business formation is shaped by the nature of prior beliefs held by individuals and the stronger the beliefs the greater the likelihood of such action. Policies for intervention then should promote individuals' perceptions of the desirability and feasibility of this kind of enterprising action, thus increasing their propensities in such direction.

In effect Jovanovic is saying that intervention can increase the propensity of individuals to be enterprising and thus increase the supply of entrepreneurs. This view is supported by Lundstrom and Stevenson.[23]

Baumol[24] reflects a contrasting view which contends that there is no shortage of entrepreneurs. Indeed, he claims, almost paradoxically, that the supply of them is constant but their distribution across productive, unproductive and destructive activities is affected by institutional arrangements and the social pay-off structure. What can happen is that they utilise their abilities in different ways and in different occupations. The task of policymakers is to 'set the rules of the game' so that that 'productive entrepreneurship' is the 'rational and informed choice for individuals with entrepreneurial talent.[25] It is, he would argue, a waste of time to seek attitudinal change since that is not the root cause of the problem. Instead 'society should align its incentives (i.e. taxation and the regulatory framework) to support legitimate and socially beneficial entrepreneurs'.[26]

In effect, Baumol is saying that there is a plentiful supply of entrepreneurs, the challenge being to activate them and in the desired direction. Issues of whether they are born or made, therefore, become irrelevant.

Source: Based on S. Bridge, K. O'Neill and F. Martin, *Understanding Enterprise, Entrepreneurship and Small Business* (Basingstoke: Palgrave Macmillan, 2009), pp. 62–4.

The conclusions of the debate?

> Entrepreneurs may well be born with the psychological apparatus to behave entrepreneurially in later life, but the strong social component suggests that there is a role for social learning and personal development.[27]
>
> Entrepreneurship is the result of the interaction between individual attributes and the surrounding environment.[28]

The summary above indicates that the discussion about whether entrepreneurship is due to nature or nurture may have been stimulated by the suggestion that entrepreneurship could be the result of genetically determined traits. Despite some considerable investigation, that hypothesis does not seem to have been conclusively demonstrated, but neither has it been entirely disproved although it might now seem unlikely. Nevertheless some people appear to have concluded that if it is not therefore clearly nature, it must be nurture, presumably on the basis that it has to be one or the other. Others, some of whom do not appear to be aware that there has been a debate on this issue, still insist that entrepreneurs are born that way.

The evidence presented here appears to indicate that both those conclusions are wrong and that neither side can be said to have won because both aspects are relevant. In other words both nature and nurture could have an influence and, although nature may be influential, nurture too is important and it should thus be possible to influence people's tendency towards entrepreneurship.

On the question of whether it is possible to influence people's entrepreneurial tendencies, it may also be relevant to note that many models of the determinants of entrepreneurship, such as those in Chapter 3, suggest that there is an environmental influence. Of course if it is assumed that entrepreneurship is solely due to nature, then no subsequent influence would be relevant and there would be no logic for models showing what it might be. Nevertheless the existence of the different models shows that many theories do support the relevance of at least some aspects of nurture.

The persistence of the 'Heroic' myth?

> One of the great myths of entrepreneurship ... [is] the notion of the entrepreneur as a lone hero, battling against the storms of economic, government, social and other environmental forces.[29]

Although the evidence thus appears to indicate that entrepreneurship is not due entirely, or even mainly, to genetic traits, the concept persists of the 'heroic' entrepreneur as an individual who somehow stands out from the rest of society. As Drakopoulou Dodd and Anderson comment:

> The popular vision of the entrepreneur has been shown to be profoundly individualistic; people may have difficulty in understanding the concept of entrepreneurship, but they readily identify with an entrepreneur.[30]

In his contribution to a book *Mastering Enterprise*, Kets de Vries suggested that many entrepreneurs are 'misfits' who are unable to accept authority and organisational rules and who need therefore to create their own environment. He suggests that

> the heroic myth begins with the hero's humble birth, his rapid rise to prominence and power, his conquest of the forces of evil, his vulnerability to the sin of pride and finally his fall through betrayal or heroic sacrifice.
>
> The basic symbolic themes here – of birth, conquest, pride, betrayal and death – are relevant to all of us. Some entrepreneurs act out the same myth, as we have seen, with a Greek chorus in the background applauding their achievements but warning them about pride.
>
> Perhaps the myth explains why so many entrepreneurs live under a great amount of tension. They feel they are living on the edge, that their success will not last (their need for control and their sense of distrust are symptomatic of this anxiety) but they have also an overriding concern to be heard and recognized – to be seen as heroes.[31]

Drakopoulou Dodd and Anderson suggest that the persistence, despite considerable evidence to the contrary, of this idea of the entrepreneur 'operating as an atomised individual – sometimes maverick, often nonconforming, but single-handedly relentlessly pursuing opportunity – is an ideological convenience', the endurance of which is an example of 'mumpsimus': 'someone who sticks obstinately to their old ways, despite the clearest evidence that they are wrong'.[32] They have examined the 'individualistic myth' and suggest that it is underpinned both by the popular image, often reinforced by newspaper journalism, of the entrepreneur as a solitary battler, and by academic studies which echo the individualistic explanations of psychology and economics[33] and use the individual as the unit of analysis. Such studies, they also suggest, 'remain superficially attractive because of the conflation, perhaps even confusion, of description of entrepreneurial behaviour and cause'.[34]

> One possible explanation lies in the issue of the most appropriate unit of analysis for developing explanatory theory. Entrepreneur*ship* is often talked about as the embodiment of those enterprising qualities and activities that are held dear, such as change and development, so that we expect progress in the modernist sense that somehow tomorrow will be better than today. But entrepreneurship thus conceived is what Nisbet[35] calls a very broad unit idea. It is both vague and elusive and at this level often defies definition. Yet the thematic power of the concept that embraces its capaciousness also masks its teleological qualities. This is why we so often hear the politicians appeal for more entrepreneurship; entrepreneurship appears both as a descriptor and an explanation. It presents a quasi-explanation and a demonstration, but drained of specificity and *a priori* true.[36]

When names are offered as examples of heroic entrepreneurs, people like Alan Sugar or Richard Branson often feature. When they first started business, their entrepreneurship was that which would be categorised no higher than E2 although some of their subsequent ventures may have been E3 or possibly E4. If some famous explorers are included as examples of heroic entrepreneurship, then that entrepreneursip can be as low as E0. Therefore heroic entrepreneurship, if it exists, is not necessarily high E-number entrepreneurship: what gets it noticed is its extent and its apparent success, and not a particularly high E-number focus.

The implications

If the debate about entrepreneurial traits has been going on for at least 25 years, why has it not yet been conclusive? Or, if it is possible to conclude that, while genetics may play a part, environmental factors are at least as important, why does the 'heroic myth' persist?

Perhaps it depends on what is meant by an entrepreneur. Is the perceived heroic entrepreneur in the same category as anyone else who starts a business? Many people believe that they know a 'heroic' entrepreneur when they see one and can probably name some famous examples, but those judgements appear to be subjective and not susceptible to scientific measurement. In contrast the act of starting a business is relatively easy to measure and so is often what is reported in statistics on the levels of entrepreneurship. If 'heroic' entrepreneurship is, however, a different category, what precisely distinguishes it and how might it be measured?

There is also a distinction between the process and the end result. Should an activity be classified as entrepreneurship because of the way it is done or because of its result, such as a new business? True entrepreneurship, it has been said, often results in failure. Among entrepreneurs, according to Handy, the successful ones have nine failures for every success but it is only the successes that you will hear about, and the failures they credit to experience. Oil companies, he reports, expect to drill nine empty wells for every one that flows and thus getting it wrong is a key part of getting it right.[37]

In his book on entrepreneurship Shane explained that

> A central premise of this book is that the failure of academics to offer a coherent conceptual framework for entrepreneurship has resulted from a tendency of researchers to look at only one part of entrepreneurial process – the characteristics of the entrepreneurs themselves, the opportunities to which they respond, their strategies, their resource acquisition or their organizing processes – without consideration for whether the explanations that they offer have any explanatory power for, or even relationship to, the other parts of the entrepreneurial process examined by other researchers.
>
> Perhaps the largest part of this problem lies with the division of the field of entrepreneurship into two camps: those who want the field of entrepreneurship to focus exclusively on individuals and those who want the field of entrepreneurship to focus exclusively on external forces.[38]

This review of the nature versus nurture argument does not indicate any very precise findings but it does suggest that it would be reasonable to conclude that entrepreneurship is not exclusively genetically determined. That conclusion implies that nurture has a part to play and that a human tendency to entrepreneurial behaviour is open, to at least some extent, to environmental influences, although it does not indicate precisely what those other influences might be. It seems, therefore, that it should be possible to promote more entrepreneurship if the right influences can be identified, and thus efforts to promote it are not necessarily going to be wasted. Nevertheless, it does seem that nature may also play its part and, while the 'heroic' entrepreneur has been described as 'mythical', the persistence of the feeling that some people are going to be entrepreneurs, almost whatever the environment, should also be recognised.

References

1. E. Chell, *The Entrepreneurial Personality: A Social Construction* (London: Routledge, 2008), p. 83.
2. D. Deakins, *Entrepreneurship* (London: McGraw-Hill, 1999), p. 9.
3. M. Brown, 'Risky Business', *Holland Herald* (the in-flight magazine of KLM)
4. From an article titled 'Encouraging Youthful Enterprise', *RSA Journal* 1/6, 2002, p. 28.
5. Newspaper report, Independent, 6 June 2006.
6. D. Deakins, op. cit., p. 18.
7. S. Shane, *A General Theory of Entrepreneurship* (Cheltenham: Edward Elgar, 2003), pp. 2/3.
8. E. Chell, op. cit.
9. Ibid., pp. 82–3
10. Ibid. – see pp. 101 and 200.
11. Ibid., p. 87.
12. E. Stam, 'Entrepreneurship, Evolution and Geography', *Papers on Economics and Evolution*, edited by the Evolutionary Economics Group, Max Planck Institute, Jena, 2009, p. 8.
13. NESTA, *Creating Entrepreneurship: Entrepreneurship Education for the Creative Industries*, written and published by the Higher Education Academy Art Design Media Subject centre and the National Endowment for Science, Technology and the Arts, 2007, p. 26.
14. E. Chell, op. cit., p. 83.
15. S. Shane, op. cit., p. 3.
16. D. Goleman, *Social Intelligence* (London: Arrow books, 2007), p. 156.
17. M. Gladwell, *Outliers: The Story of Success* (London: Allen Lane, 2008).
18. See, for instance, D. Goleman, op. cit., pp. 154–61.
19. N. Nicolaou and S. Shane, 'Can Genetic Factors Influence the Likelihood of Engaging in Entrepreneurial Activity?', *Journal of Business Venturing*, 24, 2009, p. 2.
20. Ibid., p. 17.
21. S. Drakopoulou Dodd and A. Anderson, 'Mumpsimus and the Mything of the Individualistic Entrepreneur', *International Small Business Journal*, Vol. 25, No. 4, August 2007, p. 342.
22. B. Jovanovic, 'Selection and Evolution of Industry', *Econometrica*, Vol. 50, No. 3, 1982, pp. 647–70.
23. A. Lundstrom and L. Stevenson, 'Entrepreneurship Policy: Theory and Practice', Swedish Foundation for Small Business Research, Stockholm, 2005.
24. W. J. Baumol, 'Entrepreneurship: Productive, Unproductive and Destructive', *Journal of Politcal Economy*, Vol. 98, No. 5, 1990, pp. 893–921.
25. F. J. Greene, K. F. Mole and D. L. Storey, *Three Decades of Enterprise Culture* (Basingstoke: Palgrave Macmillan, 2008), p. 247.
26. Ibid., p. 14.
27. E. Chell, op. cit., p. 200.
28. E. Stam, op. cit., p. 2.
29. T. Cooney, 'Editorial: What is an Entrepreneurial Team?', *International Small Business Journal*, Vol. 23, No. 3, 2005, pp. 226–35.
30. S. Drakopoulou Dodd and A. Anderson, op. cit., p. 352.

31. M. Kets de Vries, in S. Birley and D. Muzyka (eds), *Mastering Enterprise* (London: Financial Times Prentice Hall/Pearson Education, 1997), p. 8.
32. S. Drakopoulou Dodd and A. Anderson, op. cit., pp. 341–2.
33. Ibid., p. 349.
34. Ibid., p. 349.
35. R. Nisbet, *The Sociological Tradition* (London: Heinemann, 1970).
36. S. Drakopoulou Dodd and A. Anderson, op. cit., p. 347.
37. C. Handy, *The Age of Unreason* (London, Arrow, 1990), p. 55.
38. S. Shane, op. cit., p. 2.

8
Comparisons

Part I concluded that many government attempts to raise levels of enterprise and entrepreneurship have not worked. It also concluded that many of the current models of what determines levels of enterprise and entrepreneurship, and which largely support those government attempts, are not correct either. Therefore new models are needed, but to develop them new approaches may have to be found from new ways of looking at things. Part II therefore has considered some perspectives which are available.

The analogy with medicine

An analogy with medicine was introduced in Chapter 1 because, it was suggested, being an applied science and one of the least deterministic subjects, the field of medical understanding might offer valid comparisons with the development of understanding in enterprise and entrepreneurship. In medicine it would seem that improved practice came from an openness to the possibility of improvement along with new insight and an improved understanding of the nature of the human body and of how its normal functioning might be adversely affected, causing it to become ill. That new understanding in turn came from discoveries such as that of the circulation of the blood and new ways of seeing what leads to ill health and what therefore might promote good health. For instance, understanding the existence and impact of germs, and how they were transmitted was a significant, albeit slow, development which led to an understanding of the need for cleanliness. Such discoveries, together with a perception that germs affected the body in different ways from that of bad diet or poison, and identifying the body's ability, given appropriate encouragement, to heal itself, were all inconsistent with the old balance-of-humours model. The eventual rejection of the supremacy of that model facilitated the adoption of new concepts of what was happening which in turn led to better treatment.

Medical history thus provides a good example of the prevalence of myth, despite the availability of apparent evidence to the contrary. For medical understanding to develop, it required an openness to a different perspective of what a healthy body is. This has been a slow process of understanding, and it is still ongoing, but it has led to new practices. These have included not just new cures, but also new prevention measures. In many countries much of the health budget is spent on hospitals which have become, and remain at, the core of the medical system, and today's hospitals, it has been said, are to medicine what cathedrals are to religion. They are the sites where medicine is practised at its most advanced, specialised, innovative, complex – and costly.[1] However if the overall health of a population is poor, then it has been suggested that the provision of hospitals would be a very expensive and ineffective way of improving it. In the developing world in particular, investing in public health measures, environmental hygiene and better nutrition would be a far more cost-effective way to use a 'health' budget if the aim is to raise the overall level of the country's health.

Our efforts to improve our health have benefitted therefore from different ways of looking at our bodies and at what can have an impact on them. So the preceding three chapters have looked at aspects of enterprise and entrepreneurship from a number of different perspectives, which have in turn suggested some points which might help in the search for a better understanding of how to influence them. That does not mean that all current approaches are without relevance. Bleeding may now have been rejected as a general cure-all for the symptoms of fever but bleeding, it seems, can sometimes do some good. Hemochromatosis is a hereditary disease that disrupts the way that the body metabolises iron with the result that the body accumulates too much iron.[2] Bleeding removes some of that iron and thus reduces the effects of hemochromatosis. Although it does not to cure hemochromatosis, nevertheless, in such circumstances, bleeding can help.

A review of the points raised

Chapter 5 reviewed different aspects of enterprise and entrepreneurship, of small businesses and/or associated behaviour, and suggests that these are not single dimension issues which can be fully understood from just one perspective. Therefore, without the insight provided by multiple perspectives, it may not be possible to see how different aspects of enterprise and entrepreneurship might be influenced.

For instance, different perspectives may indicate that the views of people actually practising entrepreneurship are not the same as those 'professionals' who are hired to promote it. The 'professionals' may assume that people make logical choices, but in many aspects of consumer selection, issues of 'fantasies, feelings and fun' appear to play a big part, and social example clearly influences choices of fashion goods and status symbols. Could this be the case also with enterprise and entrepreneurship?

Chapter 6 looked at the evolution of the present range of definitions of enterprise and entrepreneurship. It shows that, like it or not, there is now a wide range of meanings of these words and suggests that sometimes initiatives to promote them have not made clear which particular definition, if any, they were using. A further complication is that some entrepreneurship initiatives are now adopting a very narrow definition of entrepreneurship based, it appears, more on what they would like to see, which is more high-tech high-growth businesses (E4 entrepreneurship), than on observations of what entrepreneurship might actually be. This raises the question of whether the process of new venture creation does in reality consist of a number of separate strands each with its own different destination, rather like aeroplanes flying to different cities, or is it one network of activity with multiple possible entry and exit points, like a city's metro system? If the latter is a better analogy for reality, then assuming that it is the former and/or refusing to use programmes which do not assume the former are unlikely to help.

This appears to be a variation of the professional versus business proprietor difference in perspectives described in Chapter 5. Professionals often seem to base their models on what they have been taught, what they think should exist and/or what they would like to exist, whereas those who actually do something are more likely to have approaches based on what they have actually seen or experienced. It is understandable that governments and their economic development agencies might want a process that produces only or mainly high-tech businesses (although it might be argued that such a strategy is misguided) but that does not mean that all entrepreneurship is, or should be, E4 and can be shaped to fit such a requirement. If there is a difference in this area between the desired and the real, basing development efforts on the real is more likely to lead to useful results.

Chapter 7 then reflected on the nature versus nurture debate about the relevance of entrepreneurial traits which has been going on for at least 25 years without deciding in favour of exclusively either nature or nurture. Chapter 7 suggests that there is no single clear conclusion from the debate but that the reality might be that it is a combination of the two. If, however, it is concluded that, while genetics may play a part, environmental factors are at least as important, why does the 'heroic' myth persist? It does seem reasonable to suggest that it is not nature alone and that environmental factors do play some part, which means that it should be possible to do something to encourage more entrepreneurship.

This conclusion may owe more to demolishing the case for the primacy of inherited traits than it does to demonstrating a specific case for nurture based on the efficacy of any particular influences. Nevertheless it does imply that nurture has a part to play and that a human tendency towards entrepreneurial behaviour is open, at least to some extent, to environmental influences, although it does not indicate precisely what those other influences might be. It seems, therefore, that it should be possible to promote more entrepreneurship if the right influences can be identified, and that efforts to promote it are not necessarily going to be wasted. However, as Chapter 7 suggests, nature may also play its part and the feeling persists that some people are going to be entrepreneurs whatever influence the environment might have on them.

Another perspective: The gap between policy and research

> 'The politician's job is to tell us where to go and research can tell us how to get there'.
>
> Anders Hoffman, Director Entrepreneurship Policy, Danish Ministry of Economic and Business Affairs[3]

The three preceding chapters look at different perspectives on some key aspects of enterprise and entrepreneurship but there is another area in which a different perspective might help and that is in recognising, and then trying to understand, the gap between policy and research.

It may seem strange to talk of a gap in this area. After all, as Chapter 2 makes clear, governments have had a considerable interest in this area for some time and have made available significant resources for its exploration. The result, according to Allan Gibb, is that 'since the 1980s ... there has been an explosion of research into entrepreneurship and the small and medium enterprise'.[4] Surely, it might be supposed, governments' need for information and researchers' ability to supply it should lead to fruitful co-operation. However, Gibb goes on to say that

> despite the increase in academic knowledge, indeed perhaps because of it, there has been a growth of ignorance. ... A major manifestation of this growth of ignorance is the emergence of a number of outstanding 'mythical concepts' and 'myths' which are considerably influencing the establishment of policy priorities.[5]

Another reason for suggesting the need for a different perspective on this area is the finding, reported in Chapter 4, that, over a 10-, 20- or even 30-year period, much policy in this area has not worked. But, if research was effectively informing policy, would that have happened and would most governments and enterprise development agencies for some time have pursued policies which appear to have been ineffective? Indeed would they, in many cases, still be pursuing the same or similar policies despite their cost, if they had asked for, and listened to, the right research?

Yet there have been, and still are, many attempts to link policy and research, in both directions. In small business and entrepreneurship conferences, researchers are frequently asked to include, in the papers they present, the policy implications of their research and those conferences are frequently attended by a scattering of policymakers. In the UK the Small Business Service, when it existed, consulted researchers when it produced *The Evidence Base*[6] for a government action plan for small business (also referred to in Chapter 2). Many researchers talk to policymakers, maybe not often, but there is communication. So why should the relationship between these two sides appear to be more like a division than a bridge?

One reason might be that it is not perceived as a divide. If it is assumed that there is no divide, then no questions will be asked about it. Thus, if it has problems, they will not be discovered and nothing done to correct them. Could it be that few people have actually attempted to sound its depths? Because policymakers and researchers talk to each other, they may assume that they are communicating or, if in their particular case the communication has not led to any new understanding, they may assume that they are the exception. Is this an example of the Emperor's new clothes in which, even if their own experience does not actually support it, people are prepared to accept the apparently prevailing view? They assume that generally there are good bridges to the other side, even if they personally have not crossed them.

When the situation is actually examined, however, a different picture may be revealed. To what extent do policymakers and researchers want different things? Policymakers in theory, or at least to start with, want the right result and want to know what to do to get it, but in practice what they actually want to know is that they are doing the right things, and they do not want to hear that they are not. Commercial researchers often want repeat business and so, as Curran reports (see Chapter 4), they will try to give the policymakers what they want. Academic researchers may be more inclined towards objective research, but they often want Ph.D.s and/or papers and publications, all of which seem to put an emphasis on following the right process rather than getting the right result. Despite attempts to link research to policy, there rarely seems to be a meeting of minds. How many instances are there of a new policy being based on research commissioned for that purpose instead of on supposed 'best practice'? How much new innovative research is designed to inform policy, instead of being carried out primarily to earn a Ph.D.? How much policy evaluation is carried out by researchers with insight, instead of by consultants with cost-effective proposals for addressing the limited terms of reference given (and who are therefore unlikely to rock the boat with new ideas)?

If there is a divide why should this be? Could it be that converting research into policy is a far harder task than is usually recognised, because what researchers can produce and what operators want are different things and getting from one to the other involves a significant transition? This problem may not be unique to the field of enterprise and entrepreneurship and Illustration 8.1 presents an example based on the failure of military intelligence to produce what military operators want.

Illustration 8.1 An example of bridging the research–practice divide

> In the final phase of a revolutionary campaign as envisaged by Mao Tse Tung, armed insurgents come out into the open and fight the forces of the government by conventional methods, but in the earlier stages the war is fought by people who strike at a time and place of their own choosing and then disappear. Sometimes their disappearance is achieved by the physical process of movement into an area of thick cover such as a jungle, and at other times by merging into the population. In either case those who are supporting them by the provision of money, food, recruits, intelligence, and supplies

rely for their security on remaining anonymous. The problem of destroying enemy armed groups and their supporters therefore consists very largely of finding them. Once found they can no longer strike on their own terms but are obliged to dance to the tune of the government's forces. It then becomes a comparatively simple matter to dispose of them. ...

If it is accepted that the problem of defeating the enemy consists very largely of finding him, it is easy to recognize the paramount importance of good information. As a rule those taking part in counter-insurgency operations do quickly recognize it, and stress the need for a good intelligence service to be built up. It is even common to find commanders at every level laying the blame for such failure as may have attended their efforts on the shortage of good information given to them. But there is a fatal flaw in the thinking of those who put down their lack of success to the shortage of information given to them, which is that the sort of information required cannot, except on rare occasions, be provided on a plate by anyone, not even by the intelligence organization. If there was a system whereby an intelligence organization could do this, it would have been devised years ago, and there would be no such thing as insurgency: because enemy armed groups and/their supporters would at once be found, harried, tracked down and destroyed by the army and the police.

The fact is that although intelligence is of great importance, it does not usually come in the form of information which will immediately enable a policeman or soldier to put his men into contact with the enemy. The reason for this is inherent in the way in which intelligence organizations work, collecting information as they do by operating informers and agents, or by interrogating prisoners to mention only a few of their methods. Information collected in this way is immensely valuable for providing data on which policy can be worked out, and it forms the background to operational planning. But only occasionally can it be used to put troops directly into contact with the enemy because material about enemy locations and intentions is usually out of date before it can be acted upon by the soldiers. The sort of information which intelligence organizations produce has to be developed by a different set of processes to those used by the organizations themselves before it can be used for putting government forces into contact with insurgents. A cow can

> turn grass into milk but a further process is required in order to turn the milk into butter.
>
> Two separate functions are therefore involved in putting troops into contact with insurgents. The first one consists of collecting background information, and the second involves developing it into contact information. To over-simplify the full process it could be said that it is the responsibility of the intelligence organization to produce background information and that it is then up to operational commanders to develop it to the extent necessary for their men to make contact with the enemy, using their own resources. Undoubtedly this is an over-simplification because, as will be shown, operational units have a function in producing background information, and the intelligence organization can help in the business of developing it, but it is absolutely necessary to understand the fact that the main responsibility for developing background information rests with operational commanders and not with the intelligence organization. Once this fact is accepted it is possible to look at the two functions involved and view the straightforward military techniques which have been developed over the years in their correct perspective. No matter how proficient soldiers and policemen become at using these techniques, they will achieve no more than isolated successes unless they can use them as part of an efficient system for handling information.

Source: F. Kitson, *Low Intensity Operations* (London: Faber and Faber, 1971), pp. 95–6.

It may be interesting that the conclusion presented in Illustration 8.2 is that the task of bridging the gap falls not to the researchers but to the operators. Cows produce milk: that's what they do – and it requires a different process, which they cannot undertake, to convert it into the butter – or cheese, or yoghurt, or extra thick double cream – which the consumer requires. In the field of enterprise and entrepreneurship, researchers can, and do, produce potentially useful information such as Birch's finding that small businesses were net creators of new jobs. Nevertheless what policy operators then wanted to know was what to do to promote more and better small businesses, and the research could not tell them that. Research could have told them something about how small businesses behave but policy operators would then have had to convert that into practical ideas for stimulating them to react in the desired manner.

So, if it is known that the problem is one of conversion, why has it not been done? Two reasons can be suggested: firstly because, although the possibility of conversion is known, it is not widely known, so in many cases milk is still being offered on the grounds that it is all there is; and secondly because, even when it is realised that a conversion is necessary, it is a very hard thing to do, especially when it has not been tried before. Knowing that it is necessary does not automatically lead to an indication of how it can be done and little attempt will be made to address that problem unless, and until, it is admitted that there is a problem. The difficulty of conversion is also increased if few policymakers, and policy implementers, really understand enterprise and entrepreneurship. Might they then be like travellers who do not know the terrain and who, if they are provided with maps, cannot read them, and so are constrained to follow pre-determined routes instead of finding more appropriate paths?

Could there be another parallel between military intelligence and small business research? It is a recognised requirement in the intelligence field that care should be taken to examine the results objectively because intelligence often has the chameleon-like quality of taking on the appearance of the background against which it is viewed. It does seem to be the case that if the intelligence on a military or political issue, such as the presence of weapons of mass destruction in Iraq, is viewed against the background of a preconceived notion of what the situation is, then the people concerned are likely to conclude that the available intelligence supports their existing assumptions. In other words they are not asking what the intelligence is telling them but asking if it supports their views. Could a similar problem afflict those government departments and agencies concerned with enterprise and small business? In theory they would like to have an objective assessment of the performance of their programmes but could it be that, in practice, and as suggested above, what they actually want research to tell them is not whether their programmes are making a difference, but that they are making a difference? That might be a subtle distinction in the requirement, but is it a distinction which colours their perceptions of the answers they hear? As a result, because research results cannot provide an absolute certainty of proof, policymakers find that they can discount findings which are contrary to what they would like to hear. Consequently they can fail to appreciate that there is evidence that their programmes are not working. Then they see no need for a better approach.

To give the Emperor a proper set of clothes, there has to be both the perception that the present clothes are inadequate and the knowledge of how to make a set of clothes which would be appropriate. If neither of those conditions is met, then there is not likely to be much change.

Illustration 8.2 What is the basis of policy?

It is suggested above that, in the field of enterprise, there has in reality been relatively little interchange between research and policy. In addition Chapter 3 suggests that although much policy is consistent with current models supposedly arising from, or used by, research, it is not actually based on those models. Instead Chapter 3 suggests that the substance of much policy has been derived, in the main, from apparent 'best practice'.

Best practice might provide the substance of policy, but not the justification (the 'rationale for intervention' in Figure 2.1 and Table 2.1). So, if policy has not been stimulated by research-based models, what have been its origins? Chapter 3 mentions the market failure approach, and there are a number of other factors which have also been suggested as having an influence on the decisions to pursue intervention policies. Those identified have included the public choice model, the economic theory of bureaucracy and more radical approaches focusing on the power relation between different interest groups and those which emphasise the ideological dimension policy.[7] Thus a summary of the key *de facto* reasons for the choice of intervention policies could include one or more of the following:

Market failure. Market failure has been described as a situation in which markets, left to themselves, 'cannot always be relied on to deliver outcomes which are optimal from society's perspective or to achieve equity objectives that ensure prosperity for all. Where this is the case there is a role for government to intervene'. It is suggested that, in the field of enterprise, there are four broad types of market failure which 'act to constrain new business formation and growth':[8]

Imperfect and asymmetric information
Externalities and incomplete property rights
Imperfect market structure
Poor regulation

> *Public choice and the role of politicians.* It is argued that politicians will consider their own welfare and so will favour policies that will maximise their chance of remaining in office through re-election. Thus they will tend to select policies which they think will appeal to their electorate.
>
> *The economic theory of bureaucracy.* State civil servants and officials can also have vested interests. They like to be associated with success so they will favour initiatives which they think are likely to be both prominent and successful.
>
> *Power relations, pressure groups and ideology.* It is also recognised that power relations exist within society and it is suggested that frequently the direction of policy is ultimately determined by the interplay of tensions between different powerful vested-interest and/or ideological groups

Source: Based on S. Bridge, K. O'Neill and F. Martin, *Understanding Enterprise, Entrepreneurship and Small Business* (Basingstoke: Palgrave Macmillan, 2009), pp. 337–41.

Conclusion to Part II

In order to advance the development of a possible new model of the influences on enterprise and entrepreneurship, Part II has looked at aspects of the subject from several different perspectives. These different views, while they do not directly lead to a new understanding, do nevertheless suggest some ideas to consider in the search for a better model. They also provide some criteria against which to compare possible models by indicating aspects of entrepreneurship which do not fit well with current models and which a new model should therefore explain, or at least not contradict.

References

1. R. Porter, *Blood and Guts: A Short History of Medicine* (London: Penguin Press, 2002).
2. See S. Moalem, *Survival of the Sickest* (London: Harper, 2008), Ch. 1.
3. Forum Report prepared by L. Stevenson, Pre-conference Policy Forum, 53rd Annual ICSB World Conference, Nova Scotia, Halifax, 2008.
4. A. A. Gibb, 'SME Policy, Academic Research and the Growth of Ignorance, Mythical Concepts, Myths, Assumptions, Rituals and Confusions', *International Small Business Journal*, Vol. 18, No. 3, April–June 2000, p. 13.
5. Ibid., p. 13.

6. Small Business Service (SBS), *A government action plan for small business: Making the UK best place in the world to start and grow a business – the evidence base*, (London: Department of Trade and Industry, HMSO, 2004).
7. Derived from S. Johnson, 'Public Policy and the Small Firm', book proposal reviewed by author and colleague (2006), p. 17.
8. Small Business Service, op. cit., pp. 5 and 6.

Part III
An Alternative Model

Introduction

Part I of this book suggested that the current models of the factors which influence enterprise and entrepreneurship are of little use to those who want to promote more of those qualities because the models do not work. An alternative proven model is not readily available however and so, if one is required, it will have to be developed. Part II therefore considered a variety of different perspectives on or about enterprise and entrepreneurship and the factors influencing them in order to identify possible starting points for another approach. Part III now seeks to build on some of the observations developed in Part II to develop a new understanding and model.

Among the perspectives explored in Part II are those considering enterprise and entrepreneurship from the position of the people involved. In Part III therefore Chapter 9 looks at how enterprise and entrepreneurship might relate to people and to their objectives in life. Chapter 10 considers what might influence the choice among options in people's lives and Chapter 11 examines in particular the relevance of social issues. Chapter 12 attempts to distil this into an explanation of how enterprise is influenced to provide a model which is consistent with the observations of enterprise. Finally Chapter 13 looks at some of the possible implications of this explanation and at what might be the next steps for those who want to build a greater understanding of this subject.

Part II also suggested a way of categorising the different meanings that are sometimes assigned to, or assumed for, the words enterprise and entrepreneurship (see Chapter 6 – especially Table 6.1 and Figure 6.2), which will, it is hoped, help to make it clearer which meaning is being used on any particular occasion. Applying this categorisation retrospectively is not always easy because it may not always have been clear originally which was the relevant meaning. This applies, for instance, to the government efforts to encourage the development of more entrepreneurship which have been reviewed in this book. Often it was not readily apparent whether the policy was following a broad (E0 or E1) approach to enterprise and entrepreneurship or a narrower (E2 or E3) approach.

Now, as indicated in Chapter 6, some initiatives do make it clear that they are aimed at stimulating a very narrow high-tech high-growth range of entrepreneurship: the high-potential start-ups (E4). Sometimes they appear to assume that this is not just a branch of the more general entrepreneurship tree, but a different plant altogether, the growth of which can therefore be separately encouraged. That assumption does not, however, appear to be clearly stated, which makes it hard to challenge it.

Part III of this book, in looking for a new model of the factors that influence entrepreneurship, assumes that all forms of entrepreneurship come from the same roots and that, as suggested in Figure 6.2, the narrower forms of entrepreneurship, such as E3 and E4, are subsets of the broader forms, and not separate, unrelated sets. That does not mean that, if more E0 is encouraged, it will automatically also include more E4, as something else may be required in addition to encourage the more specialised forms, but it does suggest that E0 and then E1 are foundations which are necessary if there is to be more E4. Therefore, while it is not wrong to wish for more E4, efforts to promote more enterprise and entrepreneurship should encourage more E0 and E1 together with any subsequent efforts to build narrower forms on that foundation. Thus, in considering models of the possible influences on entrepreneurship, Part III assumes that the wider E0 and E1 definitions of entrepreneurship are the relevant ones.

9
An Enterprise is a Goal-Realisation Device

Introduction

Chapter 5 considered the different perspectives of the business professional and the business owner. It suggested that although much research into small businesses has taken the business as its unit of analysis, nevertheless the behaviour of many small businesses depends on the characteristics and aims of their founder-owners. Similarly, starting with Cantillon, many explorations of entrepreneurship have developed from the identification of the entrepreneur as the key component in the process of creating a new business venture. This chapter though looks at entrepreneurship from a people perspective and considers the position of new venture creation, or of other forms of enterprise, in the process of a person's life. It considers how enterprise might fit into the life of the person involved, instead of how the person might fit into the life of the enterprise.

Life goals

'An enterprise', it has been said, 'is a goal-realisation device'[1] and the goals that it can help to realise are the life goals of people. Figure 5.2 suggested a possible context for considering what individuals might want in their lives. This viewpoint is compatible with the approach indicated by Maslow who suggested that many of our actions are motivated by unmet needs and that these needs can be placed in a hierarchy in which the lower-order ones predominate until they are satisfied whereupon the high-order ones come into operation. These needs can be presented as:

Self-actualising needs
Esteem needs

Belonging and love needs
Safety needs
Physiological needs – such as for food and water

Figure 5.2 also indicated some of the goals that people might have in life, including surviving, belonging, raising a family, having influence, acquiring a fortune, being famous, achieving a certain status, making a contribution and even preparing for an easy retirement. It also suggested that achieving any of these, if they are people's goals, might help to make those people happy, or at least happier than they would have been had they not achieved them. Other things that might be on such a list of goals, or components of goals, are autonomy, meeting a challenge, having a sense of achievement or finding a sense of identity.

Many people might say that what they want to make them happy is money, but money does not feature in Maslow's list. That can be explained by assuming that people do not need money itself and that instead they need things that money can buy, which is why they might ask for money. Money, for instance, can buy food and housing, and can therefore help to satisfy lower-order needs, but the higher the need is in Maslow's list, the less effective money is as a medium of exchange for addressing that need. Indeed at the top it is hard to see that money can directly buy any degree of self-actualisation. Those people who are fortunate enough to inherit, win or marry significant amounts of money, or who are in receipt of an income such as pension or unemployment benefit payments, can use that money to satisfy lower-order needs. For everyone else, however, satisfying their needs requires the expenditure of effort in some form, a process often referred to as work. Even those with money have to work at things like esteem and self-actualisation, although having money can give people more time or inclination to concentrate on self-actualisation because they do not have to worry about earning enough to feed or house themselves. Some people might seem to achieve self-actualisation by making lots of money but it can be argued that, in those situations, the amount of money they acquire acts as a sort of score for their efforts, just as the number of goals can indicate the extent of a football team's efforts. Thus money is still a means to an end, even if that end is a higher earning score.

Most people therefore have to work. Given the right conditions they can satisfy their hunger by working to hunt or gather food, by working to grow food, by working to earn money with which to buy food or by working to steal food. Some of these may be longer-term solutions than others, but they all involve work. Crime may be illegal, but it still requires a certain amount of work. Thus people work to satisfy their needs and to try to achieve what they want out of life, whether that is short-term survival or longer-term achievement. People might say that they want happiness, but the pleasure and/or contentment that brings happiness usually comes from work in some form.

On the assumption that people generally work to get what they want, what are the things that motivate and direct their working lives? Table 9.1 presents a possible list of the things that motivate people and therefore the reasons why they might want to work.

There are some things that people might do which would help to address their needs directly, like stealing or growing food to satisfy a short- or long-term survival need, whereas other things they might do would indirectly help by earning them money which they can use to address a variety of needs. However the list suggested in Table 9.1 has parallels with Maslow's original list as in both cases unsatisfied lower-order needs may take precedence over higher-order needs. Also, the higher the need is in the order, the less easy it may be always to use money to address it.

Neither the list in Table 9.1 nor the individual's view of the world suggested in Figure 5.2 includes entrepreneurship. That is because, instead of being an objective in its own right, it is suggested that entrepreneurship is instead a form of, or an approach to, work and therefore, like other work, it is a means to an end. If it were to be added to Figure 5.2, it could be shown as a route or a means of travelling from where someone is to where they want to be. Therefore it provides additional choices for that journey.

Table 9.1 Reasons why people might want to work

- To make a contribution to society and to other people.
- To discover something, for instance in science or exploration.
- To create art and/or to express themselves through art.
- To be famous and/or to have status.
- To make a fortune.
- To be respected and to have influence.
- To achieve success in sport, or in other activities.
- To belong to a group or community.
- To have a secure future and retirement.
- To raise a family.
- To obtain pleasure and gratification.
- To survive.

Resource acquisition options

Not all work is done to live, whether to acquire directly the resources needed for life or to earn money to exchange for things such as food and shelter. However there do seem to be examples of people who seem, on the contrary, to live to work. Many athletes spend a lot of time working hard to improve their performance, and there are artists who work hard refining their technique to achieve the effect they are seeking. It has been suggested, for instance, that 'ten thousand hours of practice time is required to achieve the level of mastery associated with being a world-class expert – in anything'[2] and not everyone aspires to such a level of expertise just for the money. Even among those people who cannot, or do not, show such levels of commitment, there are still many examples of people pursuing activities such as art or sport with no expectation of a financial return.

Nevertheless a lot of work is done primarily in order to gain resources and, at least in the more developed economies, most people probably expect to get the resources they need by working in some form of employment. About 40–50 years ago, when there were relatively high levels of employment, many people in such economies might have expected to have a job for life either in a large private company or in the public sector. They might also have considered that if they were unlucky, they might be unemployed and might have expected that if this happened, they would be in receipt of benefit of some kind. Either way, for many people, employment or unemployment probably seemed to be the only two alternatives. It was thought that self-employment, or enterprise, did not occur to many people then as a possibility and therefore it was promoted as representing a third option: that of people doing something themselves to create their own economic activity. In reality, however, there is a much wider variety of possible ways of obtaining the resources needed for a satisfactory life although they are not all necessarily open to everyone. Table 9.2 lists some of them.

Not all the means listed in Table 9.2 necessarily involve a significant amount of work. Pensions and annuities are not themselves a form of work, although they may have been earned by prior work, and betting requires a stake which has to be obtained somehow. Similarly receiving unemployment or sickness benefit does not directly involve work, and neither does inheritance. Marriage might also be considered to be in that category. The latter sources of resource are, however, only open to a minority of people and for the majority getting the resources needed to sustain or develop life means work in one form or another. It is also,

Table 9.2 Some of the means by which people can obtain resources for life

- Acquiring a pension or annuity
- Begging, or living off friends or relatives
- Crime
- Employment
- Entrepreneurial venturing (entrepreneurship and/or self-employment – E2)
- Hunter-gathering
- Inheriting wealth
- Marrying wealth
- Self-sufficient agriculture
- Sponsorship
- Unemployment or invalidity benefit payments
- Winning the lottery, or other forms of gambling

of course, clear that these means are not mutually exclusive, and it is possible to try more than one at the same time, such as is done by those who combine part-time employment with a form of self-employment. There is, in any case, some overlap between the categories. Much crime, for instance, can be considered to be a form of entrepreneurship, albeit illegal and often-destructive entrepreneurship, and hunter-gathering and having a farm might be considered to be forms of self-employment (although they might not necessarily be considered to be entrepreneurial if all that is done is to continue what was done by a previous generation). Nevertheless the point is that for many people life involves work, and enterprise and entrepreneurship should be considered in the context of the options for that work.

But there is also work to self-actualise – and for some the form of work chosen might be one that combines resource acquisition with self-actualisation. Even within enterprise/entrepreneurship, there can be different forms with the potential to deliver different proportions of resources (money) and self-actualisation.

Different forms of entrepreneurship

If an enterprise is a goal realisation device, then all E0 entrepreneurs might be considered to be people who want something enough to do something about it and to organise it for themselves when no one else will do that for them. This might happen in the fields of sport, of discovery, of learning, of the arts, of peace-making or of many other areas of activity including, but not limited to, work for economic benefit (E1). However, even when entrepreneurship is applied to work then, just as employment can take many different forms, entrepreneurship does

Table 9.3 Different kinds of entrepreneurs

- Capitalist entrepreneurship (à la Richard Branson)
- Lifestyle entrepreneurship
- Innovative, growth entrepreneurship (and intrapreneurship)
- Academic entrepreneurship
- Spin-off entrepreneurship
- Social entrepreneurship (non-profit, social goals, 'causes')
- Socially responsible entrepreneurship (Ben & Jerry, Anita Ruddick, Paul Hawkins)
- Nascent entrepreneurship
- Wanna-be entrepreneurship

Source: Based on L. Stevenson, presentation to 35th International Small Business Congress, Belfast, November, 2008.

not have to represent just one way of working. Table 9.3, for instance, presents one list of its different forms.

Although some of the narrower definitions of entrepreneurship considered in Chapter 6 might seem to exclude some of these activities from entrepreneurship, it is generally recognised that entrepreneurship can take a wide variety of forms, and these forms are also consistent with the wider definitions of enterprise. Other aspects of entrepreneurship might be added to the list such as political entrepreneurship or environmental entrepreneurship. Indeed viewing entrepreneurship in the context of life options suggests that it might encompass the creation of one's own transport towards one or more life goals instead of hoping to work one's passage on a vessel created by someone else. Sometimes there is indeed a suitable vessel going in the right direction on which it might be a pleasure to work, but often working for someone else might keep you alive but might mean that the place at which you eventually get off is not quite what you had in mind. Also trying to create and sail your own boat can be hard work, especially when travelling against the prevailing wind, and, while you can then select your own destination, there is always the danger of shipwreck on the way.

Preparation for enterprise

In choosing from the possible 'goal realisation devices' preparation can be relevant, but which comes first: the preparation or the option? People may not choose options for which they are not prepared, and they may not prepare for options which they have not seen as being available or desirable. Is there, however, a set of assets which people might try to acquire in order to be ready for any eventuality (the life-goal equivalent of the Swiss Army knife)?

For instance, in work, as in the rest of life, the following can be useful:

education (and qualifications),
experience,
ideas,
social capital,
opportunities,
luck (but luck favours those who are prepared?),
resources to invest in a venture,
passion,
self-confidence, and
an understanding of the options and possibilities.

It obviously also helps if people have the freedom to choose appropriate work, which depends on the availability of choices, options and opportunities for work, and freedom to prepare for those choices, options and opportunities. But, even if they are free to do it, how often do people add all these assets to their life toolkit? The formal education system may encourage people to acquire some of these assets, such as qualifications, and provide them with opportunities to do so, but encouragement and opportunities to acquire other assets, such as social capital, are likely to come from their social setting.

Looking beyond the obvious

Another aspect of enterprise and/or entrepreneurship in the context of progress towards life's goals is that it is not always clear what the entrepreneurship path is or how or where it is going, and often there are not clear distinctions between some of the categories of entrepreneurship listed above. Presenting entrepreneurship as a form or means of work helps to suggest that it need not necessarily be focused exclusively, or even mainly, on making money, although some have tended to see it in that context. For instance initiatives to introduce entrepreneurship education into university curricula have sometimes been resisted by those for whom entrepreneurship had adverse connotations associated with the baser aspects of capitalism. However such views have relaxed once it became clear that a wider meaning of entrepreneurship (E1 or E0) was being applied which could be relevant in a number of areas, including

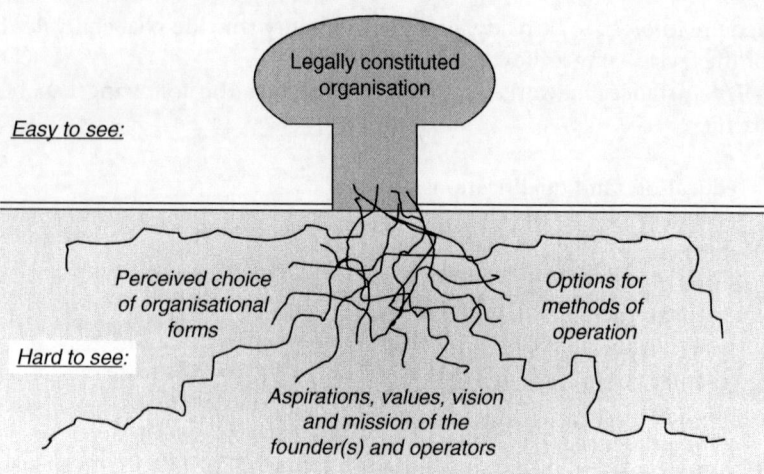

Figure 9.1 What you see is not everything
Source: S. Bridge, B. Murtagh and K. O'Neill, *Understanding the Social Economy and the Third Sector* (Basingstoke: Palgrave Macmillan, 2009), p. 39.

the arts, because what was being proposed was entrepreneurship as enterprise for life, not just for the creation of new business ventures.[3] Also, even when entrepreneurship does lead to the formation of private-sector businesses, it might be because no other options for a legal organisation were seen, rather than because the founders specifically desired to start a venture which would maximise their own financial returns.

Bridge et al. use the analogy of mushrooms to suggest that there is more to many ventures than just the legal registration.[4] Just as the mushrooms we see above ground are not the whole of the fungus but only the fruiting bodies of an extensive branched underground mycelium, so the business organisations we encounter are not the totality of the aspirations of their founders (see Figure 9.1). Instead the legally constituted bodies, the existence and activities of which can be reported and recorded, are the result of the interaction of a number of more or less hidden factors including:

- the visions, aspirations, ideas and ambitions of their founders
- the selection by those founders of methods of operating to realise their purposes
- the choice by those founders, from the options perceived to be available, of which legal form to use to give their organisations an official existence.

Conclusion

This chapter has presented enterprise and entrepreneurship, not as an end goal, but as a means towards such a goal. It suggests that the rightful place to see enterprise and entrepreneurship is in a wider goal-attainment spectrum.

In contrast others appear to treat entrepreneurship as an end result and Shane, for instance, sees entrepreneurship as the outcome of an individual–opportunity nexus.[5] That nexus however is only going to occur for those individuals who are favourably disposed towards entrepreneurship and are looking for entrepreneurship opportunities. Policymakers often want more people to be in that position, but Shane's model, by assuming that people are already there, does not indicate how more people might be encouraged to look for entrepreneurship opportunities.

This chapter has looked at enterprise and entrepreneurship as an option, or rather as a range of options, for the journeys that individuals might take towards their current, and future, goals. Enterprise, it suggests, essentially is, and should be seen as, a goal-realisation device. Enterprise and entrepreneurship can be seen therefore as a possible route in life, although it may not be chosen if it is not perceived to be among the options available. Traditionally enterprise and entrepreneurship have been seen in the context of the ventures that are created in their name, instead of from the view-point of the people who might create those ventures. Some of the differences between these perspectives are suggested in Table 9.4.

Table 9.4 How enterprise (and entrepreneurship) might be viewed from venture and people perspectives

	Seen from a venture perspective	Seen from a people perspective
Where does enterprise fit in?	Enterprise is an essential component of any new venture creation, which is the outcome sought.	Enterprise is one option among several for gaining resources and/or satisfaction. Enterprise is not an end, but a means to a life end.
Will there be enterprise?	It is taken for granted that enterprise is present.	There is no guarantee that enterprise will even be considered.

(Continued)

Table 9.4 Continued

	Seen from a venture perspective	Seen from a people perspective
What is the genesis of enterprise?	Enterprise will occur when an individual meets an opportunity.	Enterprise will occur if it is the best route for the individual at that point in time – but only if the individual is looking for enterprise opportunities.
How will enterprise be assessed?	It is presumed that enterprise will be assessed logically.	In assessing enterprise feelings probably matter more than any logical analysis.
What is the goal of enterprise?	The goal is generally supposed to be to secure the maximum financial return and that is relatively fixed.	The goal is generally to realise a life ambition, which may change so the goal is moveable.
How permanent is the enterprise?	Enterprise is realised in a venture which, once started, is expected to continue.	Enterprise will be used only if and when it might be appropriate.
How valid and desirable are different forms of enterprise?	Some forms of enterprise are more valid than others (at least in the eyes of policymakers) with private-sector business being the most valid and high-tech, high-growth, high-value added businesses (E4) often being seen as the most desirable.	All forms of enterprise are equally valid, but different forms are appropriate to different aims. The most desirable form of enterprise is therefore that which is most appropriate to the individual's aim at that time.

Another difference between ventures and people is that ventures cannot chose for themselves, whereas people can. Ventures cannot choose to be formed but people can, and sometimes do, choose to form ventures. That choice of whether or not to form a venture is crucial to the existence of the venture and Chapter 10 therefore explores the factors which might influence it.

References

1. For instance L. Hunter speaking at a University of Ulster seminar on 'Developing a strategy and vision for social entrepreneurship', Coleraine, 10 September 2007.

2. David Levitin quoted in M. Gladwell, *Outliers: The Story of Success* (London: Allen Lane, 2008), p. 40.
3. See, for instance S. Bridge, C. Hegarty and S. Porter, 'Rediscovering Enterprise: Exploring Entrepreneurship for Undergraduates', a paper presented at the 31st Institute for Small Business and Entrepreneurship Conference, Belfast, November 2008.
4. S. Bridge, B. Murtagh and K. O'Neill, *Understanding the Social Economy and the Third Sector* (Basingstoke: Palgrave Macmillan, 2009), pp. 38/9.
5. S. Shane, *A General Theory of Entrepreneurship: The Individual Opportunity Nexus* (Cheltenham: Edward Elgar, 2003).

10
The Basis of Choice

> Going to work is arguably the biggest transaction we ever undertake.[1]
>
> The key question is why in a given (opportunity) environment some individuals are more likely to start a firm than in another environment.[2]

Chapter 9 suggested that enterprise should be seen as one of the options for people for trying to get what they want out of life. This chapter looks at the possible influences on the choice people make between it and the other options.

If, as quoted in Chapter 9, 'an enterprise is a goal-realisation device', it might be relevant to consider each of the three key words in that statement:

- *'Enterprise'*: This book has recognised that there are different forms of enterprise, and of enterprising behaviour. For some people an enterprise means a business, and in particular one which has been formally created by incorporation as a limited company, or by registration as a partnership or sole-tradership. The process of enterprise (in its narrow sense) or entrepreneurship then is the process of enterprise formation and incorporation (E2 and higher). Others see enterprise and entrepreneurship as having a wider application than just private-sector business (i.e. E0 or E1) but an enterprise generally has to take some form. However, the form chosen, such as a private-sector company limited by shares or a third-sector company limited by guarantee, will depend on the entrepreneur's goals, the methods chosen for meeting those goals and the forms of incorporation/registration perceived to be available.

- *'Goal'*: An enterprise is a device, a means to an end and, if an enterprise or entrepreneurship might provide a possible contribution towards the achievement of people's goals, Chapter 9 considers the sort of goals that people might have. Those goals might be short-, medium- or long-term and people can, and do, have multiple goals, either sequentially or simultaneously, and either equally or in a hierarchy. However people might not always be clear about what their goals are and, in any case, their goals can change over time. Nevertheless goals do motivate people and so people will seek ways of achieving them.
- *'Device'*: Whether they see it in those terms or not, people do need goal-realisation devices and it is therefore relevant to consider what goal-realisation devices are available to people and what possible reasons they might have for selecting the one(s) to use. Some of the different devices are listed in Table 9.2 and this chapter now considers the possible influences on people's choices between the devices they perceive to be available.

Some possible influences

What are the possible influences on people's choices of occupation and/or their means of trying to achieve their life goals? This section reviews some of them.

Availability and practicality

Chapter 9 suggests that among the goal-realisation devices open to people are the following:

- Employment
- Crime
- Farming
- Sponsorship

- Enterprise/entrepreneurial venturing
- Hunter-gathering
- Begging, or living off friends or relatives
- Unemployment or invalidity benefit payments

- A pension or annuity
- An inheritance

- Marrying wealth
- Gambling

These devices are not however all open to everyone. Often particular methods are limited in their availability. For instance:

a) Relatively few people inherit enough wealth, or marry someone who is rich enough, to obviate the need to work.

b) A pension or annuity generally has first to be earned somehow.
c) Betting also requires an initial stake and, by its nature, is unlikely to be profitable. Nevertheless lots of people try it although very few succeed by it.
d) Many people do not have access to the land or resources needed to live by agriculture or hunter-gathering.
e) Sponsorship is very unlikely to be an achievable except for a few venturers in the fields of sport, art, science or exploration.
f) Benefit payments for those who are unemployed or unfit for work are not available in every country and, when they are offered, they are only available to those eligible for them. However, in countries with state welfare systems, they may remain as a safety net.
g) Begging might not be seen as a practical means for anything more than a last resort for basic survival.

Therefore, from an initial list of 12 or more theoretically possible devices, most people are, in practice, reduced to only three or four available choices, and even some of these may not be perceived to be suitable. Many people probably do not consider crime as an option for them or, if they do see it as theoretically available, they eschew it on moral grounds. Therefore, for many people in the more developed countries, where there is enough employment, or at least where there is a social security safety net, the remaining choice is often between employment and some form of entrepreneurship. People will select, though, not from the means that are available, but from the means that they perceive to be available and some people may not perceive entrepreneurship as being, for them, a feasible option. Perceptions of availability thus significantly limit the choices for many people.

Dislike

Closely related to availability and practicality is dislike, because some people's dislike for an option is such as to render it, in practice, unavailable to them. It is suggested above that many people will eschew crime on moral grounds and so, for them, it is not in practice considered to be available. Entrepreneurship can also come into this category because, in some situations, where it has 'become tainted with charges of profiteering, speculation, violence and criminality it has not been well received. This has been evidenced in the likes of Chicago in the 1930s and in a number of the transition economies of Eastern Europe in the 1990s'.[3] It might be argued that because some criminals are entrepreneurs, it does not mean that all entrepreneurs are criminals and we do not assume, for instance, that, because some people are murderers, all people are murderers. Nevertheless, whether it is logical or not, the word entrepreneurship has been so tainted, and it should be recognised that this does affect the reaction of some people to even legitimate activities which are given that label.

Necessity – no perceived choice

For reasons such as those considered above, some people perceive employment to be the only practical means available to satisfy their needs. For such people the choice is necessarily made for them and if they can't find employment they have to fall back on benefit payments. Others may see a very limited choice, none of which they really like, and their decision amounts to selecting the least worst from a bad selection of choices.

For instance a view of entrepreneurship, not as one of two or more valid alternatives, but as something only to be considered when there really is nothing else, seems to be behind the Global Entrepreneurship Monitor (GEM) concept of 'necessity' entrepreneurs. In some of its work GEM has divided entrepreneurship into the two categories of 'opportunity' and 'necessity' entrepreneurship. Necessity entrepreneurs, it suggests, 'are pushed into entrepreneurship because all other options for work are either absent or unsatisfactory' whereas opportunity entrepreneurs 'want to exploit a perceived business opportunity'.[4] At first GEM suggested that all entrepreneurs fell into either one or the other of these two categories, but latterly it suggests that some people could be in both.

GEM has suggested that necessity entrepreneurship is particularly prevalent in countries with low levels of income and low levels of social security[5] although it is interesting that, when Rosa et al. looked for necessity entrepreneurship in two countries in which GEM suggested that it would be most prevalent, they did not find it. They concluded that their results showed 'little support for the "necessity" hypothesis, i.e. that necessity motivates people strongly to start a business'.[6]

However, despite GEM's suggestion that many follow entrepreneurship only out of necessity, in other countries, albeit those with a social security safety net, many appear to have seen employment as the only option, with the lucky finding jobs and the unlucky being unemployed and 'on the dole'.

Preparation and timing

The comment has been made that 'students on leaving university usually don't have the social capital needed successfully to go into entrepreneurship immediately'.[7] This suggests that preparation and timing can affect perceptions of the feasibility of options, and it is suggested in Chapter 9 that aspects of preparation can be socially influenced, especially during someone's upbringing. The choice of whether or not to opt for entrepreneurship is not one that a person makes every day, and it could be that the few occasions on which it might be made often do not occur at times when people are well prepared to make it.

When do people have the option to choose any form of entrepreneurship as their route? In theory they could do this at any time but in practice, if it is contemplated at all, it is only likely to be given serious consideration at times such as the following:

- *When people first look for employment.* When people first look for employment, unless they have a particular inclination or have had specific encouragement, they may not be ready for entrepreneurship. They may have little relevant experience or social capital and, rather than having some resources to invest in a venture, if leaving university they may have student loans to pay off instead.
- *After a period in employment when people wonder what else they might do.* However after a period in employment people might be used to that system and might not wish to give up the sort of safety zone provided by a reasonably secure job which provides them with the company of a team of colleagues and the comfort of a regular income. A regular job in particular can be attractive to someone who is trying to raise a family and wants a reasonably secure source of income.
- *When there is a particular trigger.* Triggering events, such as being made redundant, can force people to contemplate alternative courses in life, but they are only then likely to chose entrepreneurship if they are ready for it and open to such opportunities. Unless people have had a long period of warning in which to prepare for redundancy, their priority may be to replace their income stream as quickly as possible and a new enterprise, which will take time to become established, is less likely to do that.

Thus, it might be argued, unless people are conditioned to consider and prepare for entrepreneurship, the occasions on which they might nevertheless consider it are often likely to be the least auspicious.

The balance of attractiveness: Risk–return considerations

Different options have different pros and cons. Among the advantages of an option might be its suitability to the person's skills and abilities and its appropriateness for the person's desired outcomes (such as the money it might bring), thus apparently offering the best potential returns in the short or long term. However that has to be balanced by the risk that the projected results might not be obtained. Those who analyse this logically may distinguish between risk, for which the odds can be determined and provision made to change the odds, and uncertainty, which is more fear of the unknown.

Some may choose an option to minimise the risk and uncertainty because they feel that they have more to lose from some choices than they have to gain. Thus, it is suggested that, for those considering enterprise and employment, there can be an age window in which such a choice might be most attractive because it is between the age by which they might have accumulated enough attributes and resources to give the venture a reasonable chance and the age by which they might have so many commitments that they cannot afford to risk losing their income for a period. Having a young family for which they might wish to have a more reliable source of sufficient income is one example of such an inhibitor.

Destiny, upbringing and family encouragement

Some people seem to be predestined for certain occupations. An obvious example, although one affecting few people, is found in hereditary monarchies in which the heir is expected to assume the position of ruler when it becomes vacant. However in other situations a person's heritage, upbringing, preparation, training and/or abilities may apparently predestine, or at least prepare, him or her for a particular route. Family businesses, whether a small family farm or a large family-owned-and-run business empire, are a clear case but there are others in which families apparently prepare children for occupations which they think will be particularly attractive or suitable.

Others

There are also other influences that are thought to apply in some situations. Some enterprise and business support agencies, wishing to increase the number of people selecting the enterprise option, have used advertising to try to influence people, either by promoting the attractiveness of starting their own businesses or at least by trying to make more people aware that it is available as a potential option. Another influence might be the availability of training and/or support for a particular option. Again enterprise agencies have sought to encourage people to consider entrepreneurship by promoting the availability of free or subsidised advice, training and/or mentoring.

The basis of the entrepreneurship decision

It has already been suggested that, in many developed countries, the occupational possibilities for a lot of people often seem to be employment or unemployment and that such people probably do not give the possibility of entrepreneurship much consideration. Traditionally it would seem that the assumption was that people only opted for the entrepreneurship choice after a logical assessment of the potential risks and returns had indicated that entrepreneurship should provide them with a better return than any of the other available options. Examples of this assumption are quoted in Illustration 10.1, and Chapter 3 indicated that this assumption is consistent with many of the available models of the influences on entrepreneurship, even if it is not formally incorporated into some of them.

Illustration 10.1 Examples of the assumption of individual risk–return analysis

The following quotes illustrate the prevalence of the assumption that the entrepreneurial choice is made on the basis of logical risk–return assessments carried out by the individuals concerned:

'One of the canonical theoretical models in the Economics of Entrepreneurship is of occupational choice. ... Occupational choice models partition the workforce between individuals who do best by becoming entrepreneurs, and those who do best by choosing an alternative occupation', ... (for instance) modelling entrepreneurial choice as trading off risk and return.'[8]

'Scholars have generally framed the decision of an individual (*homo oeconomicus*) to become an entrepreneur in terms of the model of occupational choice, where the income generated is compared to the wage earned as an employee.'[9]

'In recent years, most research on entrepreneurship has focused on employment choices and on the alternative motivations that cause some individuals to start new businesses. In these studies, an individual's choice to become an entrepreneur is the result of a decision in which the individual in question compares the returns from alternative income-producing activities and selects the employment opportunity with the highest expected return. In short, the person becomes an entrepreneur because he or she can earn more.'[10]

> 'Individuals are assumed to have a choice between operating a risky firm or working for a riskless wage. There are, of course, many factors which should influence this choice. The most important ones would include entrepreneurial ability, labor skills, attitudes toward risk, and individual access to the capital required to create a firm.'[11]

Governments and enterprise/business support agencies, which would like more people to follow the entrepreneurship route, have therefore attempted to persuade people on the basis of this logic. The policies they have pursued have in many cases been consistent with the prevailing models of, and assumptions about, entrepreneurship which tend to suggest that people generally make individual decisions to start businesses, based on a logical assessment of issues such as the perceived desirability of the goal, the ease of pursuing it, the help available and the perceived chances of success. Initiatives such as reducing red-tape, encouraging the availability of more capital, providing business training and mentoring, ensuring the availability of suitable and affordable premises and developing export sales initiatives have therefore been tried. Such steps have been designed to make entrepreneurship more attractive by making it easier, by increasing the potential return from it and/or reducing the risk associated with it. They are thus supposedly increasing the likelihood that people will opt for entrepreneurship.

> We spend most of our waking lives at work, in occupations that are often chosen by our unthinking 16-year old selves. And yet we rarely ask ourselves how we got there.
>
> Alain de Botton[12]

This book, however, is suggesting that many people do not decide on a logical, risk–return-assessment basis. As the quote above from Alain de Botton indicates, often the choice of occupation is made relatively early in life and is not subsequently changed. Also it is done without apparently a great deal of thought, or at least without the rational analysis which later people might wish to think they would have applied. So on what basis are such early choices made?

In many cases the career choices people made were influenced by tradition. In rural societies the sons and daughters of farmers often went into farming, the latter often by marriage, and in coal-mining communities the sons of miners usually went into mining. In other cases an early selection may have had a large element of chance in which, for instance, a part-time holiday job led to an interest and/or opportunity which was pursued without looking at the alternatives. Rarely, probably, have such choices been made on the basis of a rational analysis of risk and return to indicate which, of all the possible choices, might be the best longer-term option.

Behavioural economics and the social brain

> 'For every problem there is a solution that is simple, clean and wrong', wrote H. L. Mencken, and the *Homo economicus* model is all that. Unlike *Homo economicus*, *Homo sapiens* is not perfectly rational. Proof of that lies not in the fact that humans occasionally make mistakes. The *Homo economicus* model allows for that. It's that in certain circumstances, people always make mistakes. We are systematically flawed. In 1957, Herbert Simon, a brilliant psychologist/economist/political scientist and future Nobel laureate, coined the term bounded rationality. We are rational, in other words, but only within limits.

Source: Dan Gardner, *Risk* (London, Virgin Books, 2009), p. 46.

In recent years it has been increasingly recognised that there are limitations to the traditional economic assumptions about separate individual decision making (see Illustration 10.2). For instance it has been said that

> the models used to plan our economies were based on simplified individualistic assumptions about how human beings make decisions. Namely, that their decisions are wholly rational, coalesce in various forms of equilibrium (such as that between supply and demand), and are motivated solely by self-interest.
>
> These individualistic assumptions were originally adopted not because they gave a true description of human nature, but because they were thought to provide the best model for predicting behaviour. However, given the recent credit crunch, it is doubtful whether this is in fact the case. ... So perhaps we should think about policies that reflect our cognitive shortcomings rather than vainly hoping we will rid ourselves of them? This is a tall order, as governments and citizens alike are inured to the individualistic assumptions of neo-classical economics.[13]

'It is no exaggeration', another observer has stated, 'to say that orthodox economics is based on the idea that people can be treated, for economic purposes, as if they are selfish, independent calculating machines'.[14] The recognition of the limitation of that assumption has lead to the development of what has been called 'behavioural economics' for which, Daniel Kahneman, an Israeli academic at Princeton, won the Nobel Prize for economics in 2002.

> The award was unusual, indeed controversial, because Kahneman is not an economist but a psychologist. In the 1970s he became intrigued by the list of assumptions traditional economics made, and still makes, about people's nature. As Kahneman put it in the 2003 *American Economic Review*, 'I found the list quite startling, because I had been professionally trained not to believe a word of it'. As a psychologist, instead of assuming how people behave, Kahneman decided to look at how we actually behave ... (and) has become arguably the biggest name in what is now 'behavioural economics'.[15]

Thus, even in economics, it is being recognised that people do not always make important decisions on the basis of rational logical analysis but that, even if only subconsciously, their decisions are influenced by their social surroundings. Therefore, in 2009, the RSA (Royal Society for the Encouragement of Arts, Manufacturing and Commerce) launched its project 'The Social Brain', designed 'to contribute to constructing the successor paradigm to the individualism of "economic man"' (and see Illustration 10.2). In introducing the project the RSA explained that

> in recent years the 'economic man' conception of human decision-making employed in neo-classical economics – a conception where decisions are thought of as only informed and motivated by rational self-interest – has come under increasing pressure. One direction of pressure emanates from the quite dramatic failure of the conception as a short cut for predicting and modelling economic activity. Another comes from new knowledge in neuroscience and the behavioural and social sciences. These two directions are rather obviously connected: the new knowledge shows that the 'economic man' conception provides us with a limited and biased understanding of human decision-making.[16]

Illustration 10.2 The social brain

There are three main strands to the idea that the brain is essentially social:

1. The brain, now it is finally beginning to be understood, turns out to unconsciously execute many of the decision-making processes that were previously thought to be self-consciously produced. The idea that all decisions flow from an executive rational subject, in principle capable of operating in isolation from others, now appears to be at worst false and at best unhelpful.

2. The brain has evolved to develop and function within social networks. For example, a deficit in the neurotransmitter Serotonin (which, amongst other things enables self-control) will result from unstable social environments lacking in qualities like empathy. Or, another example: mirror neurons are designed to enable (amongst other things) altruistic behaviour that facilitates social cohesion and allows an agent to successfully engage with others (and thus to achieve her own goals).

3. Even when we do make self-conscious decisions these are partly constituted by systematic biases that are fundamentally social. For example, behavioural economists have shown that people often indulge in herd behaviour. Game-theorists have also shown that it can be optimally rational to act altruistically because an agent's good reputation amongst her fellows is massively important for her ability to successfully negotiate the social world. And as neuroscientists like Antonio Damasio have shown, these kinds of socially motivated biases have their basis in the neurology of the brain.

Source: RSA Projects, Project Briefing, *The Social Brain* (London: RSA, 2009).

One area in which some thought has been given to the extent to which logic might, or might not, apply to issues of individual choice is the field of consumer research. As is reported in Chapter 5, researchers in this area have questioned the hegemony of the 'information processing model' which regarded the consumer as a logical thinker who solved problems to make purchasing decisions. It is not suggested that information processing logic never plays a part in decisions but that consumers are socially connected beings and that consumer behaviour is more complex than such rational models assumes. Theories of consumer behaviour therefore also need to allow for the subjective and emotional dimensions of consumption – characterised as 'fantasies, feelings and fun'.[17]

One particular influence allied to fantasies, feelings and fun is fashion. The producers of many fashionable consumer goods know that the key to selling their products is persuading people that it is the acceptable thing to have and to be seen in or with. Although, if challenged, those same consumers might claim that the item in question was logically the best thing for them to buy. How many people, for instance, actually buy a BMW car because they have made a comparison which shows that, of all the cars available, the model of BMW which they bought best addressed their needs? Smart producers know that people often buy for reasons of kudos or prestige, even if they persuade themselves that there is another rationale for their choice.

Being influenced by fashion is a form of peer-pressure which often makes people do things that they might not have done had they made the decision on their own. How many young people would take up smoking if they thought about it logically? Yet, despite all the evidence that it is both costly and very harmful, many do it because their peers are doing it. If forms of social encouragement such as fashion and peer-pressure are that powerful, could they also affect people's choices of occupation?

The importance of social influence

A number of studies have shown that more unemployed people find employment through friends and personal contacts than through any other single route.[18]

Acting entrepreneurially must be perceived as a desirable thing to do, not simply to oneself but to significant others.[19]

America has found the transition to a more entrepreneurial economy easier than its competitors because entrepreneurialism is so deeply rooted in its history.[20]

Entrepreneurialism has become cool.[21]

Chapter 5 also includes a summary of some aspects of the science of collective behaviour which seeks to use some of the laws of physics to make predictions about society. It suggests that in many aspects of human behaviour, while people may be free to make their own individual decisions, they still tend to act as a group and to follow what the social group as a whole is doing. Although the people concerned may not be conscious of it, there is a group social influence on individual behaviour.

In many such situations, the apparent application of individual free will can tend, nevertheless, to produce consistent behaviour across much of the group. This suggests that most people are more influenced by social pressure than they might admit, or even be aware of.

The influence of fashions, considered above, is one such example of a social influence leading to many individuals making similar purchasing decisions, even when the people concerned might still feel that they are making their own rational choices. The work of researchers such as Klucharev in the field of neuroimaging 'reveals the brain activity behind our tendency to "follow the crowd"' and has shown 'how human behaviour can be guided by the perceived behaviour of other individuals' and 'why we automatically adjust our opinions in line with the majority opinion'.[22] Therefore, this approach would suggest, in many aspects of human behaviour, that the social influence of peers and others might have a more significant effect on people's actions than the application of their own rational analysis. Could the choice of career be one such example of a behaviour which is often socially influenced?

A piece of research by Nanda and Sorensen[23], for instance, does support such a view. They found that 'the career experiences of peers in the workplace play an important role in defining the informational and normative environment within which individuals reach the decision to become entrepreneurs'. Their results indicated that people are more likely to become entrepreneurs if they work with people who have recently been self-employed than if they work in an environment where no one has entrepreneurial experience. Nanda and Sorensen suggest that 'entrepreneurial peers are important because they change co-worker attitudes and beliefs about entrepreneurship' and that two mechanisms of peer influence are 'deeply rooted in the entrepreneurship literature – opportunity identification and socialization to entrepreneurship'. Thus they conclude that 'the social environment of the workplace has a substantial impact on individual rates of entrepreneurship'. In addition Stanworth and Gray looked at people in selected service sectors and found that

> overall some 43.5 per cent ... had fathers and/or mothers who had been self-employed ranging from 56 per cent for the owners of free houses, wine bars and restaurants down to 33.3 per cent for the owners of both advertising, marketing and design companies and computer services business. This finding thus strongly supports the contention that parental experience of self-employment in general, and small business ownership in particular is the best single predictor of the propensity to enter into small business ownership.[24]

A social influence model

> Entrepreneurs are hardly lone individuals who rely primarily on their extraordinary efforts and talents to overcome the difficulties inherent in the formation of a new firm. The process of starting a new firm is eminently social.[25]
>
> Entrepreneurship, like all business, is a social activity.[26]

One of the possible options identified above for accessing the resources needed for life is crime. Crime might even be considered to be a form of enterprise or entrepreneurship as many criminals undertake their own criminal initiatives, instead of simply working to implement the criminal plans of someone else. Nevertheless, if crime is enterprise, it is illegal enterprise and it is its illegality which separates it from other enterprising actions.

It might be supposed that the extent to which people resort to crime would be proportional to the level of temptation and/or the level of incentive from factors such social and/or economic deprivation, offset by the risk of detection and punishment, and that the decision of whether or not to engage in crime is essentially a risk–reward decision. In that case the relationship between the level of crime and the strength of an influence might be like that portrayed in Figure 10.1.

In his book *Critical Mass*,[27] Philip Ball illustrates the potential of the science of collective behaviour by reference to studies of criminality. He relates how the economists Michael Campbell and Paul Ormerod have considered the relationship between social deprivation and the potential of people to become criminals. They assumed that the population could be divided into three groups: those who are active criminals, those who are immune from the temptations of crime and those who are, in effect, 'floating voters', who might become criminals under the right

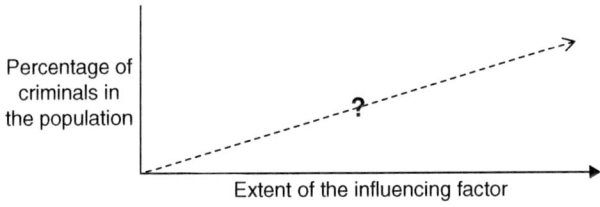

Figure 10.1 A 'default' model of the impact of an influence on crime

conditions. Individuals, they then suggest, can switch from one group to another and do so as the result of a form of peer pressure. Thus those who are in the susceptible group will look around them and if they see a lot of other people engaging in crime will follow their example, whereas as if they see few others so employed, they too will desist from crime.

The result of members of that susceptible group following the majority is that they then become part of the majority in turn influencing others. As a result, instead of the level of crime rising steadily as factors such as social and/or economic deprivation increase, the level of crime will be relatively stable at either a high or a low state, almost whatever the level of deprivation. Whether it is high or low during the period in question will depend, not on the level of deprivation, but whether the level of crime was high or low at the start of the period. Further it will then persist at that stable level until there is sufficient cumulative pressure to tip it into the other state. This is illustrated in Figure 10.2 and, Ball suggests, it is a very similar picture to the phase change between the liquid and solid forms of a pure substance. If the solid substance is heated then, once melting occurs, all the molecules change state at the same temperature, but if the substance is then cooled again, it can remain liquid until a lower temperature before starting to refreeze.

The Campbell and Ormerod model of crime is based on a few simple credible assumptions and it predicts, not a single progression line, but two alternative states, each stable over a wide range of conditions because, despite individual choice, it assumes that crime is socially influenced. This suggestion that levels of crime might be influenced by social example rather than being proportional to need explains, for instance, why looting suddenly become prevalent after incidents such

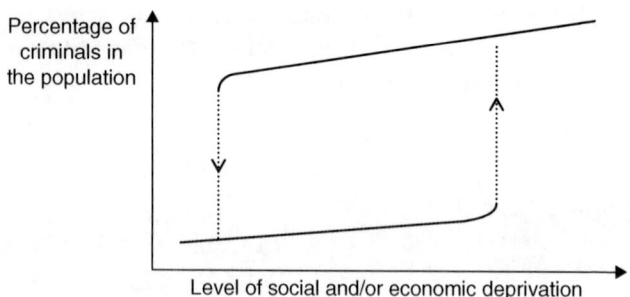

Figure 10.2 Predictions of the incidence of criminality in a society
Source: from P. Ball, *Critical Mass: How One Thing Leads to Another* (London: Arrow Books, 2004), p. 400. Reprinted by permission of The Random House Group Ltd.

as riots or shipwrecks. It is not that those involved suddenly need to turn to crime but that they see others so engaged and feel a sort of obligation to claim their share of the booty apparently on offer.

Conclusion

This chapter has considered a number of possible influences on the choice of entrepreneurship as an appropriate means for realising people's goals. In particular it has considered the potential importance of social influence. A model based on social influence, and its possible implications for encouraging more entrepreneurship, are explored further in Chapter 12. Before that, however, Chapter 11 explores the potential for social influence on entrepreneurship, not least in the context of social capital.

References

1. P. Lunn, *Basic Instincts* (London: Marshall Cavendish, 2008), p. 125.
2. E. Stam, 'Entrepreneurship, Evolution and Geography', *Papers on Economics and Evolution*, edited by the Evolutionary Economics Group, Max Planck Institute, Jena, 2009, p. 4.
3. A. Morrison, 'Entrepreneurship: What Triggers It?', *International Journal of Entrepreneurial Behaviour & Research*, Vol. 2, No. 6, 2000, p. 63.
4. N. Bosma and R. Harding, *GEM 2006 Results* (Babson College and London Business School), p.18, at www.gemconsortium.org, accessed on 4 July 2009.
5. M. Minniti, W. Bygrave and E. Autio, *Global Entrepreneurship Monitor: 2005 Executive Report* (Babson College and London Business School), p. 23, at www.gemconsortium.org, accessed on 4 July 2009.
6. Peter Rosa, Sarath Kodithuwakku and Waswa Balunywa, 'Reassessing Necessity Entrepreneurship in Developing Countries', 29th ISBE Conference, Cardiff, November 2006.
7. Said by Paul Westhead in presenting his paper on Graduate Employment in SMEs at the ISBA 27th National Conference at Newcastle 2004.
8. S. C. Parker, 'The Economics of Entrepreneurship: What We Know and What We Don't', *Foundations and Trends in Entrepreneurship*, Vol. 1, No. 1, 2005, pp. 5–7.
9. D. A. Audretsch, W. Boente and J. P. Tamvada, *Religion and Entrepreneurship* (Germany: Jena Economic Research Papers, 2007–075), p. 4.
10. M. Minniti, 'Entrepreneurs Examined', *Business Strategy Review*, Vol. 17, Issue 4 (London: London Business School, Winter 2006), p. 79.
11. R. E Kihlstrom and J-J. Laffont, 'A General Equilibrium Entrepreneurial Theory of Firm Formation Based on Risk Aversion', *Journal of Political Economy*, Vol. 87, Issue 4, 1979, p. 720.
12. Reported in the Belfast Telegraph on 19 March 2009.
13. M. Grist (Director of the RSA's Social Brain project), 'After Individualism: Activating the Social Brain', at www.thersa.org, accessed on 10 February 2009.

14. P. Lunn, op. cit., p. ix.
15. Ibid., p. 42.
16. RSA Projects, Project Briefing, *The Social Brain* (London: RSA, 2009).
17. See for instance M. Holbrook and E. Hirschman, 'The Experiential Aspects of Consumption: Consumer Fantasies, Feelings and Fun', *Journal of Consumer Research*, 9, September 1982, pp. 132–40.
18. Performance and Innovation Unit, *Social Capital: A Discussion Paper* (London: Cabinet Office, April 2002), p. 20.
19. E. Chell, *The Entrepreneurial Personality: A Social Construction* (London: Routledge, 2008), p. 170.
20. A. Wooldridge, 'Special Report on Entrepreneurship', *The Economist*, 14 March 2009.
21. A. Wooldridge, op. cit.
22. 'Brain Mechanisms of Social Conformity', at www.eurekalert.org/pub_releases/2009-01/cp-bmo010909.php, accessed on 27 September 2009.
23. R. Nanda and J. B. Sorensen, *Peer Effects and Entrepreneurship* (Harvard Business School, Entrepreneurial Management Working Paper 08-051, 2007).
24. J. Stanworth and C. Gray (eds), *Bolton 20 Years On: The Small Firm in the 1990s* (London: Paul Chapman Publishing Ltd, 1991), p. 174.
25. E. Stam, op. cit., p. 4.
26. A. Wooldridge, op. cit.
27. P. Ball, *Critical Mass: How One Thing Leads to Another* (London: Arrow Books, 2004).

11
The Social Dimension

Traditional economic thinking has assumed that human beings make rational economic decisions. Similarly many of the models of the influences on entrepreneurship reviewed in Chapter 3 also seem to be based on the assumption that people make individual decisions to start businesses, based on a logical risk–return assessment incorporating issues such as the perceived desirability of the goal, the ease of pursuing it, the help available and the perceived chances of success.

In contrast to this assumption of individual, logical, risk–reward assessments, Chapter 5 alluded to the science of collective behaviour which finds that, while the people in a group may each be free to make their own individual decisions, the behaviour of the group overall can still follow consistent and predictable courses. Chapter 10 referred to recent developments in behavioural economics and neuroscience which suggest that, whereas people might be supposed to make decisions based on individual rational evaluations of the available options, and might even think and indicate to others that this is what they have done, in reality that is often not the case. Social influence can and does play a big part in their choice, whatever their subsequent explanations. As Gardner comments in his book about our perceptions of risk: 'humans are compulsive rationalisers'[1] and 'we don't review information about risks with cool detachment and objectivity. We screen it to make it conform to what we already believe. And what we believe is deeply influenced by the beliefs of the people around us and of the culture in which we live'.[2]

Chapter 10 then asked if, for this reason, whatever people might say, or even think, about their motivation, there might nevertheless be a social dimension to people's choice of occupation and, in particular, to whether they might consider entrepreneurship to be a valid option for them. This chapter examines further the potential role of social factors in entrepreneurship to see if such a suggestion might be credible. It might have been thought that the social impact on business would be minimal as business decisions were supposed to be motivated by the prospect of personal financial gain and to be subject to the market forces of supply and demand. However businesses are run by, and for, human beings and humans are social animals so social interaction has always played a part in business. This has been recognised in recent years, for instance, in the concept of social capital which has received increasing recognition as one of the essential requirements for economic success.

Is there a social dimension to entrepreneurship?

> Organisational scientists, economists and sociologists especially are focusing on (entrepreneurial) networks as a vehicle for understanding how work gets done.[3]
>
> The remainder of (this) article is structured first by examining the case for understanding entrepreneurship as socially embedded.[4]
>
> Entrepreneurship emerges dynamically in social interaction between people.[5]

Is entrepreneurship an individual activity, a social activity or an individual activity in which social influence is nevertheless crucial? Few of the models of entrepreneurship described in Chapter 3 overtly indicate that it might have a social dimension. Shane, for instance, in his model, portrays alert individuals discovering opportunities, and the attributes and resources model does not mention a social aspect, unless it is implied in 'network', and Stevenson does not include it in her portrayal of the entrepreneurship system. It is not included in the suggested hierarchy of enterprise needs and, while Peterson and Rondstadt's formula for entrepreneurial success is one model which does include 'entrepreneurial know who', that has been interpreted as having the contacts needed to run a business rather that any social encouragement to be in business:

> The problem, as we see it, is that many network approaches imply an instrumental rationalization of social relations – friendship and other social contacts are studied as tools used by entrepreneurs in order to obtain financing and succeed with their business plans.[6]

But because it is not mentioned does not mean that a social dimension does not exist, or is not important, and some models, such as the GEM conceptual model and the Danish analysis, do include reference to the cultural context of entrepreneurship. Krueger also acknowledges a social dimension by specifically including perceived social norms as a key factor in his intentions model of entrepreneurial potential and Gibb's suggestion of the layers of the support network highlights the strong influence of close friends, relatives and family.

Other commentators also suggest that there is a social aspect. Behavioural economics, briefly referred to in Chapter 10, acknowledges that there is a social dimension to economics generally. It seeks to base economics, not on how people have been assumed to behave, but on how in reality they do behave. It recognises, for instance, that marketing can influence buyer behaviour, even if the response to marketing is not a logical reaction, and that advertising which seeks to persuade people that by buying a particular product they will become part of a social elite, while being nonsense, can nevertheless be effective. It suggests that

> much of our behaviour is strongly influenced by other people's behaviour. Examples include the clothes we wear or whether we haggle when shopping. Social learning is a process by which we subconsciously take in the behaviour of others to learn how to behave. In more complex situations with which we are unfamiliar, we consciously watch and learn from the behaviour of others – known as 'social proof'. ... When we must make a conscious decision on how to behave, our sense of social identity is important – we think: how would other people from 'my group' behave in this situation? In situations where there is high social capital (i.e. where there are strong networks between people and a high level of mutual trust), other people's behaviour and our sense of social identity may be extremely important in influencing our own behaviour. We are particularly open to influence from people in authority or from people whom we respect or like. The influence of people's behaviour on social norms – which themselves influence yet more people's behaviour – gives rise to an ever-evolving system of shifting social norms. Illustrations of the importance of other people's behaviour abound, including fashion, the films we watch, stock market prices and the pursuit of status, which is always socially defined and changes through time.[7]

Behavioural economics may refer to wider economic responses, rather than specifically to entrepreneurship, but entrepreneurship is unlikely to be an exception. In 2008 a special issue of the journal *Social Influence* examined 'how social influences can affect such outcomes as creativity, innovation, originality, and inventiveness',[8] all of which are related to entrepreneurship. In 2007 a special edition of the *International Small Business Journal* addressed social capital and entrepreneurship because 'relationships clearly matter to entrepreneurs, but understanding how they function requires an appreciation of social capital'.[9] Thus it seems to be relevant to consider how social influence fits with social capital: whether as a part of it or as a partner to it.

The concept of social capital

In the context of economics the word capital usually refers to the availability of something, usually money, needed to start or run a business. Traditionally it was suggested that the three things which needed to be combined for a successful business were investment, materials and labour. In *The Wealth of Nations*, Adam Smith identified four types of capital: machines and instruments, buildings, land, and 'the acquired and useful abilities of people'. Since then variations and further capitals have been identified: such as natural capital (natural resources such as land, minerals or forests); physical, manufactured or infrastructural capital (anything made by humans for use in, or by, a business such as machinery for manufacture, roads for distribution and telephone systems for communication) and human capital (encompassing both the skills and the knowledge that humans can apply). Other capitals have also been proposed such as cultural capital, intellectual capital and infrastructural capital.

The application of such ideas to apparently deprived communities, whether in less developed regions or in the poorer neighbourhoods of otherwise thriving cities or regions, suggested that what they usually lacked was money (financial capital). They seemed to have as much access to natural capital as wealthier areas and things like road networks were in place. Often people had some skills and/or could be trained, so with money they could invest in such training and in the means of production such as buildings or machinery which was what was apparently missing for wealth creation. That appeared to leave a lack of money as the explanation for their problems but, in cases in which money was then made available to such communities, for instance through development grants, the experience was often that it did not seem to lead to any significant improvement.

It was suggested therefore that something else was also missing. Just as starving people need food which includes not just the basic components of proteins, fats and carbohydrates, but also vitamins, so too it was argued that communities needed more than just investment of money, training and infrastructure and that additional something was social capital:

> If one asks what distinguishes successful from unsuccessful communities and why it is that some communities facing similar economic, social and demographic issues cope better than others, it soon becomes apparent that the more successful communities have greater levels of such social capital.[10]

Towards the end of the twentieth-century, development studies[11] suggested that five capitals were needed for the sustainable development of communities and regions, and they were financial capital, human capital, manufactured or physical capital, natural capital and social capital. This recognised that money (financial capital) is not alone enough to ensure development success because although businesses might use money to buy or hire other things, that is only possible when those things are available. In similar ways the development studies suggested that the potential to substitute one of the five capitals for another was very limited.

Such studies helped to highlight the need for social capital, but the concept of social capital had been introduced much earlier. A description of it was given by Hanifan in 1916[12] although the term did not start to get much recognition until it was used by people like Bourdieu in the 1970s.[13] It then became the subject of a World Bank research programme in the 1990s and was popularised by books such as Putnam's *Bowling Alone* in 2000.[14] It has been applied by both economists and sociologists. In a community context it has been described as increasing the confidence and capacity of individuals and small groups to get involved in activities and mutually supportive networks that hold communities together.

Indeed the importance of social capital has been recognised, not just in a development context, but also in business and entrepreneurship. A number of commentators have pointed out, for instance, the relevance and importance of social contacts and networks to entrepreneurship and entrepreneurial performance:

> The presence or absence of social capital is likely to influence the very nature of the entrepreneurial venture. Social capital involves social interaction and would appear to reside in and between connections to others. It could even be regarded as representing 'networking capital' since in essence it is really a relational phenomenon and a term that actually refers to the social connections entrepreneurs use to obtain resources they would otherwise acquire through expending the human or financial capital.[15]

What is social capital?

Although identified as a necessary ingredient in development and entrepreneurship, social capital has not been closely pinned down. One paper suggests:

> Social capital is a widely used concept in the social sciences, but its precise meaning is elusive. It has been variously and broadly defined as involving the building and maintaining of networks and the norms of behaviour that underpin them; the goodwill that is engendered by the fabric of social relations and that can be mobilised to facilitate action; and taken to be the sum of the resources that accrue to an individual or group by virtue of possessing networks.[16]

There is, therefore, no agreed standard list of the constituents of social capital, of its varieties, its domains and its components. Nevertheless sometimes definitions of social capital include lists of components such as the following:

> 'Networks, norms, and trust ... that enable participants to act together more effectively to pursue shared objectives.'[17]

> 'The institutions, relationships and norms that shape the quality and quantity of a society's social interactions.' [18]

> 'Networks together with shared norms, values and understandings that facilitate co-operation within or among groups.'[19]

> 'Work-based networks, diffuse friendships and shared or mutually acknowledged social values can all be seen as forms of social capital.'[20]

> 'Shared norms or values that promote social co-operation.'[21]

One summary of the main components of social capital identifies them in the following terms:

> *social networks* – who knows who;
> *social norms* – the informal and formal 'rules' that guide how network members behave to each other; and
> *sanctions* – the processes that help to ensure that network members keep to the rules.[22]

Another summary states that social capital comprises four elements:

1 'Bonding' and 'Bridging'. Bonding is where social capital is concentrated within the group, allowing the development of trust and agreed norms of behaviour that enable the group to more easily attain its goals. Bridging focuses on the individual's external ties; social capital is used as a resource to explain how the entrepreneur uses his/her contacts to bring about personal gain.
2 Social capital benefits the entrepreneur through access to information and sources of influence. Entrepreneurs may, where they are on the edges of several networks, have the power to exploit different sources of information, by being able to put together apparently disconnected information in a way that an individual without his or her 'silo' cannot do.
3 A further dimension of social capital is relational and concerns the development of trust. Trust facilitates the network connections because it suggests beneficial relations and continuing reciprocity of arrangements. This suggests that the network ties and relations are strong.
4 There is a cognitive dimension to social capital, which concerns the shared understandings that develop between the different parties. This, ironically, limits the range of possibilities whilst providing a stronger basis for the preferred, probable way forward.[23]

Social capital can also be observed in different areas of activity or aspects of life. Table 11.1 presents a list of what have been called the 'domains' of social capital.

Then there are thought to be different types of social capital, with at least three forms now being identified:[24]

- Bonding social capital – characterised by strong bonds (or 'social glue'), for example, among family members or among members of an ethnic group.
- Bridging social capital – characterised by weaker, less dense but more cross-cutting ties ('social oil'), for example, with business associates, acquaintances, friends from different ethnic groups, friends of friends etc.
- Linking social capital – characterised by connections between those with differing levels of power or social status, for example, links between the political elite and the general public or between individuals from different social classes.

Table 11.1 Some domains of social capital

Domain	Description
Empowerment	People feel they have a voice which is listened to, are involved in processes that affect them, can themselves take action to initiate changes
Participation	People take part in social and community activities; local events occur and are well attended
Associational activity and common purpose	People co-operate with one another through the formation of formal and informal groups to further their interests. Developing and supporting networks between organisations in the area
Supporting networks and reciprocity	Individuals and organisations co-operate to support one another for either mutual or one-sided gain; an expectation that help would be given to or received from others when needed
Collective norms and values	People share common values and norms of behaviour
Trust	People feel they can trust their co-residents and local organisations responsible for governing or servicing their area
Safety	People feel safe in their neighbourhood and are not restricted in their use of public space by fear
Belonging	People feel connected to their co-residents, their home area and have a sense of belonging to the place and its people

Source: Based on R. Forrest and A. Kearns, 'Social Cohesion, Social Capital and the Neighbourhood', *Urban Studies*, Vol. 38 (2001), p. 2140.

Therefore, it is said, the distinction between bonding and bridging capital, or between strong and weak ties, is crucial. The impacts of social capital, for good or ill, depend on the form it takes in different circumstances and individuals also have needs for different types of social capital at different points in their lives.

Illustration 11.1 Measuring social capital

Another way of examining social capital is to try to measure it. If social capital is a necessary component for economic development then it should be possible to establish a link between them. An incentive for measuring social capital therefore has been to compare the levels of social capital in different areas with the corresponding levels of economic development and growth and to see if there is any correlation between the two. One approach to measuring social capital encapsulated the key parts of definitions of it under six headings, thus suggesting that there might be six components or dimensions to it:

- Trust.
- Reciprocity and mutuality.
- Shared norms and behaviour.
- Shared commitment and belonging.
- Both formal and informal social networks.
- Effective information channels.[25]

Financial capital is probably most people's default model of a capital. It can come in several forms such as founders' investments, outside shareholder funds, term loans, overdrafts, credits, informal investments and grants. Although these forms often have different uses and conditions, it is nevertheless possible to measure each of them in money terms and then all add those amounts together to present one measure of all the capital in a business.

However some other capitals are clearly different. Human capital, for instance, includes skills, knowledge, ability to labour and good health and even if each of those could be scored they could not then be added together to produce just one overall measure of human capital. Even in the case of financial capital adding together the different parts of it may not always be helpful because often they cannot be substituted for each other and it is sometimes important to know how much of each one there is.

So, even when the different dimensions of an issue can be measured in the same units, it is not necessarily relevant to combine them into one overall score. For instance the width, depth and height of an object can be all be measured in units of length and those measurements can be used to describe the object. But, just because the measurements can then be added together to produce one figure, it does not mean that that figure provides a meaningful comparison. For instance summing the three dimensions of a 4.5 inch cube of concrete, a 12 inch ruler and a piece of A5 paper would in each case produce a similar combined measurement, although in reality the three objects are very different.

Social capital, as often described, is multi-dimensional and has different components which apparently cannot be substituted for each other. For instance it is conceivable that, in a society divided into warring tribes, each tribe could have a lot of bonding social capital but no bridging social capital. Would it be relevant to equate that to a society which had very weak family ties but relatively good work relationships? A deprived society may be highly bonded but is it relevant to equate the bonding social capital of a mafia society with the bridging social capital of a society which trades on the basis of trust (which Fukuyama has suggested has been the basis of high economic growth)?[26] In those circumstances one form of social capital might contribute to economic development but the other probably does not. Any attempt therefore to provide a single measure of social capital must either treat all dimensions as equivalent, which they are not, or ignore some of them, which is arbitrary and misleading. If a single measure is sought then the alternative is to define only one dimension as social capital and the other components as something else, but that is contrary to most current views.

Halpern[27] has used a vitamin model in the context of social capital. Trying to determine the relationship between social capital and economic growth may therefore be like exploring the relationship between vitamins and health. It is not the case that the total amount of vitamins correlates with good health but that the body manufactures or receives enough of each vitamin for the purposes for which it is needed. (See Illustration 11.2.)

Thus social capital appears to have a very diverse nature, being comprised of a variety of components and domains as well as potentially existing in different forms which have different effects and are needed at different times or for different stages or in connection with different issues. Take, for instance, trust and network contacts. They are both generally acknowledged to be part of social capital but knowing people and trusting them are different things, and they do not necessarily go together. It is quite possible to trust people but not to know who to go to for advice and guidance on a particular issue, just as it is possible to know the person who is responsible for the particular issue but not to trust them. Adding more trust will not help in a situation in which a lack of contacts is the problem, just as adding more contacts will not help if the issue is that they are not trusted. Thus both of these most basic components of social capital may be needed and, if a person or organisation is short of one, having or adding more of the other will not be a suitable substitute, and neither will adding more of one automatically increase the level of the other.

Illustration 11.2 An analogy with vitamins?

As proposed in Illustration 11.1, and following the suggestion of Halpern,[28] could the role of social capital in development be comparable, in some ways, to the role of vitamins in diet? Without vitamins the other components of food, such as proteins, fats, carbohydrates and salts, are not sufficient to maintain life. In a normally varied diet the foods we eat usually include sufficient vitamins so it is only when that diet is limited or deficient in some way that they need to be supplemented. There are different vitamins, some of which may have different forms, and they have diverse biochemical functions. Although the potential of citrus fruit to prevent the deficiency disease scurvy was first discovered in the middle of the eighteenth century, the need for vitamins in diet, and the existence of different vitamins, was not fully established until the first part of the twentieth century, and vitamin B_9 was not identified until 1941. Depending on the circumstances, it is now thought that humans need up to 13 vitamins, most of which have multiple functions, but they cannot be substituted one for the other.

Although having enough vitamins is essential for a healthy body, in some cases too much of a vitamin can be harmful. Also measuring the total amount of all vitamins in a diet is relatively meaningless as what matters is not the total amount of vitamins but that there is enough of each of the relevant ones.

Similarly social capital appears to be necessary for successful enterprise and development, along with the other traditional capitals, and it seems to exist in different forms or dimensions. Could those different forms or dimensions potentially contribute in different ways and therefore not be capable of substituting for each other? In that case it would be important to have a range of forms of social capital and measuring the total amount of all social capital in an organisation, if it were possible, would be meaningless.

Traditional views seem to consider social capital to be a single entity which may have different aspects but can nevertheless be defined as an entity because each portion of it is substitutable for another portion. The vitamin analogy suggests instead that it may be a group of components which have aspects of human relationship in common, but which nevertheless have different effects and cannot be substituted for each other. Looking at social capital in this way could explain why it does not yet seem possible to agree a single clear definition of what it is and why efforts to introduce it often do not seem to have the beneficial effects expected because, by failing to understand the need for different components, they do not introduce all the aspects needed. It is also consistent with the suggestion by Audretsch and Keilbach (summarised in Illustration 11.4) that what they have identified as entrepreneurship capital should not be confused with social capital but is instead a subset of it.

This analogy with vitamins might stimulate attempts to identify different components of social capital, each with different properties, instead of assuming that they are just different aspects of a single entity. It could also suggest that, like the requirement for certain vitamins during growth, some aspects of social capital might be particularly important during an enterprise's formative years. It might also explain why social capital sometimes needs to be supplemented. Just as people can get enough vitamins from natural food, but may need vitamin supplements if they rely too much on some processed food, is it also possible that when business funding comes from social or professional contacts, it is often accompanied by aspects of social capital which can be missing from officially constructed, impartial and arms-length business funding schemes?

NB: It does seem that, like vitamins, social capital can also have a direct impact on our health. In his book *Outliers* Malcolm Gladwell reports on an investigation into the reason why the inhabitants of the town of Roseto in Pennsylvania have had significantly better levels of health than the US as a whole, including having roughly half the average death rate from heart disease. The conclusion was that this difference was not due to factors such as diet or exercise, because they did not differ from the norm for the area, but was instead due to the nature of the relationships within the community which were still like those of the town in Italy from which the ancestors of many of the town's residents had once come. In other words Roseto's social capital was the factor which made its citizens healthier.[29]

Is social influence a form of social capital?

None of the comments on social capital quoted above seems specifically to include forms of social influence, such as peer pressure, as a form or component of social capital. Instead it might be argued that, as peer pressure can be negative or harmful, such as the influence which seems to persuade many people to take up smoking, it should not be seen as part of a capital because that is generally seen as something positive. However bonding social capital is sometimes seen as having a negative influence, for instance apparently making some communities insular and exclusive with limited external connections, and surely being susceptible to peer influence is a form of bonding. Similarly one of the six headings quoted in Illustration 11.1 is 'shared commitment and belonging' which must also embrace peer influence, and in the domains of social capital listed in Table 11.1 'collective norms and values' is described as including 'norms of behaviour' which must also be peer influenced. If the norm of behaviour espoused by someone's family and friends is that it is respectable to enter one of the traditional professions but questionable to start another form of business, especially one which trades, then that is clearly a social influence against many forms of entrepreneurship. It is also this sort of peer pressure which Baumol suggests was responsible in other times for directing

Table 11.2 The components of social capital?

Which comes first in considering social capital: the concept or the observation of its aspects? Instead of trying to define social capital and then see what components might be consistent with that definition, social capital might be described as the collective word for those aspects of human contact which seem to be relevant to enterprise and development. Based on what seems to help in real life case studies, such a list might include:
    Encouragement
    Mentoring
    Vouching for the entrepreneur
    Contacts
    Connection
    Endorsement
    Guidance
    Reinforcement
    Trust
    Approval
    Example and role models
And social influence, including peer influence, also fits well with such a list?

much entrepreneurship into unproductive or even destructive forms (see Chapter 6).

Therefore, it might be argued that social capital gets so close to embracing peer and other social influences that such social influence should be explicitly included (as Table 11.2 suggests), especially if it is correct to assume that it does have a considerable influence on entrepreneurship. Is that peer influence, the possible sources of which are suggested in Illustration 11.3, the essence of the 'entrepreneurship capital' referred to in Illustration 11.4?

Illustration 11.3 Who are a person's peers?

Who are a person's peers? In the context of peer pressure, it has been said that 'peers are the individuals with whom a child or adolescent identifies, who are usually but not always of the same age group. Peer pressure occurs when the individual experiences implicit or explicit persuasion, sometimes amounting to coercion, to adopt similar values, beliefs, and goals, or to participate in the same activities as those in the peer group'.[30]

While a person's 'peers' are usually from the same age group, it is suggested that in the context explored in this chapter the influences come from a somewhat wider group. It may include all those members of a person's family, relatives, friends and/or acquaintances with whom that person tends to identify and whose suggestions and example that person might be accustomed to consider and/or follow.

Illustration 11.4 Entrepreneurship capital

Audretsch and Keilbach have suggested that entrepreneurship capital should be added to the list of factors which drive economic growth. They describe entrepreneurship capital as 'a milieu of agents and institutions conducive to the creation of new firms ... such as social acceptance of entrepreneurial behaviour, individuals willing to deal with the risk of creating new firms, and the activity of bankers and venture capital agents willing to share risks and benefits.[31]

Audretsch and Keilbach identify entrepreneurship capital as a specific subset of social capital because, while 'not all social capital may be conducive to economic performance, let alone entrepreneurial activity, ... entrepreneurial capital, by its very definition, will have a positive impact on entrepreneurial activity'.[32] Therefore, they suggest, what has been called social capital in entrepreneurship literature may instead be this particular sub-component.

Using the number of start-up businesses in a region relative to its population as an indicator of entrepreneurial capital, Audretsch and Keilbach found that in Germany there is a positive link between entrepreneurship capital and regional economic performance, measured by labour productivity. However they report that their findings do not enable them to shed any light on what exactly constitutes entrepreneurial capital, although they speculate that it 'would include a broad spectrum of institutions, policies, historical, social and cultural traditions, as well as personal characteristics associated with the particular region'.[33]

Conclusions

This chapter has looked at the social dimension of entrepreneurship to see if something akin to peer pressure could be a relevant factor. The conclusions from this exploration might be summarised in the following terms:

- Contrary to what some models seem to indicate, it is sometimes acknowledged that there is a strong social dimension to economics in general and, more specifically, to enterprise and entrepreneurship. An example of that acknowledgement is the adoption of the concept of social capital and the recognition of its application to entrepreneurship and business.
- Social capital is not fully defined or described. It is multi-dimensional and appears to be an embracing concept – a label given to a loose range of social connection issues with a number of different aspects and which have a diverse, somewhat indeterminable, but nevertheless significant impact. It might be said of social capital that there is something which is influential but that it is not clear precisely what it is (rather in the way that morale is known to be important for team performance but cannot be precisely identified and measured).
- Social capital and social influence are clearly related. Social capital could include example and peer influence, although that does not so far appear specifically to have been acknowledged. Social influence, in terms of norms and pressure to conform to them, seems to fit well with the other aspects of social capital necessary for entrepreneurship to thrive. At least in that context, it could therefore be recognised that

'bonding social capital' includes, or is at least closely associated with, peer group and wider social example, encouragement and/or pressure.
- In any case, even if peer and wider social influences are not specifically included in social capital, that does not mean that they are not relevant influences on entrepreneurship (at any level from E0 upwards). Could it be that, like the importance of vitamins in a diet, entrepreneurship needs the right form of social influence and its lack cannot be compensated for by raising the levels of other possible contributory factors?

References

1. D. Gardner, *Risk* (London: Virgin Books, 2009), p. 166.
2. Ibid., p. 148.
3. Drakopoulou Dodd and A. Anderson, 'Mumpsimus and the Mything of the Individualistic Entrepreneur', *International Small Business Journal*, Vol. 25, No. 4, August 2007, p. 345.
4. Ibid., p. 343.
5. M. Lindgren and J. Packendorff, 'Social Constructionism and Entrepreneurship', *International Journal of Entrepreneurial Behaviour and Research*, Vol. 15, Issue 1, 2009.
6. Ibid.
7. nef, *Behavioural Economics: Seven Principles for Policy Makers* (London, new economics foundation, 2005), p. 3.
8. M. Turner, 'Introduction – Social Influence and Creativity: Setting the Stage for Inventiveness', *Social Influence*, Vol. 4, Issue 3, 2008, p. 223.
9. J. Cope, S. Jack and M. Rose, 'Social Capital and Entrepreneurship: An Introduction', *International Small Business Journal*, Vol. 25, No. 3, 2007, p. 214.
10. R. Putnam quoted by H. Frazer (Director of the Combat Poverty Agency in Ireland) in 'Capital Common Sense' in *Scope* (Belfast: NICVA, September 1999).
11. As summarised, for instance, in the Department for International Development (DFID), *Sustainable Development Guidance Sheets* (London: DFID, 1999).
12. L. J. Hanifan, 'The Rural School Community Centre', *Annals of the American Academy of Political and Social Science*, 67, 1916, pp. 130–8.
13. For instance P. Bourdieu, *Outline of a Theory of Practice* (1972).
14. R. Putnam, *Bowling Alone: The Collapse and Revival of American Community* (New York: Simon and Schuster, 2000).
15. J. Cope, S. Jack and M. Rose, op. cit.
16. Ibid., p. 213.
17. R. Putnam, 'Turning In, Turning Out: The Strange Disappearance of Social Capital in America', *Political Science and Politics*, Vol. 28, 1995, pp. 1–20.
18. World Bank, www://go.worldbank.org?C0QTRW4QF0, accessed on 22 May 2010.
19. OECD, *The Well-Being of Nations: The Role of Human and Social Capital* (Paris: OECD, 2001).

20. Based on Performance and Innovation Unit, *Social Capital: A Discussion Paper* (London, Cabinet Office, 2002), p. 10.
21. F. Fukuyama, 'Social Capital and Development: The Coming Agenda' in *SAIS Review* Vol. XXII No.1 (2002).
22. Performance and Innovation Unit, op. cit., p. 11.
23. E. Chell, *The Entrepreneurial Personality: A Social Construction* (London: Routledge, 2008), pp. 164–5.
24. Based on Performance and Innovation Unit, op. cit., pp. 11–12.
25. J. Pearce, *Social Enterprise in Anytown* (London: Calouste Gulbenkian Foundation, 2003), pp. 74–5.
26. See F. Fukuyama, *Trust: The Social Virtues and the Creation of Prosperity* (New York: Free Press, 1995).
27. D. Halpern, *Social Capital* (Cambridge: Polity Press, 2005), p. 35.
28. Ibid.
29. M. Gladwell, *Outliers* (London: Allen Lane, 2008), pp. 3–11.
30. From the *Psychology Encyclopaedia* entry on 'Peer Pressure' at http://psychology.jrank.org/pages/479/Peer-Pressure.html, accessed on 8 July 2009.
31. D. B. Audretsch, M. C. Keilbach, and E. E. Lehmann, *Entrepreneurship and Economic Growth* (Oxford: Oxford University Press, 2006), p. 60.
32. D. S. Audretsch and M. Keilbach, 'Does Entrepreneurship Capital Matter?', *Entrepreneurship Theory and Practice*, Vol. 28, Issue 5, (USA: Baylor University, 2004), p. 420.
33. Ibid., p. 424.

12
An Alternative Approach

> A long habit of not thinking something is WRONG, gives it a superficial appearance of being RIGHT, and raises at first a formidable outcry in defence of custom.
>
> Thomas Paine in *Common Sense*
>
> Doing the same thing over and over again and expecting different results is insanity.
>
> Attributed to Albert Einstein
>
> The only question is how much resources the US will commit to its 'war on drugs' before trying something that works.
>
> A newspaper comment on the US approach to its drug problem[1]
>
> The UK government is committed to evidence-based policy but ... often the available evidence base is only partial, and [it] can easily revert to 'opinion-based' policy.
>
> Senior Researcher in Enterprise and Small Business, UK Department of Business, Enterprise and Regulatory Reform[2]

The previous chapters in this book have looked at current assumptions about the factors which might influence enterprise and entrepreneurship and the apparent inability of current models, based on those assumptions, to explain the poor results of much entrepreneurship policy. This chapter presents an alternative model in the hope that it might provide a better understanding leading to better policy. It does not, however, present a definitive conclusion because, while the case for a lot of current strategy appears to have been disproved, the case for this suggested alternative has not been proved. Indeed scientific method suggests that such theories can never be proved: only accepted as apparently workable until such time as they may eventually be disproved. So there can never be a final conclusion to such arguments and this model, having only just been advanced, has not yet been tested.

The argument so far

Illustration 12.1 Enterprise and deprivation: The rationale for UK public policy

> Our reading of UK government literature suggests there are five logical steps implicitly linking the contribution of enterprise to the addressing of disadvantage in local areas, each of which is "evidence-based". This section ... *also points to other evidence which suggests the "evidence base" for the statements is more ambiguous than is implied in public documents.*
>
> 1. Enterprise Rates are low in Deprived Areas;
> 2. Low Enterprise Rates are one of the causes of poverty;
> 3. Promoting Enterprise is a key route out of disadvantage and deprivation;
> 4. The promotion of Enterprise requires a range of public funded programmes to support "conventional businesses, social enterprises and community businesses";
> 5. The effectiveness of policy is reflected in increased business formation and SE employment rates.

Source: J. Frankish, R. Roberts and D. Storey, 'Enterprise: A Route Out of Disadvantage and Deprivation?', paper presented at the 31st ISBE conference, Belfast, November 2008 (with emphasis added).

Measures designed to stimulate enterprise and entrepreneurship (usually E2 or E3) often form an important part of economic development policies. The first part of the book explores those policies and suggests that, while they are not all identical, they do often seem to be based on the same menu of options which, in turn, are based on a set of assumptions consistent with standard economic theory. What evidence there is suggests that those policies are not working. Governments and other agencies want more enterprise, but it seems that current policies are not delivering it. This is not therefore a question of whether more enterprise and entrepreneurship will help economic development but of how more enterprise and entrepreneurship might actually be achieved – because, until that is done, it will not be possible to assess how effective they would be in addressing economic problems. Thus this book is not concerned with the efficacy of the prescribed medicine but about how that medicine can actually be administered to the patient because, until it is, its efficacy cannot be assessed.

Governments generally feel a need to do something: 'there are strong pressures on politicians to show that they are actively and regularly introducing new policies that meet perceived problems in the economy'.[3] However, in reviewing entrepreneurship policies, Karlsson and Andersson quote a remark from Verheul et al.[4] that 'there is very little that generates consensus in the field of entrepreneurship' and then develop this into their own claim that 'there is very little that generates consensus in the field of entrepreneurship policies'.[5] They also state that

> an analysis of entrepreneurial decisions as pure economic decisions does not imply that economic factors are the only factors determining such decisions. On the contrary, there is a rich literature convincingly showing that other factors influence such decisions ... However, we claim that these other factors are either difficult or impossible to influence by economic policies alone and that entrepreneurship policies, to the extent they are needed, should focus on the involved economic factors.[6]

Current entrepreneurship policies do generally ignore those other possible factors and follow received economic wisdom. They largely follow, or are similar to, received 'best practice', often because copying best practice seems to be a cheaper and quicker option than engaging in the innovative exploration of potential new methods. As a result they follow, or are at least consistent with, the same, mainly economic, models. Therefore, if the policies do not work, it implies that those models also do not work and that they are based, in turn, on incorrect assumptions about what influences the level of entrepreneurship in a population. However, instead of accepting the failure of policy and the need to look for a new understanding and new models, it seems that often the models continue to be accepted and/or similar policies continue to be pursued, although possibly after some repackaging.

Indeed, if the indications are that much enterprise policy is not working, it would seem that, instead of evidence-based policy, what many people are following is assumption-, or opinion-, based policy. If the proof of the pudding is in the eating, it seems that many of those assumptions about what influences the level of entrepreneurship are wrong because applying policies based on them does not lead to the desired result. If that analysis of the situation is not accepted, then there is little that this book has to offer. On the assumption, though, that the analysis might be correct, this book has tried to examine some of the current theories about entrepreneurship to see if there are alternatives which are consistent with the evidence and which might lead therefore to more effective policy.

A scientific approach?

The basic process of scientific exploration might be summarised as:

- Observe a phenomenon.
- Develop a hypothesis for the phenomenon which is consistent with the observations of it.
- Test that hypothesis by using it to make new predictions about the phenomenon and then conducting experiments to check their accuracy.
- If the hypothesis appears to work, use it until it is shown to be wrong.
- If and when it is shown to be wrong, look for a different hypothesis which is consistent with the evidence, and then test that.

Assumption-based approaches are not necessarily a bad thing: what is not helpful is to continue to use them when the evidence indicates that the assumptions are wrong. Assumption-based approaches which are not properly tested and/or continue to be used after they have been shown to be wrong are a waste and a delusion. And it may only need one contrary observation to upset a long-standing theory: just one 'black swan'.

> Before the discovery of Australia, people in the Old World were convinced that all swans were white. ... The sighting of the first black swan ... illustrates a severe limitation to our learning from observation or experience and the fragility of our knowledge. One single

observation can invalidate a general statement based on millennia of confirmatory sightings of millions of white swans ... all you need is one single ... black bird.[7]

A significant difficulty in finding a new scientific hypothesis is that, by its nature, it will be contrary to received wisdom and so contrary to at least some of the assumptions behind that wisdom. But we tend to be both somewhat attached to received wisdom and cautious about questioning its foundations because we are unsure where to start and/or, if part of the foundation is suspect, because we do not want to bring down the whole edifice by removing the wrong part.

> We associate truth with convenience, with what most closely accords with self-interest and personal well-being or promises best to avoid awkward effort or unwelcome dislocation of life. We also find highly acceptable what contributes most to self esteem. ... Economics and social behaviour are complex, and to comprehend their character is mentally tiring. Therefore we adhere, as though to a raft, to those ideas which represent our understanding.
>
> John Kenneth Galbraith[8]

A hypothesis is easier to develop if some sort of model of the phenomenon is first constructed (like the natural-selection-by-survival-of-the-fittest model which Darwin developed to explain evolution). But that model by its nature will be new, and different from conventional views.

We use models all the time, sometimes more consciously or extensively than others. Aircraft designers make models of their designs and place them in wind tunnels to see how they will behave, and structural engineers make models of things like bridges to test them with various load combinations. In that way they use those models to predict how the real thing would behave in specific circumstances. If we throw a rubber ball at a wall in order to catch it when it bounces back, we have in our heads a model of how that ball will behave when thrown in that way because we would not expect to be able to catch a paper ball or a snowball when thrown in the same way. A snooker player expects that the snooker balls will respond in a particular way and adjusts his or her shots accordingly. Such a player does not have to test each stroke first on real balls to get the right amount of angle and spin: he or she has a mental model from which to assess how a shot should be played to get the desired result.

At their simplest form such models can be reduced to formulae. Newton's Law of Gravity provided a formula for gravitational attraction which explained how planets behave in a way which could be used to predict their future moves, and even to use minor differences between their predicted and actual moves to find previously unobserved planets, the existence of which explained those differences. The same formula could then be used successfully to predict how much thrust a space rocket would need to escape from the earth's gravity and take a spacecraft to the moon.

That is the essence of a scientific law or a model. It is a simplified, accessible and usable way of predicting how the real thing will behave. Scientific theories are tested by making predictions about new conditions and circumstances and then testing those predictions. For a given set of inputs they will predict an outcome and if experiments show that prediction to be wrong, then a new theory has to be sought. If, on the other hand, the predictions are found consistently to be correct, then the theory is assumed to be correct and can become a 'law'. If theories are shown in this way to be sound and become laws, engineers can then use them to indicate how the inputs should be adjusted to achieve a desired outcome. In that way they use scientific theory not just to predict the future, but also to guide changes to make future results more to our liking. In that way we use models, not only to tell us the destination to which our path is likely to lead, but also to suggest which path we should take in order to get to the destination we want.

However scientific theories can never be conclusively and permanently proved; they can only be disproved. A theory is tested by comparing its predictions with reality and once a difference is found between predictions and reality, the theory fails. So, until a difference is found, the theory remains on probation. Even the gravitational theories of Newton, which proved reliable enough to be referred to as a law, were eventually shown to be less accurate than the later theories of Einstein. That does not mean that they now have no use. Despite having been disproved in this way, they still remain accurate enough to guide trips to the moon. Nevertheless such developments do show that even scientific laws of the highest pedigree and with a long history of successful use can eventually succumb to new theories which prove to be more accurate. It also suggests that, unless established laws continue to be questioned and tested, further developments in knowledge will not be made.

Illustration 12.2 The bias of the 'classic' dissertation

Many of the dissertations in the business sciences follow an archetype. It assumes that "good" research follows a fixed sequence. First we select a theory; from that we deduce models from which testable hypotheses can be developed. Then we develop instruments to test those hypotheses on a data base with statistical tools – preferably regression analysis. The 'classic' dissertation is seldom the most suitable format for an emerging paradigm such as entrepreneurship because it is too rigid.

The history of science teaches us that in emerging paradigms, successful science rarely follows the sequence of the 'classic' dissertation. Darwin did not have a theory until he 'happened to read for amusement Malthus on *Population*' seven years after he embarked on his field work, and fifteen months after he began his systematic enquiry into the variations of animals and plants. ... Thus at the beginnings of a paradigm, inspired inductive logic (or more likely enlightened speculations) applied to exploratory, empirical research may be more useful than deductive reasoning from theory. Natural science has recognised this for three centuries.[9]

An alternative model of enterprise

> Explanations give you power. They give you power to change.
>
> Jared Diamond[10]

Scientific method highlights the need to question and test assumptions and to look for new approaches when evidence no longer supports the old ones. And it also suggests that it is not necessary to wait until that contrary evidence is totally overwhelming: even a few contrary examples can be enough. Science can also sometimes help in the development of new models by providing analogies from approaches in other fields and this book thus considers analogies from medical science and, in Chapter 10, it borrows the example of phase change from physics.

The argument in this book is that most of the policies in use throughout the world to stimulate more entrepreneurship appear not to work. They seem to have been derived largely from apparent best practice elsewhere, and so repeat earlier approaches instead finding new ideas, and those earlier approaches are consistent with the traditional economic

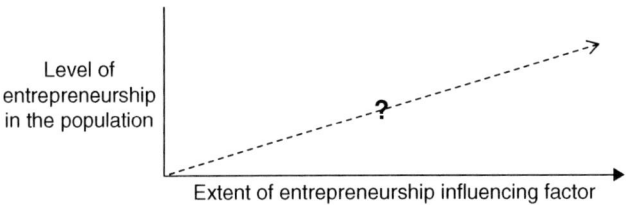

Figure 12.1 The 'default' assumption about influencing entrepreneurship?

belief that people take an individual rational approach to economic choice. It appears to have been assumed that people will engage in entrepreneurship after individually made, logical, risk–return assessments which indicate that, for them, entrepreneurship is likely to produce better returns than any alternative occupations. Therefore the policies have been based on doing things which will have the effect of reducing the risk and/or increasing the expected returns from entrepreneurship, in the expectation that this will lead to more people making positive assessments of entrepreneurship and then engaging in it.

Such a view of the entrepreneurship decision is consistent with the questions posed in GEM's attitude survey such as: 'Will there be good opportunities for starting a business?', 'Do you have the knowledge, skills and experience required to start a new business?' and 'Would fear of failure prevent you from starting a business?'.[11] The models also seem to imply, or at least be consistent with, the sort of default model of the impact of influences on entrepreneurship, illustrated in Figure 12.1 (which is also the basis of Figure 10.1), which is probably the default assumption about the impact of a supposed influence on entrepreneurship.

However this book suggests that the assumption of individually made, logical, risk–return assessments is wrong and that, instead of following logic, people often follow social example. Therefore it is likely that in many cases, the key factor determining whether or not people engage in entrepreneurship will be social influence. Chapter 10 highlights the importance of social influence in activities such as clothes shopping, smoking and crime. If they are socially influenced, why not also a person's choice of occupation?

Among others, Drakopoulou Dodd and Anderson argue that although 'much of the debate concerning the essence of entrepreneurship has placed the individual at the centre, depicting entrepreneurship as the individual adventurously projecting',[12] the entrepreneur is a social animal. If, they suggest, 'one ignores the milieu that supports, drives, produces and receives the entrepreneurial process, how is it possible

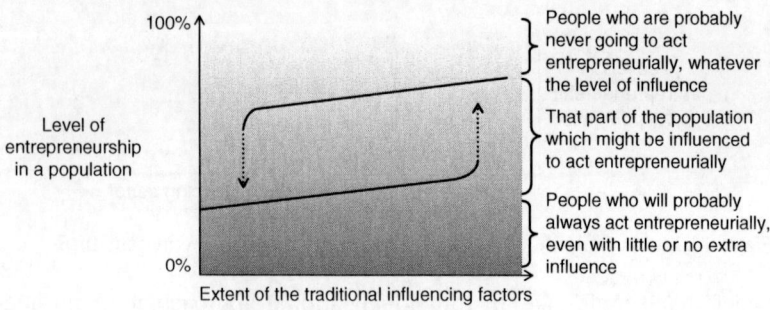

Figure 12.2 A possible model of the level of entrepreneurship

for effective policies and educational programmes to be developed?'.[13] This book adds the suggestion that, if there is a social dimension to entrepreneurship, then a similar analysis to the study of crime reported in Chapter 10 might also apply.

Entrepreneurship is not the same thing as crime (although some criminals may be entrepreneurs). It seems reasonable, though, to assume that, as in the analysis of levels of criminality, in entrepreneurship terms a population could also be divided into three groups: a group that is immune to the temptations of entrepreneurship, a group of active entrepreneurs and a third group who are 'floating voters' and are susceptible to becoming entrepreneurs under the right circumstances but who might instead decide not to act entrepreneurially (E0). Then, if social influence is added to the model as the factor which most influences the 'floating voters', a two-state picture of the extent of entrepreneurship in a population could be projected. This is the picture shown in Figure 12.2 which projects the impacts of the factors traditionally supposed to influence levels of entrepreneurship, such as individual necessity and/or the availability of finance.

The assumptions

The model suggested in Figure 12.2 is based on just two assumptions:

1. First it is assumed that, in entrepreneurship terms, a population can be divided into three groups: a group of people who are in practice immune to the temptations of entrepreneurship, a group of people who are active entrepreneurs and a third group of people who are 'floating voters' and are susceptible to becoming entrepreneurs under the right circumstances but who might instead decide not

to act entrepreneurially. In other words, instead of assuming that people are either entrepreneurs or not entrepreneurs (a sort of black or white approach consistent with the 'entrepreneurs are born that way' viewpoint) or assuming that everyone has an equal potential to be an entrepreneur (everything is a uniform 'colour'), it is assumed that there is a gradation: a sort of spectrum. At one end of the spectrum there are those who will almost always act entrepreneurially and at the other those who will almost never act entrepreneurially, with those who might sometimes act entrepreneurially in the middle.

2. Second, consistent with the social influence idea introduced in Chapter 10 and then explored further in Chapter 11, it is assumed that the major factor that determines whether those in the middle group will act entrepreneurially is not logical, individually made, risk–return assessments but the example of whether or not their peers and other influential people are acting entrepreneurially. Thus if, because they see their peers acting entrepreneurially, people in the middle group act entrepreneurially, they will themselves become part of that influence and a high level of entrepreneurship will thus be self-reinforcing. Alternatively, if those in the middle do not act entrepreneurially, there will not be enough examples of people acting entrepreneurially to persuade others, and the level of entrepreneurship will remain low. Entrepreneurship then will be pursued only by that section of the community who were going to do it anyway.

(NB: This model takes a wide view of entrepreneurship and assumes that all forms of entrepreneurship have the same roots and therefore that low E-number entrepreneurship is a foundation for all the other narrower forms of entrepreneurship at higher E-numbers. These who have tried to limit the application of the label entrepreneurship only to the higher E-numbers, thereby implying that other forms of activity covered by the lower E-numbers are not entrepreneurship, may feel that their entrepreneurship has different roots. But they have yet to prove their case.)

These two assumptions lead to a model in which the key influence is social, not individualistic or based on logic. In it the key influence comes from people's social circles comprising, it might be said, the four Ps of their pals, peers, parents and other persuasive people. In any particular social circle those in the 'middle' group will tend to follow the majority, or a rapidly growing minority, and, in doing so, become part of the majority, thus reinforcing its influence. Switching the position of the majority will thus require a sufficient cumulative pressure for change to persuade people more or less simultaneously to switch: a sort of critical mass' leading to a 'tipping point'. That might be rare, but it is not without precedent.

The old 'traditional' models assume that factors such as an agency support structure, training, the availability of finance and a reduction in red tape should all have an effect on levels of entrepreneurship, because they will make it easier to engage in entrepreneurship and thus reduce the risk element of the individual risk–return assessments that people are supposed to make. This alternative model does not suggest that these factors have no connection with entrepreneurship, just that, if they do have an effect, it is marginal. They might help people once they are persuaded to look seriously at entrepreneurship but the influence of these factors on the entrepreneurship decisions that people make is much less than the influence of those people's peers.

This assumption of peer influence does not presume that this influence is applied just on the occasion when a decision is made. Peer influence may also encompass aspects of encouragement and preparation. It might predispose people to look for an enterprise opportunity, to prepare for such an eventuality, and give more attention to the enterprise option when it does occur or when the possibility for it is triggered. It might not only encourage people therefore to look for enterprise opportunities, but it might also predispose them to consider such opportunities more positively when they do occur, not least because they may also have been encouraged, and given the opportunity, to prepare for them.

Examples and implications

> More entrepreneurship begets more entrepreneurship.
>
> Lois Stevenson[14]
>
> Encouragement for enterprise is generally lacking and young entrepreneurs have to contend with cynicism, a dearth of useful advice and the burden of complex legislation. The main source of encouragement for an entrepreneur comes from other entrepreneurs. Perhaps, unsurprisingly, young people who come from families in which a parent runs their own business are much more likely to set up in business.
>
> RSA report on young entrepreneurs[15]

This model does seem to explain a number of observations about entrepreneurship. Because it assumes that there are some people who are almost always going to act entrepreneurially, whatever the apparent logical risk–return assessment, it explains why the so-called 'myth' of the heroic entrepreneur still persists. Because it is a two-state model in which either a relatively high level of entrepreneurship could be stable, or a relatively low level, but not an intermediate level, it explains why increases in the factors which are supposed to influence entrepreneurship, such as official encouragement, the availability of finance and the provision of agency support, seem to have little or no effect on levels of entrepreneurship. It explains why some areas can appear to have high levels of entrepreneurship without any official encouragement of it, whereas it is actively encouraged in other areas which nevertheless have persistently low levels. It also explains why levels of entrepreneurship can be high in immigrant communities, even though their access to official support, finance and training is no higher than for other people in the same geographic area, because the immigrants and the others are influenced by different social circles.

Bolton and Thompson, in their book on entrepreneurship, take as one of their case studies Silicon Valley which, they suggest, is 'an example of what happens when a community taps into its well of entrepreneurial talent – it simply takes off!'.[16] The concept of entrepreneurship taking off because it feeds on itself, without the need for additional support or encouragement, is consistent with this model.

In Chapter 4 this book reported a number of observations on entrepreneurship which, it suggested, were incompatible with traditional models. It reported, for instance, Storey's comment that 'despite (the Tees Valley) being an enterprise laboratory with pretty much every imaginable potion being administered to promote enterprise, the new businesses and their performance looks remarkably similar over three decades'.[17] It also reported a study by Audretsch and Keilbach of entrepreneurship capital in Germany in which they found that 'entrepreneurship capital shows significant spatial autocorrelation and does not spill over into neighbouring regions' from which they concluded that 'the capacity to generate entrepreneurship is in fact a local phenomenon'.[18] Both these observations could be consistent with the new model which suggests that levels of entrepreneurship are likely to remain low in areas where they start low, as in the Tees Valley, but where they are high in people's social circles, they will remain high in those circles. It could be relevant that the German study was based on units of area which might be small enough to reflect the effects of the social circles within them.

This points, however, to one implication of the new model. The model suggests that people's social circles are the key factor influencing levels of entrepreneurship and most people's social circles are not spread out over a whole country. The level of entrepreneurship could vary therefore across a country because different social circles will predominate in different areas. Yet many strands of research into different levels of entrepreneurship, such as GEM, only consider levels of entrepreneurship at country, or sometimes regional, level. This is too high a level to reflect any heterogeneity in a population or to highlight any differences in levels that there might be among different social circles in a country. So, if the new model is correct, GEM may not have observed a key factor in entrepreneurship. Because the model is based on people's social circles, it also means that any changes to a particular circle may not go beyond that circle. Thus policies targeted at particular circles may only address the circles targeted and not have a more general effect.

In addition to examples in which the model seems to explain the maintenance of the *status quo* despite efforts to change it, are there any clear examples of a situation where the opposite seems to have happened: where there does seem to have been a step-change, a phase-shift, in the level of entrepreneurship? That is harder to find both because such shifts seem to be rare (as the model would suggest) and where present levels suggest there might have been a change, clear evidence of a different earlier level is lacking. However the example of Silicon Valley is suggested above – but was that due to a relatively sudden rise in entrepreneurship in people living in Silicon Valley or a move to Silicon Valley by people who were already entrepreneurially inclined? Another example might be found in areas of China. It does seem that, recently, there has been a significant rise in the levels of entrepreneurship in China, shown, for instance, in the number of businesses being founded. Yet this has happened at a time when China seemed to have few if any of the conditions which were thought to support or encourage entrepreneurship. Thus Allan Gibb and Jun Li have argued both that there was very significant growth in the GDP of China between 1980 and 1995 and that, 'in an economy known for state ownership, remarkably this growth has been led by the non-state sector composed of community/collective enterprises, co-operatives, individually owned businesses, private corporations, and foreign joint ventures'.[19] However, they suggest, this was despite the absence of factors which were thought to underpin Western economic development such as private property rights, clear forms of ownership and a clear regulative environment, an adequate banking system and the support of a government small business support agency.[20] Thus China might be an example of a phase change in entrepreneurship, and could the same also be said of regions of India?[21]

Illustration 12.3 Entrepreneurship and the Theory of Planned Behaviour

It is acknowledged in Chapter 11 that Krueger's Model (see Figure 3.5) is one of the few models considered in Chapter 3 which might suggest that social acceptability could be an influencing factor in entrepreneurship. That is because Krueger specifically includes the perception of social norms as one of the antecedents of intention, even though it does not suggest that it is the prime factor.

Krueger's model was derived from the 'planned behaviour' approach. Considerations of planned behaviour followed from the failure of trait theory to provide reliable predictors of behaviour. In theory personality traits, which might be defined as relatively enduring behavioural dispositions, should help to predict behaviour in a variety of different situations. Thus, for instance, it was suggested that individuals who cheat on their income tax are dishonest and might therefore be supposed to have a dishonesty trait which would lead them to be dishonest in other situations. Research, however, has not found this to be the case and people who do cheat on their taxes do not appear also to be more likely than non tax-cheats to shoplift or to lie to their friends. Also personality traits might be supposed to be related to attitudes, but when attitudes are assessed through questionnaires, they do not seem to correlate closely with observed behaviour.

A development of the trait approach had considered whether traits, if they do not predict single actions very well, could nevertheless predict actions in aggregate, or whether other factors could be identified which moderated the consistency between dispositions and actions. However neither aggregating behaviour nor a search for moderating variables seem to help link dispositions to actions and, in any case, personality traits are inferred from behaviour and so do not help explain that behaviour. Suggesting that someone has a trait, or traits, for entrepreneurship because they behave entrepreneurially, does not help to predict entrepreneurial behaviour before it occurs.

The thinking behind the planned behaviour approach was not that traits are irrelevant, but that there are other factors which influence behaviour. Ajzen, in developing his Theory of Planned Behaviour[22] (the Theory), suggested that of all the behavioural dispositions, it is intentions which are most closely linked to the corresponding actions. According to his theory a person's intentions are assumed to capture the motivational factors that have an influence on that person's

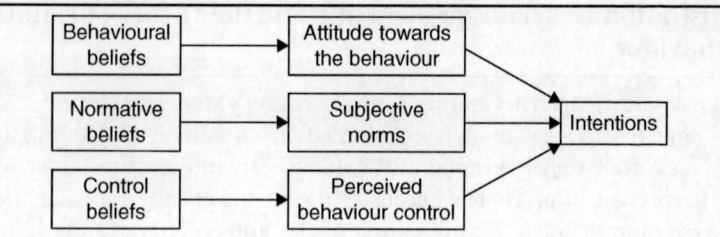

Figure 12.3 Diagrammatic presentation of Ajzen's Theory of Planned Behaviour
Source: Reprinted from N. Krueger, M. Reilly and A. Carsrud, 'Competing Models of Entrepreneurial Intentions', *Journal of Business Venturing*, Vol. 15, Issue. 2, p. 416. Copyright 2000, with permission from Elsevier.

behaviour. Those factors act directly to determine intentions which in turn affect actions and thus, although there is a connection between the factors and the actions, it is indirect. Further intentions do not necessarily lead to immediate action and, once they are formed, intentions initially remain as behavioural dispositions until, given an appropriate time and opportunity, they translate into actions.

The Theory also suggests that there are three independent determinants of intentions: attitudes towards the behaviour in question, subjective norms and perceived behavioural control. Behaviour, according to the Theory, is thus the result of salient information or beliefs: behavioural beliefs which are assumed to influence attitudes towards behaviour, normative beliefs which are the underlying determinants of subjective norms and control beliefs which are the basis for perceived behavioural control (see Figure 12.3). Global attitudes and personality traits thus play no direct role in the Theory. They may influence some of the beliefs but are too general to have significant predictive validity.

Krueger, in developing his model, started with the assumption that much of what is considered to be entrepreneurial activity is planned behaviour and that 'planned behaviours such as starting a business are intentional and thus are best predicted by intentions towards the behaviour, *not* by attitudes, beliefs, personality or demographics'.[23] 'Empirically', he and his colleagues state, 'we have learned that situational (for example employment status or informational cues) or individual (for example demographic characteristics or personality traits) variables are poor predictors'.[24] Krueger, together with Reilly and Carsrud,[25] compared the predictive ability of two intentions models, that of Ajzen from social psychology and the Entrepreneurial Event model of Shapero from entrepreneurship research, and concluded that their 'results offered strong statistical support for both models',[26] with the Shapero model being slightly superior for assessing entrepreneurial intentions.

The implications

What implications does the Theory of Planned Behaviour therefore have for the theme of this book and, in particular, does it contradict the suggestion that, for a part of the population, social influence might be the prime factor in influencing a tendency towards entrepreneurship?

The focus of this book is on efforts to encourage the development of more entrepreneurship, which means encouraging more people to take up the entrepreneurship option. In the terms of the intentions approach does that mean helping more people to realise an entrepreneurial intention or helping more people to have that intention in the first place? If, as the Theory suggests, intentions are the best indicator of eventual action, then many of the people who already have the intention will carry that through into action and there may not be much scope to increase that conversion rate. Therefore, the Theory suggests, instead of trying to encourage more people with an entrepreneurial intention to carry it through into action, it might be more productive to encourage other people, who do not yet have an entrepreneurial intention, to acquire one.

However, knowing that the best indicator that someone will follow the entrepreneurship route is his or her intention so to do, is only helpful if it is possible to stimulate more people to have that intention. Both the Theory of Planned Behaviour and Krueger's model indicate that what influences intentions are:

- Behavioural beliefs, which are assumed to influence attitudes towards behaviour (personal desirability);
- Normative beliefs, which are the underlying determinants of subjective norms (perceived social norms); and

  } and which together then determine perceived desirability

- Control beliefs, which are the basis for perceived behavioural control (perceived self-efficacy leading to perceived feasibility).

Therefore both the theory and the model include not only social influence but also perceptions of efficacy, and the latter might be assumed to come from some form of risk-benefit analysis. Kruger's testing of the Ajzen and Shapero intention models[27] appeared to support the inclusion of such efficacy considerations. That testing was however done with a sample of business students who might therefore already have been relatively well disposed towards entrepreneurship and possibly were relatively less likely to admit to having it as an intention without some form of logical analysis. It could therefore be argued that, in that respect, their responses might not have been typical of the wider population.

However the model advanced by this book assumes that the population can be divided into three groups. One group consists of those people who need no external encouragement to be actively inclined towards entrepreneurship and who, if they are not already practicing it, clearly have the intention so to do. Another group consists of those people who are in practice immune to the temptations of entrepreneurship, and who therefore are not going to have the intention to do it. The third group then is those people who are potentially open to becoming entrepreneurs given the right social pressure but who, if they do have the intention to try entrepreneurship, will do so primarily because of that social influence rather than because they have independently carried out a risk-benefit assessment of all the options.

This therefore raises the question of what 'planned' means in the context of 'planned behaviour'. Planning to do something can just mean having the intention to do it, as when someone says 'I plan to go shopping tomorrow'. Planning to do something can also mean working out how to do it, as in 'I am making a plan for a shopping trip tomorrow'. In a business context, however, planning might be taken to mean producing a business plan, and that would usually be expected to include an assessment of the feasibility of the proposed venture, or at least provide the information needed for such an assessment. In a business context therefore planning might suggest an element of risk-benefit (efficacy) analysis.

This book assumes that the part of the population which might be socially influenced to try entrepreneurship will, given the right influence, 'plan' to do it in the sense that they will intend to do it. It assumes that, for them, it will then be the preferred option

> because it is the socially acceptable thing to do and not necessarily because they have made a careful assessment of the different options that might be open to them. It would support a suggestion that, instead, for many of these people business planning would be a chore to be done once the intention has been formed and not an antecedent to the formation of that intention.
>
> Therefore, for the arguments advanced in this book, the Theory of Planned Behaviour is helpful in that it suggests that intentions are much better predictors of behaviour than situational factors and it highlights the importance of social norms in forming intentions. However this book does not assume that entrepreneurship is a 'planned' behaviour in the sense that it is always influenced by considerations of efficacy. Krueger seems to have assumed that entrepreneurship is such a planned behaviour but the arguments advanced here suggest instead that sometimes it might be better described as a 'semi-planned' behaviour which is still predicted by intentions, but that those intentions are often formed less as a consequence of any formal feasibility and/or cost-benefit analysis and more as the result of social push.

Summary

Following the analysis and reflections in earlier chapters of the book, this chapter has attempted to present a model of the influences on entrepreneurship which:

- does not repeat the mistakes of the earlier models, and
- is nevertheless consistent with the various findings about the prevalence of entrepreneurship.

This model also seeks to acknowledge, not the classical economic assumption that people generally make rational responses, but the reality of human nature which means that people's actions are often much more likely to be influenced by social example than by the strict application of individual logic. This model does not say that levels of entrepreneurship cannot be changed, but that they are unlikely to be changed by many of the present policies which appear to be consistent with current models, and which, according to the available evidence, do not appear to be working. The new suggestion could therefore provide a basis for the development of new, and more effective, approaches, although it is only a model and an untested one at that.

References

1. E. Howker, writing in the *Independent*, 9 March 2009.
2. Forum Report prepared by L. Stevenson, Pre-conference Policy Forum, 53rd Annual ICSB World Conference, Nova Scotia, Halifax, 2008.
3. C. Karlsson and M. Andersson, *Entrepreneurship Policies: Principles, Problems and Opportunities*, CISEG Working Paper No. 7 (Sweden: Jönköping International Business School, 2009).
4. I. Verheul, R. Thurik, S. Wennekers and A. Audretsch, 'An Eclectic Theory of Entrepreneurship', *Timbergen Institute Discussion Paper* TI 2001-03013, 2001.
5. C. Karlsson and M. Andersson, *Entrepreneurship Policies: Principles, Problems and Opportunities*, CISEG Working Paper No. 7 (Sweden: Jönköping International Business School, 2009).
6. Ibid.
7. N. N. Taleb, *The Black Swan: The Impact of the Highly Improbable* (London: Allen Lane, 2007), p. vxii.
8. J. K. Galbraith in 'The Concept of Conventional Wisdom', the second chapter of *The Affluent Society* (Boston: Houghtom Mifflin, 1958), as quoted in S. Levitt and S. Dubner, *Freakonomics* (London: Penguin, 2006), pp. 89–90.
9. W. Bygrave, 'The Entrepreneurial Paradigm (I): A Philosophical Look at Its Research Methodologies', in *Entrepreneurship Theory & Practice*, Vol. 14, No. 1, 1989.
10. Quoted in a television programme about Jared Diamond's book, *Guns, Germs and Steel* (London: Jonathan Cape, 1997). The programme was broadcast on More 4 on 21 February 2009.
11. M. Minniti, W. Bygrave and E. Autio, *Global Entrepreneurship Monitor: 2005 Executive Report*, Babson College and London Business School.
12. S. Drakopoulou Dodd and A. Anderson, 'Mumpsimus and the Mything of the Individualistic Entrepreneur', *International Small Business Journal*, Vol. 25, No. 4, August 2007, p. 344.
13. Ibid., p. 352.
14. Said during her presentation in a seminar on 'Fostering Enterprise', organised by Invest Northern Ireland and held on 14 March 2007 at Narrow Water Castle, Warrenpoint.
15. From an article titled 'Encouraging Youthful Enterprise', in *RSA Journal* 1/6, 2002, p. 28.
16. W. Bolton and J. Thompson, *Entrepreneurs: Talent, Temperament, Technique* (Oxford: Butterworth Heinemann, 2000), p. 198.
17. D. Storey, in an e-mail communication about Greene et al., 21 January 2008.
18. D. Audretsch and M. Keilbach, 'The Localization of Entrepreneurial Capital – Evidence from Germany', Jena Economic Research Papers, at www.jenecom.de, 22 May 2010.
19. A. Gibb and J. Li, 'Organising for Enterprise in China: What can We Learn from the Chinese Micro, Small, and Medium Enterprise Development Experience', *Futures 35*, 2003, p. 403.

20. Based on comments made by Allan Gibb when making a presentation on his work in China on 20 April 2004.
21. See also A. Wooldridge, in an article titled 'The More the Merrier' in a special report on entrepreneurship in *The Economist*, 14 March 2009.
22. See, for instance, I. Ajzen, 'Attitudes, Traits, and Actions: Dispositional Prediction of Behaviour in Personality and Social Psychology', *Advances in Experimental Social Psychology*, Vol. 20, 1987, pp. 1–63.
23. N. Krueger and A. Carsrud, 'Entrepreneurial Intentions: Applying the Theory of Planned Behaviour, *Entrepreneurship and Regional Development*, Vol. 5, No. 4, 1993, p. 315.
24. N. Krueger, M. Reilly and A. Carsrud, 'Competing Models of Entrepreneurial Intentions', *Journal of Business Venturing*, Vol. 15, No. 2, 2000, p. 411.
25. Ibid., pp. 411–32.
26. Ibid., p. 412.
27. Ibid.

13
A View Forward

The earlier parts of this book have suggested that much current enterprise and entrepreneurship policy is not working and that the models of entrepreneurship which are consistent with, and thus explain, that policy are, at least to some extent, based on myth. After looking at entrepreneurship from a number of different perspectives, it is suggested that enterprise is essentially a goal realisation device and so entrepreneurship is, and should be seen as, one of a number of possible options available to people that help them to realise their life goals. This book also suggests that many people, in choosing between the options they perceive, will be influenced much more by social pressures that by any individual, logical, risk–benefit analysis.

Chapter 12 then attempted to present a model of the influences on entrepreneurship which, instead of following received economic theory, acknowledges the reality of human nature and is consistent with the various findings about the prevalence of entrepreneurship. It is however only a model, not reality itself, and it is still untested. Can it, nevertheless, help to improve our understanding of entrepreneurship and thus guide entrepreneurship policy to be more effective? Chapter 13 looks at some of the possible implications of this model for enterprise policy and other applications and at what might be the next steps for those who want to build a greater understanding of this subject.

Drawing lessons from the medical analogy

Chapter 1 introduced, and Chapter 8 further developed, an analogy between medicine and entrepreneurship. Medicine, for instance, provides an example of a situation in which an apparently evidence-based policy can be followed for some time, can appear to work, can

> (Science) is a creative process. You are trying to identify ways of thinking about a problem slightly differently. ... Mental illness is not something that can be understood by observing its symptoms, although this is still how it is diagnosed. ... You'd never diagnose something like cancer by looking at the symptoms.
>
> Dr Sabine Bahn[1]

be accepted and believed in by lots of people and can be welcomed by patients. Yet later it was shown by new discoveries to have been based on false assumptions, to have been inappropriate, and indeed to have been harmful to many of those to whom it was administered. The lessons to be drawn from this and other aspects of medicine include:

- Practice can be based on myth and yet still appear to work. For a long time the practice of medicine included bleeding people to cure them. Not only was this practice based on classical observation-based medical theory but there was probably an apparent correlation between bleeding patients and their subsequent recovery. Nevertheless it was a myth.
- Myths can prevail/persist for a long time. In medicine, apart from the myth that bleeding could cure fevers, there were other myths, such as the myth that bad air caused malaria and cholera. Still today there is a tendency for doctors in different countries to diagnose seemingly different conditions and to suggest different cures. And there are alternative medicines and fashions in medicine which are followed by many although they do not (yet) appear to have a scientific basis.
- The development of knowledge in a subject such as medicine has not come from the development of major overall general theories, as it has in physics, but through an accumulation of many smaller incremental developments.
- Despite the development of our knowledge of medical science, there are still different approaches to its application and there are different specialities with different practices within it.
- Much of our medical knowledge has come from treating illness and has led to the establishment of hospitals as places in which to practice such treatment. However governments do not just want to treat people who are ill, they want healthier populations. If, therefore, the aim is to raise the average level of health in a population, treating those who

are ill in hospitals will often be a very expensive way in which to do it. For improving health, rather than just curing those who are ill, public health measures such as health education, dietary advice, improved sewerage systems, cleaner air and water, and exercise regimes could often be far more cost-effective than building more hospitals.

So what?

In a further application of the medical analogy used in this book, the economy is seen as the patient, and enterprise and entrepreneurship are the medicine which has been prescribed to improve the health of the patient. However, it is suggested, the dispensing system has failed because the prescribed medicine has not been getting to the patient as levels of enterprise and entrepreneurship have not risen. Whether they would in practice help to improve the economic health of the patient if they did rise is not clear because, until the medicine is actually administered to the patient, it will not be possible in practice to assess its effectiveness. Attempts to deliver the prescribed medicine seem to have failed because they have followed prevalent myths about how people react economically. This reliance on myth is, in some ways, similar to the way that medical practice also has been shown to have suffered from myths about how people react medically.

This book has been written to try to identify a new model of entrepreneurship because the old models do not seem to be consistent with the evidence, and policies consistent with them do not seem to work. It has tried to look at entrepreneurship from several different perspectives and, as a result, has identified a new model which does appear to be compatible with those observations about the reality of entrepreneurship which did not support the old models.

This model looks at enterprise and entrepreneurship in the context of the choice of routes which people follow to try to get what they want out of life. It is based on two assumptions. The first is that it is possible to influence some people to choose an enterprising route amounting, in some cases, to business entrepreneurship. It is not possible to influence everyone, as many traditional models seem to assume, because the new model assumes that some people are never going to choose entrepreneurship and that others will almost always choose it without any additional encouragement. The model assumes, though, that there are other people in neither of those categories, who can be influenced. The second assumption is that what will influence these people is social example and/or pressure, which is mainly local in nature. One of the models described in Chapter 3 is that proposed by Krueger and it includes as one of its influencing factors 'perceived social norms' (see Figure 3.5). This assumption is therefore like a variance of Krueger's model in which 'perceived social norms' is the predominant influence with the other influences having only secondary effects.

The new model does not suggest that peer influence should be seen as an additional factor alongside the assumption of individual, logical analysis and decision making. Instead it suggests that peer influence is, for many people, the main factor and that the predominance of individual, logical, risk–return analysis is largely a myth. There may still be a role for some individual logical analysis, but it is only a minor one.

In medicine the four humours model was not added to by new thinking – it was replaced – albeit slowly. It is now seen to have been a myth, despite its apparent 'evidence base'. And there have been, and still are, many myths in economic development.

Implications of the model

Does the new model work? We do not know, but it does at least appear to be consistent with some observations about the prevalence of entrepreneurship. It does, for instance, explain why current enterprise promotion policies may be misguided because they seem to assume individual, logical decision making instead of allowing for the strong social influence which is characteristic of much of human activity. The model thus provides a diagnosis for the failure of current policies and suggests that they are the wrong policies rather than that they are correct but need more time in which to work. Continuing them, therefore, is not going to lead eventually to a different outcome.

However, just as in medicine, diagnosing why a supposed cure does not, and will not, work does not itself mean that an alternative prescription is already developed and available for immediate use. It does nevertheless present a number of implications such as the suggestion that continuing with the old cure is likely to waste resources and an indication of new avenues to explore in a search for working solutions.

Do not persevere with failed models

The new model suggests that the main influence on entrepreneurial intentions is peer influence, not perceptions of how rewarding or easy it is. An implication from that is that traditional approaches to encouraging more entrepreneurship, such as reducing red tape, making finance available, supplying training and mentoring and providing help with marketing will have only a marginal effect. They might encourage a few waverers, and they might help those who have decided to try entrepreneurship to do it better, but they will not have the significant effect they are supposed to have. Thus it is suggested that if the assumptions on which the new model is based are correct, and if the model does have some validity in explaining what influences levels of entrepreneurship, then continuing with policies consistent with the old models will not work, for however long they are tried. So, if budgets are not to continue to be wasted pursuing fruitless approaches, policymakers and implementers should not persevere with the old models.

Do not expect other immediate policy recommendations

Although, as suggested above, old policy should not be continued, it is not easy immediately to suggest what should be done in its place. Just because the route originally being followed has been shown to be the wrong one, it does not mean that simultaneously it is clear which is the right one: that often requires some reflection and a search for indications which had been ignored in the belief that the route followed earlier was correct. Such a lack of immediate policy recommendations from the new model should not, however, be seen as a sign of weakness in the model. That is the nature of new perspectives: they need to be used to find new ways forward, and while a new perspective may not give an immediate indication of a new way, it is indispensable to the process of finding them.

Do explore some avenues

Nevertheless there are avenues to explore. One problem for policymakers with the new model is that if the aim is still to encourage more entrepreneurship and the key influencing factor is social desirability, that cannot be manipulated by the old methods, such as the government-funded or encouraged supply of things such as finance and training. This is not to say that such forms of support will be wasted: as suggested above they might be helpful after the decision is made – but the implication is that they will not encourage more people to make the decision. Instead it may be necessary to find and/or develop possible new methods by exploring avenues such as:

- Who are the others, the 'peers' who might have the influence indicated?
- How many of them are needed to have a 'critical mass' of influence?

- When could those people be persuaded to exert an appropriate influence?
- How would their influence be felt?
- And, if market failure is a condition of government intervention[2], does a lack of appropriate social influence constitute 'market failure', or is the concept of market failure less appropriate for behavioural economics? (Market failure does not seem, for instance, to be a condition for measures to reduce crime.)

It is interesting that Krueger, in his model (see Chapter 3), talks about 'perceived social norms' because that indicates one possible policy approach. Krueger's observation suggests that it is the perception of the norm that matters, not necessarily the reality. If a perception of majority influence can be engineered, that might be sufficient to tip enough people into following it to make the perception a reality. That is what some of the people marketing fashion goods try to do: they try to persuade enough people to start to use the items in question so that it appears to others that these are now the items that everyone who matters should be seen to have. So engineering a perception of popularity might be one avenue to explore.

> If we think of culture as a network, we can begin to see how it works and what kinds of strategies can be used to help change it. Relevant policies are critical but so are the channels through which we conduct our daily affairs. These have to carry the message of enterprise. Ultimately, young people themselves have to become the messengers of the enterprise message.[3]

It is not a cure-all

This new model does not provide some sort of cure-all. It does not suggest that the addition of the right sort of social capital will encourage everyone to follow the entrepreneurship route. Greene et al. commented on the high proportion of businesses started in Teesside by individuals seeking to repair cars or service the hair and beauty needs of individuals,[4] and this model does not suggest that social influence might persuade those individuals to start high-tech high-growth E4 businesses instead. E4 businesses will still require people with the relevant human capital and access to the necessary financial capital, but the model suggests that without the appropriate social capital 'vitamin', even when sufficient human and financial capital are available, people will not put them together to form businesses. Also, while the model suggests that social encouragement might persuade more people to start businesses because that is the socially acceptable thing to do, it does not necessarily mean that all those businesses will be successful because success in business is also dependent on having appropriate business skills. However, if more people see businesses as something they might aspire to try, they might also, given suitable opportunity, decide to try to prepare for it.

Do consider the moral issues

Suggestions that it might be possible to engineer a perception of social desirability raises the question of the extent to which it is morally right to do so. Many would find it acceptable to use advertising to try to persuade people of the disadvantages, including the possible social undesirability, of smoking, which is clearly a habit which is initially taken up because of social influence. Would the same however apply to trying to engineer a perception of the social desirability of something a government wishes to encourage, such as entrepreneurship? Governments may want to promote entrepreneurship because more entrepreneurship will lead to a stronger economy which should in turn make people happier. But, if so, will encouraging people to do something which might not suit all of them be conducive to more happiness? Entrepreneurship is not always good or suitable for everyone. Then, if the tendency to enterprise and entrepreneurship depends on a perception that lots of key people are doing it, is engineering such a perception morally justified?

Do not limit entrepreneurship by the wrong associations

One aspect of entrepreneurship leads to business formation, and that is the part which had received most attention recently. Therefore entrepreneurship has been aligned academically with business, and its study and teaching has often been assigned to business faculties. But is it actually much closer to social science, and therefore subject to limiting associations and constraints when presented only in a business context?

It does not suit business plans

A business plan is supposed to provide a logical presentation and analysis of a business proposal. If people did indeed engage in entrepreneurship following logical risk–return assessments of their options, then business plans should fit in well with their approach. However the reality seems to be that the business plan approach is foreign to the attitudes of many starting-up entrepreneurs (although not all) which might be held to support the view that they are not engaging in logical analysis. Maybe they should, but the model advanced in this book suggests that they are not, and that seems to accord better with reality. The new model therefore supports the view that many entrepreneurs find it very hard to make business plans and that they think of them, not as a help, but as an awkward and unnatural obstacle to be overcome. They think that they cannot credibly produce a business plan at start-up because they will not have the information needed to complete what they are told should be in a plan until after two or three years of trading. An implication of the new model is that for many new entrepreneurs that way of thinking is the reality, not the exception. Forcing them to produce business plans at a very early stage without addressing their reservations is thus likely to be counterproductive. Instead, if business plans are really necessary, for instance to support funding propositions, then an awareness that business plans do not come naturally and that the entrepreneurs concerned probably have not engaged in any logical analysis of their initial options might help to prevent tensions and misunderstandings.

What next?

So, what are the next steps? The model has not been proved, and it never will be completely proved, and much remains to be done to explore it, to map it, to test it, to refine it and to build on it. New ways of thinking need time to sink in and replace old ones and until that happens, their full potential will not be discovered, if indeed they have potential. But, as it does appear that the current approach is wrong, we should look for a better approach and this does appear to have that potential.

Therefore we should:

- Test and explore the new model.
- Think and reflect on it and its implications.
- Re-examine our understanding and re-test our assumptions.

This is not therefore the end. Obviously there is more to come in pursuing the ideas in this book, and some suggestions for that are made above. But it is the end of this stage in putting forward a new suggestion, and therefore of this book. The next steps are another stage and, if they are taken, are appropriate therefore for another book.

References

1. Quoted in *CAM: Cambridge Alumni Magazine*, Issue 57, Easter 2009, p. 28.
2. As suggested, for instance, in GLA Economics, *The Rationale for Public Sector Intervention in the Economy*, (London: Greater London Authority, 2006), p. iii.
3. Enterprise Insight, *The Enterprise Report 2005: Making Ideas Happen – Summary* (London: Enterprise Insight, 2005).
4. F. J. Greene, K. F. Mole, and D. J. Storey, *Three Decades of Enterprise Culture* (Basingstoke: Palgrave Macmillan, 2008), p. 95.

Index

Accelerating Entrepreneurship Strategy (NI), 29, 39, 68–70, 99
Acs, Z. J. and Szerb, L., 102
Ahmad, N. and Hoffman, A., 27, 60
Ajzen. I., 207–8, 210
Armstrong, P., 45
attributes and resources model, 47–8
Audretsch, D. B. and Keilbach, M. C., 75, 188, 190–1, 205
availability of goal-realisation devices, 161–2

Bahn S., 215
Ball, P. *Critical Mass*, 90–1, 173–4
Bannock, G., 57, 71
Baudeau, N., 96
Baumol, W. J., 101, 104, 107, 111, 115, 127, 189
behavioural economics, 168–9, 177, 179, 219
Ben and Jerry, 154
best practice, xi, 4, 37, 40–1, 44, 59–60, 139, 143, 196, 200
Birch, D., 4, 24, 97, 107
black swan, 197
bleeding / bloodletting, 3, 9, 11, 135, 215
Bolton W. and Thompson J., 205
de Botton, A, 167
Bourdieu, P., 181
Branson, R., 130, 154
Bridge, S., Murtagh, B., and O'Neill, K., 18, 19, 23, 85, 156
Bridge, S., O'Neill, K. and Martin, F., 20, 42, 47, 50, 65, 82–3, 127, 144
Business Link, 66
business owners' perspectives, 83–4, 149
business plans, 34, 210, 220–1
business professionals' perspectives, 82–3, 136, 149
Bygrave, B., 49

Campbell, M., 173–4
Canada, 17, 124
Cantillon, R., 96, 112, 149
Carroll, Lewis, 95–6
Casson, M., 56, 58, 108
Chell, E., 86, 104, 119, 121–2
China, 206
  medieval China, 101–2
cholera, 8–9, 215
classic dissertation, 200
collective behaviour, 91, 171, 173, 177
compulsive rationalisers, 177
Copernicus, 12
cows produce milk, 140–1
crime, 151, 153, 161–2, 173–5, 201–2, 219
Curran, J., 64, 139

Darwin, 198, 200
Davidsson, P., 112
Deakins, D., 120
Denmark, 17, 26, 35, 52, 54–5, 60, 98, 107, 137, 179
Department of Economic Development (NI), 40
Department of Trade and Industry (UK), 45
dependency culture, 98
deprivation (social or economic), 7, 21–3, 70, 173–4, 195
destiny, 165
destructive entrepreneurship, 101–7, 111, 115, 127, 153, 190
determinants (of entrepreneurship), 26–7, 51, 60–1, 128
development studies, 181
Diamond J., 200
Drakopoulou Dodd, S. and Anderson, A., 126, 129, 201

The Economist, 100–1
Einstein A., 12, 76, 194, 199

223

Eliot, T. S., 11
entrepreneurial personality, 121–2
entrepreneurship capital, 75, 188, 190–1, 205
entrepreneurship and Education Action Plan (NI), 5, 100, 105, 107
entrepreneurship education – three roles, 99, 101
entrepreneurship indicators, 27, 60
entrepreneurship – three phases of use of the word, 103
enterprise policy – the basis of choice, 143–4
Enterprising Northern Ireland, 33, 39–40, 65–6
E-numbers, 106–7, 108, 111, 118–19, 130, 203
European Enterprise Award, 2, 28
EU, 6, 25, 26, 84
EUROSTAT, 27, 60
evaluating policy, 63–6

factors impacting entrepreneurship, 54
family business, 165
'fantasies, feelings and fun', 91–3, 136, 170–1
fashion (goods), 93, 136, 171–2, 179, 219
Filion, L. J., 31
Finland, 35
focus of entrepreneurship, 104–6
forms of entrepreneurship, 106, 109, 115, 148, 153–4, 158, 203
France / French, 9, 96, 108, 111
Franco-Prussian War, 9
Frankish, J., Roberts, R. and Storey, D., 70, 195
Fukuyama, F., 186

Galbraith J. K., 198
gap between policy and research, 137–43
Gardner, D., 168, 177
gazelles, 107, 108–10
GEM (Global Entrepreneurship Monitor), 6, 7, 48–9, 51, 68–9, 73, 75, 99, 100, 104, 107, 111, 163, 178, 201, 206
  conceptual model, 48–9
  U-shaped curve, 48, 73

genes, 119, 122, 124, 125–6
Germany, 75, 191, 205
Gibb, A. A., 56–7, 58, 100, 104, 137–8, 179, 206
Gibb A. A. and Li J., 206
Gladwell, M. *Outliers*, 124, 188
Glaeser, E. L., Kerr, W. R. and Ponzetto, G. A. M., 74
Global Entrepreneurship Index, 102
Global Entrepreneurship Monitor, *see* GEM
goal realisation device, Chapter, 9, 160–1, 214
government agency perspectives, 86–9
Green Book, 37, 63
Greene, F. J., Mole, K. F. and Storey, D. J., 71, 219

Halpern, D., 186–7
Handy, C., 131
Hanifan, L. J., 181
Hart, M., 86
Hart, M. and Roper, S., 66–7
Harvard, 96, 100
  definition of entrepreneurship, 100
Hawkins, P., 154
Heffalump, 95
hierarchy of enterprise needs, 42–4, 178
'heroic' myth, 128–30, 131, 137, 205
high (job) expectation entrepreneurship, 99
high-tech high-growth, 103, 106, 108, 114, 136, 148, 158, 219
Hippocratic doctors, 3, 8
Hoffman, A., 27, 60, 137
homo economicus, 166, 168
HPSUs (high potential start-ups), 98, 103, 107
Huggins, R. and Williams, N., 70
human capital, 180–1, 185, 219
humours, four, 8–10, 135, 217
Hytti, U. and Kuopusjärvi, P., 99, 101, 103, 111

ice hockey, 124
IDB, 39
information processing model, 91–2, 170

Industrial Revolution, 102
Invest Northern Ireland (Invest NI), 29, 39–41, 68–70, 99

Jovanovic, B., 127
Johnson, P., 70

Kahneman, D., 169
Karlsson C. and Andersson M., 196
Kepler, 12
Kets de Vries, M., 129
Keynesian economics, 4, 97
Kilby, P., M., 95
Kim, J., Weinstein, A., G., Shirley, S., E. and Melhem, I., 53
kinds of entrepreneurs, 154
Kitson, F., 141
Klucharev, 172
Krueger, N., F., 46, 59, 179, 207–11, 217, 219
Krueger N. Reilly M. and Carsrud A., 208

LEDU, 33, 38–41, 65, 66, 88
Lisbon Strategy, 17, 26
Lister, 9
local enterprise agencies (LEAs), 33, 39, 41
logical choice, 58, 91
Lundstrom, A. and Stevenson, L., 127

Malaria, 8–9, 215
Malthus, *Population,* 200
market failure, 18, 19, 59, 64, 67, 143, 219
Martin, F., xi
Maslow, 149–51
medical analogy, 3–4, 8–10, 77, 134–5, 214–6
Mencken, H. L., 168
Middle Ages, 101–2
military intelligence, 139
money supply, 106
Montreal, 29–31
'mumpsimus', 129
mushrooms, 110, 156

Nanda, R. and Sorensen, J. B., 172
narrow meanings/definitions (of enterprise or entrepreneurship), 2–3, 98, 101, 102, 103, 104, 106, 107, 111–12, 114, 136, 148, 154, 160, 203
natural capital, 180, 181
nature or nurture debate, 13, Chapter, 7, 136, 137
Naude, W., 101
neo-classical economics, 168–9
NESTA, 42, 73
meuroscience, 169, 177
Netherlands, 28, 35
Newton, 10, 12, 76, 199
Nicolaou, N. and Shane, S., 125, 126
Nisbet, R., 130
NISBI, 66
Northern Ireland, xii, 5, 26, 29, 31–33, 38–41, 45, 65, 66, 67, 68–70, 74, 88, 100
nurture (or nature debate), *see* nature or nurture debate

oak trees, 113
OECD, 6, 25, 26, 27, 52–3, 60, 63
O'Neill, K., xi, xii
Ormerod, P., 173, 174

Paine, Thomas, 194
Parker, S. C., 75
Pathfinder (NI initiative), 40
peers, and peer influence/pressure, 47, 93, 171–2, 174, 189–92, 203, 204, 217–8
people perspective, 81, 149, 157–8
personal business advisers (PBAs), 67
personality theory, 119
Peterson, R. and Rondstadt, R., 44, 178
physical capital, 181
physics, 10, 44, 90, 171, 200
   physics (of society), 91
policy benefits, 21
policy drivers, 18–21, 37
policy evolution, 24
policy framework, 18–19, 25, 34–5, 52–3
policy objectives, 18–19, 23, 37, 115
policy rationale, 18–19
policy/research gap, *see* gap between policy and research

preparation for enterprise, 105, 154–5, 163–4
productive entrepreneurship, 101–2, 104, 111, 127
private sector, 2, 31, 53, 64, 84–6, 88, 104, 107, 112, 114, 158, 160
public sector, 32, 84, 85, 100, 152
Publius Decius, 96
Putnam, R. *Bowling Alone*, 181

Quebec, 30

rationale for UK enterprise policy, 195
reasons for wanting to work, 151
regional development agency, 71, 72
Renaissance Europe, 101
resources for life, 152–3
Richard, D. (Richard Report), 72–3
risk-return analysis/assessment, 164, 166, 167, 177, 201, 203–5, 217, 220
Rome (ancient), 101
Roper (and Hart), *see* Hart, M. and Roper, S.
Roper, S. and Hewitt-Dundas, N., 67
Rosa, P., Kodithuwakku, S. and Balunywa, W., 163
Roseto, 188
RSA, 169, 170, 204
Ruddick, A., 154

Say, J-B., 96
SBS, *see* Small Business Service
Schumpeter, 101
science of collective behaviour, 91, 171, 173, 177
scientific approach, 76, 197–9
Scotland, 26, 74
self-actualisation, 150, 153
Shane, S., 45–6, 121, 123, 125–6, 131, 157, 178
Shapero, 208–10
Silicon Valley, 205, 206
Simon, H., 168
Small Business Service (SBS), 43, 66, 138
   The Evidence Base, 43, 138
Smith, A. *Wealth of Nations*, 180
Snark, 95–6
social brain, 168–70

social capital, 14, 23, 155, 163, 164, 178, 179, 180–192, 219
   bonding, 183, 184, 186, 189, 192
   bridging, 183, 184, 186
   components, 182, 185, 186, 188, 189
   constituents, 182
   domains, 182, 183, 184, 186, 189
   measuring, 184–6, 187
social context, 89
social influence, 57, 171–5, 177, 178, 180, 189–92, 201–3, 209–10, 217, 219, 220
social entrepreneurship, 88, 104, 107, 154
social norms, 46, 49, 50, 55, 179, 182, 207, 209, 211, 217, 219
stage of entrepreneurship, 104, 105
Stam, E., 75
Stanworth, J. and Gray, C., 172
Stevenson, L., 6, 24–5, 34, 35, 51–2, 127, 154, 178, 204
Sugar, A., 130
Storey, D. J, 25, 27, 71, 195, 205
sustainable development

terminology, 2–3
Teesside / Tees Valley, 71, 205, 219
The Evidence Base (SBS), *see* Small Business Service – *The Evidence Base*
Theory of Planned Behaviour, 207–11
third sector, 84, 86, 160
Thompson J. and Bolton W., 205
timing of entrepreneurship, 163–4
Total Entrepreneurial Activity (TEA)., 68–70
traits, 119–26, 128–30, 136–7, 207–8
trigger, 46, 47, 48, 164
trust, 179, 182, 183, 184–6, 189
two state model, 202, 205
Tycho Brahe, 12
type of entrepreneurship, 104, 105

upbringing, 118, 120, 126, 164, 165
UK enterprise strategy, 27–8
UK unemployment, 4, 7
unproductive entrepreneurship, 101–2, 104, 107, 111, 115, 127, 190
US war of drugs, 194

VAT registrations (UK), 74
venture perspective, 157–8
Verheul, I., 196
vitamins, 180, 186, 187–8, 192

Washington, George, 3
Wennekers, S. and Thurik, R., 101

Wennekers, S., Uhlaner, L., M. and Thurik, R., 51, 58
Winnie-the-Pooh, 95
Wisdom, 11–2, 13, 43, 196, 198
World views
   economic development agency, 89
   individual, 90